In the Malay World

Based on various archival and non-archival records, oral testimonies and travel accounts, some of which are used for the first time, this book explores the historical migration of Bengalis and their diasporic experiences in Malaysia, Singapore and Brunei, covering a period from the mid-nineteenth to the late twentieth century. Despite the tremendous historical mobility of the Bengalis in the Malay world and their contemporary salience, as reflected in the region's more-than-a-million-strong Bengali diaspora, their historical contribution remains almost unseen. This book addresses this lacuna by exploring the connections between Bengal and Malaya. The book further examines the formation of a Bengali social, political, economic and cultural space within the diverse South Asian diaspora during the colonial and postcolonial periods. The study contributes to the recent flourishing of mobility studies, cosmopolitanism, ethnic studies, connected histories and transnational histories in modern Asia.

Gazi Mizanur Rahman is assistant professor of history at BRAC University, Bangladesh, with expertise in historical migration. He is a member of different academic bodies, notably the Midwest World History Association, USA, and the Centre of South Asian and Indian Ocean Studies of Sunway University, Malaysia.

GLOBAL SOUTH ASIANS

Throughout the modern era, South Asia and South Asians have been entangled with global flows of goods, people and ideas. In the context of these globalised conditions, migrants from the subcontinent of India created some of the world's most extensive and influential transnational networks. While operating within the constraints of imperial systems, they nevertheless made distinctive and important contributions to international trade, global cultures and transnational circuits of knowledge. This series seeks to explore these phenomena, placing labourers, traders, thinkers and activists at the centre of the analysis. Beginning with volumes that seek to radically reappraise indenture, the series will continue with books on the mobility of elite actors, including intellectuals, and their contributions to the global circulation of ideas and the evolution of political practice. It will highlight the creativity and agency of diasporic South Asians and illuminate the crucial role they played in the making of global histories. As such it sets out to challenge popular misconceptions and established scholarly narratives that too often cast South Asians as passive observers.

General Editor

Crispin Bates
University of Edinburgh

Editorial Advisory Board

Sunil Amrith
Yale University

Subho Basu
McGill University

Marina Carter
University of Edinburgh

Joya Chatterji
Trinity College, University of Cambridge

Maurits S. Hassankhan
Anton de Kom University of Suriname

Ashutosh Kumar
Banaras Hindu University

Andrea Major
University of Leeds

Rajesh Rai
National University of Singapore

Goolam Vahed
University of KwaZulu-Natal

Books in the series

Fleeting Agencies: A Social History of Indian Coolie Women in British Malaya, Arunima Datta

The Indentured Archipelago: Experiences of Indian Labour in Mauritius and Fiji, 1871–1916, Reshaad Durgahee

Citizens of Everywhere: Indian Women, Nationalism and Cosmopolitanism, 1920–1952, Rosalind Parr

Uncivil Liberalism: Labour, Capital and Commercial Society in Dadabhai Naoroji's Political Thought, Vikram Visana

Passages through India: Indian Gurus, Western Disciples and the Politics of Indophilia, 1890–1940, Somak Biswas

Beyond Indenture: Agency and Resistance in the Colonial South Asian Diaspora, ed. Crispin Bates

Girmitiyas and the Global Indian Diaspora: Origins, Memories, and Identity, ed. Ashutosh Kumar and Crispin Bates

In the Malay World

A Spatial History of a Bengali Transnational Community

Gazi Mizanur Rahman

CAMBRIDGE
UNIVERSITY PRESS

Shaftesbury Road, Cambridge CB2 8EA, United Kingdom

One Liberty Plaza, 20th Floor, New York, NY 10006, USA

477 Williamstown Road, Port Melbourne, VIC 3207, Australia

314–321, 3rd Floor, Plot No. 3, Splendor Forum, Jasola District Centre, New Delhi – 110025, India

103 Penang Road, #05–06/07, Visioncrest Commercial, Singapore 238467

Cambridge University Press is part of Cambridge University Press & Assessment, a department of the University of Cambridge.

We share the University's mission to contribute to society through the pursuit of education, learning and research at the highest international levels of excellence.

www.cambridge.org
Information on this title: www.cambridge.org/9781009446099

First published 2024

Printed in India by Avantika Printers Pvt. Ltd.

A catalogue record for this publication is available from the British Library

ISBN 978-1-009-44609-9 Hardback

For
those Bengali migrants who settled and
lost their ethnic identity in the Malay world

Contents

Maps

Tables

Figures

Graph

Notes on Weighing Scale

bale | an equal to half a candy (1 candy = 690 pounds)

bolt | a unit of measurement for fabric; the length is usually either 40 or 100 yards

cattie | a unit of weight, used in Asia, traditionally equal to about 1.5 pounds but formalised as 0.5 or 0.6 kilograms in China and the Malay Peninsula

chest | a large strong box used for storage or transport

maund | a unit of weight in some Asian countries; it is equivalent to about 37.32 kilograms

Palletised Load System | a unit of measurement used for trade in the nineteenth and the twentieth centuries; it was a decimal-scales system, where every decimal may value from 5 to 20 kilograms

picul | a unit of weight, used in Asia, equal to approximately 60 kilograms

Note on Place Names

In this book, I refer to many places known by different names at different points in time. I use Bombay, Madras, Calcutta, Dacca, Siam and Burma when discussing the colonial period and the early decades after independence. When referring to these places in postcolonial times, I switch to the current nomenclature, for example, Mumbai, Chennai, Kolkata, Dhaka, Thailand and Myanmar.

Acknowledgements

An Austrian historian, Ludwig von Mises (1881–1973), expressed that human action is 'purposeful behaviour'. Like Ludwig's statement, the compiling of this book has a particular purpose. In 2014, I read a book titled *Crossing the Bay of Bengal* by Sunil Amrith, a history professor at Yale University. In the book, he suggested that following the Anglo-Dutch Treaty of 1824, some 'Free Bengalis' had been removed from Bencoolen (presently Bengkulu) to Penang and Malacca. This reference hints at the Bengali migration during the colonial period. A question appeared in my mind: presently, remittance is one of the critical sources contributing to the national gross domestic product (GDP) in Global South countries, particularly Bangladesh. Malaysia, Singapore and Brunei are the destinations of many Bangladeshi expatriates. However, what was Bengali migration to the Malay Peninsula during the nineteenth or early twentieth centuries like? This seed began the research on Bengali migration, which eventually became this book.

This book has been formed from my PhD research project, which has benefitted enormously from the guidance, criticism and encouragement of many individuals. I am fortunate to have received supervision from Dr Iftekhar Iqbal. He has gone the extra mile in seeing through the development and culmination of this book. I could barely imagine completing this research project without his extraordinary attention to detail and support. Dr Nani Suryani's close reading of the drafts and insightful comments were instrumental. At Universiti Brunei Darussalam (UBD), I would also like to register my gratitude to the following scholars for their invaluable knowledge and resources: Dr A. K. M. Ahsan Ullah, Dr Haji Awang Asbol Haji Mail, Dr Asiyah Az-Zahra Ahmad Kumpoh, Dr Johannes L Kurz, Dr Rommel Curaming and Dr Md Shafi Noor Islam.

I was able to pursue my PhD research project only because of the generous UBD Graduate Scholarship and other support from the Faculty of Arts and

Social Sciences. Also, two rounds of the Asian Graduate Student Fellowship (AGSF) at the Asia Research Institute, National University of Singapore, opened the door to my recent research in Asian Studies. During the fellowship period, my meeting with the following scholars was enriching: Sunil Amrith, Jayati Bhattacharya, Tim Bunnell, Jonathan Rigg and Michiel Bass.

I would like to express my gratitude to the staff of the following institutions where I worked for collecting research materials: the National Archives of Bangladesh; Asiatic Society of Bangladesh Library; Bangla Academy Library; National Public Library, Bangladesh; Central Library of the University of Dhaka; Universiti Brunei Darussalam Library; National Archives of Brunei; Brunei History Center; National Archives of Singapore; Lee Kong Chian Reference Library; Rare Books Collection; Singapore-Malaysia Collection and Microfilms Collection of the National University of Singapore; Institute of Southeast Asia Studies Library, and ARI Resources Room.

I would also like to thank the three anonymous readers for their insightful reading and comments so that this manuscript could reach its final stage. My recent interactions with Crispin Bates, the series editor at Cambridge University Press (CUP), have helped me to dig deeper and further nuance some research areas. I extend special thanks to him as he offered perceptive comments that generated crucial revisions to the manuscript. I am grateful to the syndicate members of CUP who approved this book project. I am also thankful for the constant support and guidance from CUP—Aniruddha, Anwesha Rana, Priya Das, typesetters and other staff who were involved to make this publication successful.

I also thank the various conference organisers and panellists between 2017 and 2022 who gave me the incredible opportunity to share my research and whose insightful comments helped me develop my arguments. Your time, comments and suggestions were precious.

I would like to recall the generous and rewarding mentorship that I received during my years at the University of Dhaka. Ahmed Kamal stirred my interest in the history of subalterns and peripheral people on the move. He remains a constant source of inspiration. I would also like to note my gratitude to my following teachers from the University of Dhaka for their foundational support and mentorship in appreciating the various windows to historical studies: Sharif Uddin Ahmed, Syed Anwar Husain, Kazi Shahidullah, Ahmed Abdullah Jamal, Nurul Huda Abul Monsur, Rana Razzaque, Surma Zakaria Choudhury, Prodip Chand Dugar and Mr Mohammad Abul Kawser.

Oral interviews with members of the diasporic community are a vital part of this book, and I am particularly grateful to the participants for sharing their memories and giving me a warm reception: Mushahid Ali, Anwarul Haque, Noorul Islam, A. K. M. Mohsin, Dolly Sinha Devanport and Shafiya Khatoon. The grandchildren of M. A. Majid, particularly Fazlur Rahman and Noorul Islam, provided me with some rare photographs. My thanks to the entire family for allowing me access to the sources at their disposal.

A few chapters are revised versions of the following articles: parts of Chapter 2 appeared in 'Transnational History and Colonial Records: Locating Bengali Mobility in the British Malaya', *Journal of Maritime Studies and National Integration* 3, no. 2 (2019): 97–112; Chapter 3 is a revised version of 'Colonising the Penal Capital: Locating the Bengali Convicts in Cosmopolitan British Malaya', *Asian Studies, The Twelfth International Convention of Asia Scholars (ICAS 12), ICAS Conference Proceedings* 1 (June 2022): 569–582. I owe grateful acknowledgement to the journals and publishers for allowing me to build on this earlier work.

Throughout the research and writing of this book, I received encouragement and feedback from my friends and colleagues in Brunei and beyond. Siti Noraqilah Binti Haji Abas was a source of practical support, and she helped me with drawing maps for this book as well as translating some Malay texts. The following friends were equally supportive and were the source of inspiration and joy: Christine Lewis and Ririn Kurnia Trisnawati of UBD, Hanee Kang of the University of London, Amit Das Gupta of Universität der Bundeswehr München and Nur Aisyah Kotarumalos of Seoul National University.

Finally, I would like to thank my wonderful colleagues at the Department of English and Humanities of BRAC University, who were constantly great support through the process of finishing this book.

Of course, any shortcomings in the book remain entirely mine.

Gazi Mizanur Rahman
July 2024

Abbreviations

BAS	Bengali Association Singapore
BLCF	Bangladesh Language and Cultural Foundation
BLLS	Bangla Language and Literary Society
BMET	Bureau of Manpower, Employment and Training
BMPC	British Malayan Petroleum Company
CIAM	Central Indian Association of Malaya
CM & HO	Chief Medical & Health Officer
DA	*Daily Advertiser*
EBR	Eastern Bengal Railway Company
EDMSMA	*Eastern Daily Mail and Straits Morning Advertiser*
EIC	British East India Company
IDM	*Indian Daily Mail*
IIL	Indian Independence League
ISEAS	Institute of Southeast Asian Studies
IYL	Indian Youth League
LMS	Licentiate in Medicine and Surgery
MaT	*Malaya Tribune*
MBA	Malayan Bengalee Association
MCP	Malayan Communist Party
MdHD	*Mid-Day Herald and Daily*
MIC	Malaysian Indian Congress
MMA	Malaysian Medical Association

MoT	*Morning Tribune*
NAB	National Archives of Bangladesh
NAM	National Archives of Malaysia
NAS	National Archives of Singapore
NLA	National Library of Australia
NN	*New Nation*
NUS	National University of Singapore
OHI	Oral History Interview
PAP	People's Action Party
POW	prisoner of war
SASF	Singapore Asian Seafarers' Federation
SBS	Singapore Bangladesh Society
SCBA	Straits Chinese British Association
SCCR	*Singapore Chronicle and Commercial Register*
SDN	*Singapore Daily News*
SFP	*Singapore Free Press*
SFPMA	*Singapore Free Press and Mercantile Advertiser*
SIA	Singapore Indian Association
SLP	Singapore Labour Party
SO	*Star Online*
ST	*Straits Times*
STOJ	*Straits Times Overland Journal*
STWI	*Straits Times Weekly Issue*
TOL	Ticket of Leave
UBD	Universiti Brunei Darussalam
UMNO	United Malays National Organisation
VOC	Verenigde Oostindische Compagnie (Dutch East India Company)

Prelude

A thousand years have I been roaming the world's pathways,
From Ceylon to Malaya in darkness of night across oceans
Much have I traveled; in the grey universe of Bimbisara, Ashoka,
Yes, I was there; deeper in the darkness in Vidarbha metropolis,
A weary soul, I, life's waves all around foaming at the crest,
A moment or two of peace she gave me, Natore's Banalata Sen.[1]

Jibanananda Das, a leading Bengali poet of the twentieth century, never travelled to the Malay Peninsula. However, in an allegorical verse in his famous poem 'Banalata Sen', an ode to the eponymous eternal woman, Das expressed that he had travelled for thousands of years from Sri Lanka to the Malay world to attain a moment of peace. His literary mind knew no bounds. Though his journey was a fantasy of love, it gives us a sense of the constant flow of Bengali mobility and culture between the two coasts of the Bay of Bengal and the Malay Sea. Factually, the Bengalis did voyage to the Malay Archipelago over the course of a thousand years. This truth fuelled the imagination of the Bengali poets, as reflected in Das's verse. With the advent of British colonialism, Bengali mobility took a new turn, and Das's verse reflects its nodal points in the eastern Indian Ocean domains during the late colonial period.

The trans-regional mobility of peoples, goods and cultures and its attendant space-making is the central theme of this book. Although studies of connected histories have flourished in the past few decades in the Global South, Bengali historical diasporic experiences have remained largely unexplored. With a focus on the historical mobility of the Bengalis from both Bangladesh and West Bengal of India, the book argues that there was robust Bengali trans-regional mobility in the Malay world,[2] a story that has been largely lost in the narrative of 'Indian' migration.

By the turn of the twenty-first century, the total number of Bangla-speaking migrants from Bangladesh in the Malay world was approximately 900,000, the vast majority being in Malaysia, followed by Singapore and Brunei Darussalam (hereinafter Brunei).[3] The number is higher if the Bengalis from West Bengal of India are included. Such a significant number of Bengali migrants reflects the long and complex history of their presence in this region. Yet there has been no substantial study of the emergence and development of Bengali migrants and their diaspora in the Malay world. This book addresses this lacuna in the history of Bengal–Malaya connections; it explores the formation of Bengali social, political, economic and cultural space within the diverse South Asian[4] diaspora during the colonial and postcolonial periods and offers a modest contribution to the flourishing studies addressing mobility in modern Asia.

Conceptualising Space-making in Transnational History

Space-making in transnational history warrants further discussion at this point. 'Space' refers to various phenomena in science, mathematics and communications, but it generally denotes a terrestrial zone that is primarily free, available or unoccupied. The idea of space was rescued from its geometric concept by Henri Lefebvre (1901–1991), a French Marxist scholar. Lefebvre's innovative idea of space was articulated in his book *The Production of Space*,[5] where he analysed space in three interrelated ways. First, he looked at 'spatial practice' or the physical or geographical form of space; this form of space is exemplified by earthly formation, such as government housing projects. The second aspect relates to the 'representation of space' or the space of knowledge, for instance, logic, cartographies, mathematics or urban planning. This is a theoretical or mental space. Third, 'representational space' is considered by Lefebvre to be social, or living space.[6] Lefebvre and his followers' contribution to the formulation of the production of space had a significant impact on our understanding of the interplay of physical space, social action and capital or assets.[7] However, in the conceptual framework of Lefebvre's idea of space, the role of transnational human mobility, particularly transnational migrants, which accompanies the 'production of space', is mostly overlooked.

In the context of migration histories, the term 'space' is very metaphoric. The migrating community creates civic associations and has been involved in the cultural and political spheres of the host society over the years. Even sometimes, they settle in a specific area of host countries, and the area is known by the particular diasporic community, for example, 'Little India' or 'Bangla Town'. In migration studies, historians consider those areas and spheres as 'spaces' in the settling country. Frances Pine studies the economic migration in two cities in Poland. She shows how these migrating communities created spaces in terms of formal and informal economic activities, kinship and the networks of care over time.[8]

Since the late twentieth century, some historians have introduced their works as transnational or global history.[9] European imperialists and capitalists invested capital globally as well as transported different ethnic groups across the world. Such migrants created space in distant places away from home.[10] Their contribution to the production of spaces in transnational domains remains understudied. This book combines Lefebvre's conceptualisation of the production of capitalist space with an analysis of the space produced through the transnational mobility of people focusing on the Bengalis in the Malay world.

Objectives and Materials

This book aims to address three core areas. First, it looks at the routes and points of connectivity between Bengal and the Malay world, which facilitated the mobility of people and commodities. This leads to an understanding of the scope of the multidimensional spatial contact points between the two regions. Second, this book demonstrates the factors behind the Bengali migration and associated issues of governance of migration in both Bengal and Malaya. Third, it critically explores the evolution and development of Bengali diasporic space and the formation of a Bengali transnational community in the colonial and postcolonial Malay world, concentrating on the contribution of Bengali merchants, workers, professionals and civil societies.

In order to comprehensively explore the themes outlined here, this book relies on a range of primary and secondary sources. The primary sources comprise population censuses, official correspondences, government records and almanacs, produced by the Governments of Bengal, the Straits Settlements and Brunei. Official correspondences include those made through interdepartmental channels, for instance, between the Home Department and Emigration Department of the Governments of Bengal (provincial) and India. Government records include administrative reports, documents of the emigration department and reports of the police department. The sources have been collected from different libraries and archives.[11]

The labour migrants themselves hardly left any written documentation of their voyages and quotidian life in a foreign land. However, their journeys and post-migration life are well documented in the accounts of two Bengali travellers, Hurrish Banarjee and Ramnath Biswas, used in this book. These travel accounts, spanning the years from 1903 to 1931, are crucial for shedding light on the experiences of thousands of Bengali migrants.

In the rewriting of historical migration, interviews with descendants or eyewitnesses are considered the primary source, filling the gap left by archival evidence. In this respect, oral testimony is crucial in writing Bengali historical mobility because the non-Bengalis were blended with them. The reminiscences of Bengali descendants about how their ancestors had come to British Malaya are important in locating the Bengalis among the 'Indian' population. For selecting interviewees, I applied an arbitrary method, snowball sampling, and used a set of questionnaires for collecting interviews from the Bengali descendants of different professionals. An open-ended question was also employed during the interview to collect more information. A good number of interviews with Bengali descendants in Singapore have been used in this book. Most of the interviewees spoke in English, and the author transcribed and translated all into English (in the case of Bangla). After transcribing the interviews, the author checked them with the interviewees. Moreover, some essential oral testimonies from Bengali descendants preserved in the Oral History Interview section of the National Archives of Singapore are used.

Various periodicals and newspapers published since the early nineteenth century in British Malaya were important sources for this book. Moreover, some newspapers have been used which were published in Australia during the early twentieth century. The National Library Board of Singapore and the National Library of Australia have digitised most newspapers. I also use a few valuable items from the British Library and German Embassy in Singapore.

Competing Literature

In terms of trans-regional connectivity and mobility, some scholars have discussed the trading networks and cultural exchange between South and Southeast Asia during the early modern and pre-modern periods.[12] Another group of scholars have shown the connections and human mobility between the two regions in the form of Indian migrations, substantially exploring topics such as Indian slave traffic, the functioning of the institution and abolition of slavery and the conditions of the Indian indentured and *kangany* labourers.[13] Other scholars have illustrated the socio-economic conditions of the Indian diasporic community during the colonial and postcolonial eras.[14] Rajesh Rai, for example, has examined the Indian diaspora's changing political ideologies in the colonial context, their encounters with communication technologies and their transnational religious and political engagement in the late nineteenth and early twentieth centuries.[15] Meanwhile, Arunima Datta has interrogated the everyday lives of Indian coolie women in plantation economies in British Malaya.[16]

Within the narrative of 'Indian' diasporic experiences, South Asian heterogeneous ethnicities, religions and cultures are often overshadowed. John Solomon suggests that the term 'Indian' hides heterogeneous religions, languages, classes and castes.[17] Even south Indian Muslims, whilst sharing a common religious faith, do not share the same communal practices as north Indian Muslims.[18] Therefore, existing scholarships on the Indian diaspora have tended to underplay the vast range of diversity within it.[19]

Dipesh Chakrabarty has problematised the idea of 'Indians' and suggested that the British represented 'Indians' through a homogenising narrative. Through a transnational perspective, he deconstructs the idea of 'Indians'.[20] Broadening the available terminology, Crispin Bates uses the term 'Pan-South Asian identity' instead of Pan-Indian identity. He highlights that members of different Indian ethnicities, castes and religious communities have informed the creation of constitutions and decision-making processes of many governments for most of the twentieth century.[21] The umbrella term 'Indian' has only recently begun to be dissected and nuanced.

Within this broader shift in studies on the South Asian diaspora, Sunil Amrith's work convincingly demonstrates how the missing identity of the Tamils among Indian migrants can be recovered. Amrith's work on Tamil experiences in the Malay world has contributed to rescuing a heterogeneous India from a homogenising narrative. Amrith's work calls for further explorations of other underrepresented cultural, economic and ethnic groups who made up the South Asian diaspora in the Malay world.[22] The Sikh community in British Malaya has also been the focus of some histories, and Mustafa Izzuddin is currently working on the migration of Dawoodi Bohras, a Shia minority sect, from India to Singapore.[23]

In keeping with the recent contributions listed earlier, I aim here to write the history of the Bengali transnational community and their space in the Malay world. The Bengalis are an ethnolinguistic community that is different from other Indians. Some interviewees of different ethnic groups, including Malayalee, Telugu, Tamil and Sikh, who were brought up in Singapore in the early twentieth century, suggested that the Punjabis should not be mixed up with the Bengalis because their language and culture are different from others. Therefore, there are sociocultural and historical distinctions between Bengali and non-Bengali or Indian identities. The Bengalis represents a language-based ethnic identity, whereas 'Indian' denotes a nation-based identity where different ethnic groups, religions, languages and cultures are amalgamated.

This book looks at multiple temporal and contextual elements to understand the historical development of the Bengali diaspora. It is curious that although the Bengali historical experiences in Southeast Asia have yet to be substantially explored, their presence in the Western world is well registered in historical literature. Therefore, before discussing the Bengali historical migration and diaspora in Malaya, references may be made to the literature on Bengali migration to other regions.

Several publications have revealed the history of Bengali migrants and the making of their transnational community in Britain, ranging from the life and time of the lascars, the Bengali crews of the nineteenth century, to their more recent experiences in British politics and economy.[24] Vivek Bald has described the history of petty business people, sailors and enginemen who travelled from Noakhali, Sylhet and other parts of Bengal to the USA. Bald tells how a small group of Muslim peddlers arrived every summer at Ellis Island with a heavy bag of embroidered silk from Bengal in the 1890s. Later, hundreds of seamen escaped from the ships that carried indentured labourers and found work in the factories of Detroit in the 1900s. These Bengalis drifted into the local communities and settled themselves.[25]

Ansu Datta examines the trans-oceanic slave trade between southern Bengal and South Africa from the mid-seventeenth century to the 1840s. He offers a historical narrative on the Bengali enslaved people who carved out a place in mainstream society. Datta found many interviewees who claimed Bengali slave ancestry in South Africa.[26] Titas Chakraborty describes the work environment of the Bengalis under the Dutch East India Company (VOC) and the British East India Company (henceforth EIC) from the pre-colonial to the colonial eras. Her study is an excellent contribution to the social, economic and trade history of South Asia and the Indian Ocean.[27]

The historical mobility of the Bengalis among other South Asians in Australia has recently been explored by Samia Khatun.[28] The history of the Bengali migration in Australia is not entirely new. During the late nineteenth century, Bengali mobility received significant attention from Devleena Ghosh.[29] However, Khatun has brilliantly enriched the writing of Australian history through her use of non-English sources.

When it comes to Bengali migration and diaspora in the Malay world, most published works focus on the current state of migration and related policy issues from an economic and sociological perspective. Except for a recent memoir of a Bengali doctor,[30] the majority of literature generally concerns Bengali skilled and unskilled labour migration, migrants' gender, health and security and their contribution to the remittance flow to their home countries.[31] Nayeem Sultana takes a sociological and anthropological perspective and explores the organisational structure, modes of networking and survival strategies of Bangladeshi migrants in the Malay Peninsula, particularly Kuala Lumpur, Penang and Johor Bahru.[32] A. K. M. A. Ullah has examined how potential migrants rationalised their earlier aspirations or decision-making with post-migration experiences in Southeast Asia.[33]

The earlier discussion demonstrates the rich range of literature on Bengali historical mobility worldwide, including in western Europe, North America and Australia. However, the recent scope of the topics in Malaya arguably shows a lack of critical historical insight. This book, in contrast, covers the period from 1830 to 1990. In 1830, the Straits Settlements came under the Government of Bengal, with significant implications for greater Bengali mobility in this region. This starting point is significant because, following the end of slavery in Malacca in 1829, the labour supply was bolstered under the indentured system from the 1830s onward, which enormously contributed to the colonial economy.[34] 1990 is the terminal year for this book mainly because it signalled a shift in migratory patterns. There was a new wave of Bengali migration to Southeast Asia away from the Middle East due to the Gulf War (1990–1991). The 1990s was about the time when Malaysia, Singapore and Brunei started massive construction and development works. Therefore, Bangladeshi migrants travelled to these countries for better opportunities, especially after 1990, foreshadowing another phase of migration and diaspora, which deserves its own treatment. The Bengali historical migrations to the Malay world occurred primarily because of the geographical proximity and the maritime connectivity between the Bay of Bengal and the Malay Sea. Therefore, before discussing Bengali historical migration, it is essential to address some crucial questions and lay out the geographical parameters of the Bengal and Malay worlds as understood in this study.

Bengal and the Malay World: Contexts of Connectivity

The Bengalis are considered the third largest ethnic family after the Han Chinese and the Arabs in terms of population size.[35] Due to colonial political contingencies, the Bengalis as an ethnic group were divided twice in modern times, once in 1905 and then again in 1947. At present, the majority of them are spread across Bangladesh, West Bengal (Map P.1) and Assam as minorities in each. This book focuses on those Bengali migrants who originated from these regions. In 2010, there were about 300 million Bengalis, including those spread across the world.[36] Bangla is the fifth-largest spoken language in the

Map P.1   Bangladesh and West Bengal, India

Source: Adapted by Gazi Mizanur Rahman from Google Maps.

Note: Map not to scale and does not represent authentic international boundaries.

world and the official language of Bangladesh, where nearly 165 million people speak it.[37] It is the official language of the states of West Bengal, Tripura, Assam (Barak Valley) and the Andaman and Nicobar Islands in the Republic of India. The number of Bangla users in India is about 90 million, of which 70 million speakers are from West Bengal.[38] It is estimated that almost 10 million Bangla-speaking diasporas from Bangladesh are spread across the world.[39]

In this book, the Malay Sea is seen to encapsulate the area of the Malay world countries. A Portuguese historian and cartographer, Emanuel Godinho de Eredia, coined the term 'Malayos' to describe the jurisdiction under the Malaccan Sultanate in the sixteenth century. The sultanate mostly covered the Malay world, which had multiple defining features, including various trading centres, a tropical climate and racial and linguistic similarities centred around different dialects of the Malay language. Thaib and Che Pa suggest that the Malay world had many trading centres during the Muslim period, which included Pasai (Lhokseumawe) and Aceh (Banda Aceh) to Cirebon, Kudus, Celebes (Sulawesi) and Ternate in Indonesia; from Pattani in Southern Thailand to Sulu in the Philippines.[40] Tarling points out that the Malay world is located in a tropical area that is distinguished from other regions of the world.[41] Beyond territorial characterisations, the majority of scholars defined the Malay world by race, culture and language.[42] As per the definition of Thaib and Che Pa, Map P.2 shows the approximate area of the Malay world; however, this book excludes the Indonesian part of the Malay world. This is why this book's theme focuses exclusively on the British-governed areas, but Indonesia was under the Dutch East Indies Company.

The Indian Ocean has been a means of connection as much as separation. It played a significant role in shaping the Malay world's social, political, religious and cultural landscape. The waters of the Bay of Bengal became a maritime highway across the Straits Settlements, South Indian colonies, African colonies and the Arabian Gulf countries. Map P.3 shows the location of the Bay of Bengal and the waterways between Bengal and the Malay world.

By the early nineteenth century, the European (namely Dutch, French and British) trading companies established their authority around the rim of the Bay of Bengal and the Malay Sea. The EIC, chartered in 1600 AD with monopoly trading rights in the eastern waters, arrived at Surat in Gujarat in 1608 and established the first trading factory in 1618. Later, they founded three presidencies: Bombay Presidency (1618), Madras Presidency (1652) and Bengal Presidency (1765). The capital city of the Bengal Presidency was Calcutta (presently Kolkata). Eastern Bengal, or today's Bangladesh, was a significant

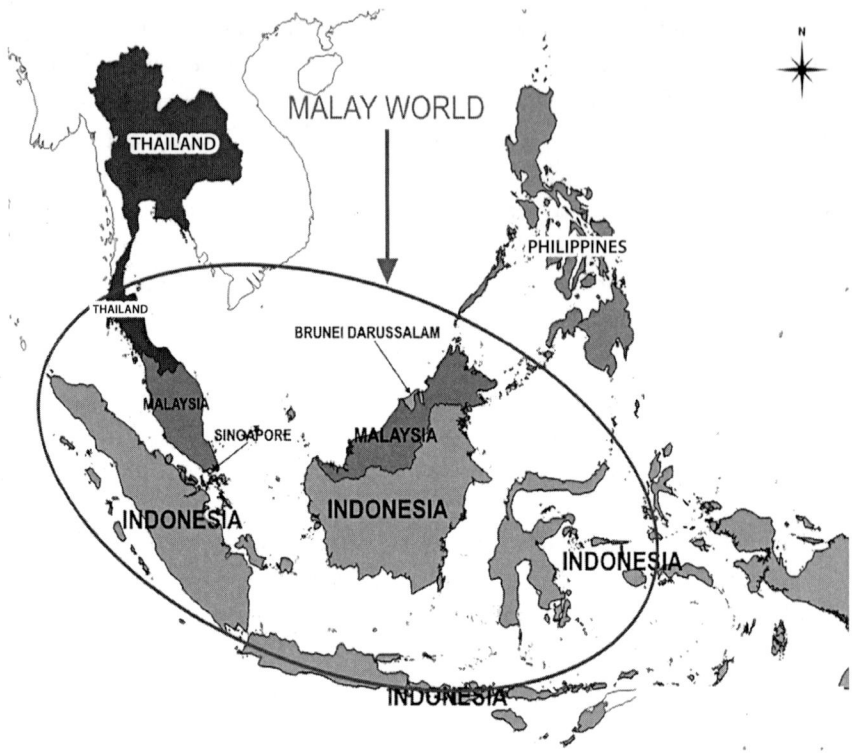

Map P.2   Malay world

Source: Adapted by Gazi Mizanur Rahman from Google Maps.

part of the Bengal Presidency. Though the Bengal Presidency was founded in 1765, the British had established a factory at Hugli in West Bengal by the beginning of 1651.

The EIC connected the Malay Archipelago and Bengal within an administrative framework. They established a fourth presidency at Bencoolen (presently Benkulen/Bengkulu) in southwest Sumatra in 1685, which was a penal settlement for Indian convicts. After a century, it was downgraded to a residency and placed under the Bengal Presidency in 1785. As the EIC was expelled from their North American colonies in the 1780s, they sought new settlements in other regions, including the Malay Peninsula. New British settlements emerged in Penang in 1786, Singapore in 1819 and Malacca (Melaka) in 1824. Using these three settlements, the EIC formed the Straits Settlements in 1826. Later on, Christmas Island, Cocos-Keeling Islands and Labuan were brought under the jurisdiction of the Straits Settlements. The

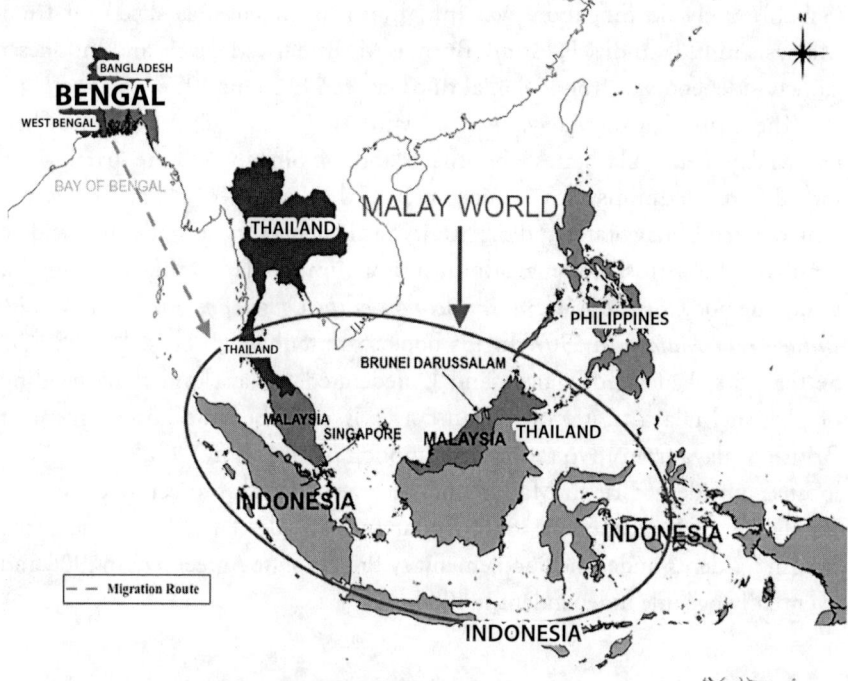

Map P.3   Bengal and the Malay world
Source: Adapted by Gazi Mizanur Rahman from Google Maps.

colonial government annexed most Malay states and North Borneo within the nineteenth century by imposing direct or indirect rule.

The British divided the Malay states into two governing zones in 1895: the Federated Malay States and the Unfederated Malay States. The first zone consisted of Selangor, Perak, Negeri Sembilan and Pahang, placed under a British resident general. It lasted until 1946. The second zone consisted of Johor, Kedah, Kelantan, Perlis and Terengganu, under indirect British control. The Straits Settlements was dissolved in 1946, and Singapore became a separate crown colony with the Cocos-Keeling and Christmas islands. The remaining states of the Straits Settlements, Penang and Malacca, joined with the Unfederated Malay States. After that, the Malayan Union was formed with the Federated Malay States and the Unfederated Malay States in 1946 and later became the Federation of Malaya in 1948. The Federation of Malaya gained complete independence from the United Kingdom in August 1957. Finally, today's Malaysia was formed in 1963 with the inclusion of North Borneo

(Sabah), Sarawak. Singapore was initially included but was sliced off from Malaysia in 1965. India, Pakistan, Burma (Myanmar), Malaysia and Indonesia gained independence from colonial rule between 1947 and 1957.

The term 'British Malaya' was initially used in the 1890s, mainly when the Malay Peninsula states and the island of Singapore were partitioned into different administrative units, such as the Federated Malay States, the Unfederated Malay States and the Straits Settlements. The term became widely familiar when British colonial administrator cum scholar, Frank Swettenham, wrote the book *British Malaya: An Account of the Origin and Progress of British Influence in Malaya* in 1907. In his book, Swettenham discussed the Straits Settlements, Federated Malaya and Unfederated Malaya under the heading of 'British Malaya'. Later on, Chan correctly described the improvement of British Malaya from 1896 to 1909 in his book published in 1964.[43] Brunei was located outside of British Malaya and became a British protectorate through the Treaty of Protection in 1888. About two decades later, Brunei accepted British residents under the Supplementary Protectorate Agreement in 1906 and eventually became independent in 1984.

Manifest of Pre-colonial Trajectory across the Bay of Bengal and Malay Sea

Although this book covers the colonial and postcolonial periods, it must be noted that Bengali connections with the Malay world go back centuries. It would be pertinent to briefly discuss this connectivity before moving on to the timeline covered in the following chapters. The Bengalis have been travelling widely in Southeast Asia since about the third century BCE at least.[44] During the pre-colonial era, the primary connections were the circulation of goods and ideas. Chittagong port was prominent for trade and cultural dissemination. Anthony Reid and R. C. Majumder have shown that Buddhism and Islam were disseminated from Bengal to Southeast Asia. Majumder and Ganguly suggested that Bengal was extensively involved in developing the cultural links between the diverse civilisations of Eastern and Southeastern Asia for nearly 1,500 years.[45] In this respect, both Chittagong and Malacca ports played a crucial role in the exchange of cultures and commodities.[46]

Around 1509, there were about 40,000 merchants in Malacca, of whom one-third was Gujarati, and the rest were of diverse ethnicities: Klings, Chuliahs, Bengalis, Persians and Malabaris.[47] No fewer than eighty-four different languages, including Bangla, were found on Malacca's streets and its bazaars in the sixteenth century.[48] Bengali merchants exported a range of manufacturing and agricultural products, including textiles, rice, wheat, salt, gram, sugar, opium, clarified butter and saltpetre. In return, they imported spices, camphor, porcelain, sandalwood, ivory, metals, conch shells and cowries.[49] In the early sixteenth century, Tomé Pires describes the pre-colonial trans-regional connectivity and the flow of commodities between Bengal and the Malay world, noting that the Bengali merchants with vast fortunes sailed by junks.[50] Apart from Malacca, Bengali merchants were found in Barus port (Sumatra), Pase, Aceh, Java coast, Banda Island and Siam (Thailand) ports during the sixteenth century.[51] Anil Das collected together source material that details the movement of Bengali merchants and commodities in the Malay world during the fifteenth and sixteenth centuries.[52]

Bengali merchants did business in the Malay Peninsula and assisted in managing the Malacca Port at some point.[53] Parameswara (1344–c. 1414), a Malay nobleman, established the Malacca Sultanate and founded a port in 1400. He was the first Sultan of Malacca, who later converted to Islam and was renamed Iskandar Shah. In order to avoid petty corruption, he established a hierarchy with four harbour managers representing Gujaratis, Bengalis, Malays and East Asians.[54] The Portuguese and Dutch East India Companies colonised Malacca in 1511 and 1641, respectively. Malacca was given to the British in 1824 through the Anglo-Dutch treaty. However, the Bengali foreign trade had already started sliding during the seventeenth century because of the stringent regulations of the Portuguese and Dutch governors in Malacca and the arrival of British merchants in Bengal.[55] The Nawab's mercantile marine consisted of about twenty ships, which annually sailed to sea from Dacca, Balasore and Pipli, some to Ceylon, and some to Tenessarim during the early seventeenth century.[56] By the late seventeenth century, the number of Bengali ships visiting Southeast Asia was reduced to between six and eight.[57]

With the arrival of the Europeans in the Bay of Bengal region, the Bengalis were introduced to Malaya through various avenues, including slaves and later as imperial subjects. Europeans introduced the Bengali enslaved people to the global slave-trading network. Hall suggested that from 1623, the Dutch frequently visited Chittagong to buy the Bengali enslaved people captured by the marauding Portuguese known as Feringhi.[58] Welif counted that approximately 100,000 enslaved people, and possibly more, were taken by the Dutch from many regions, including the Bengal–Arakan border (Map P.4).[59]

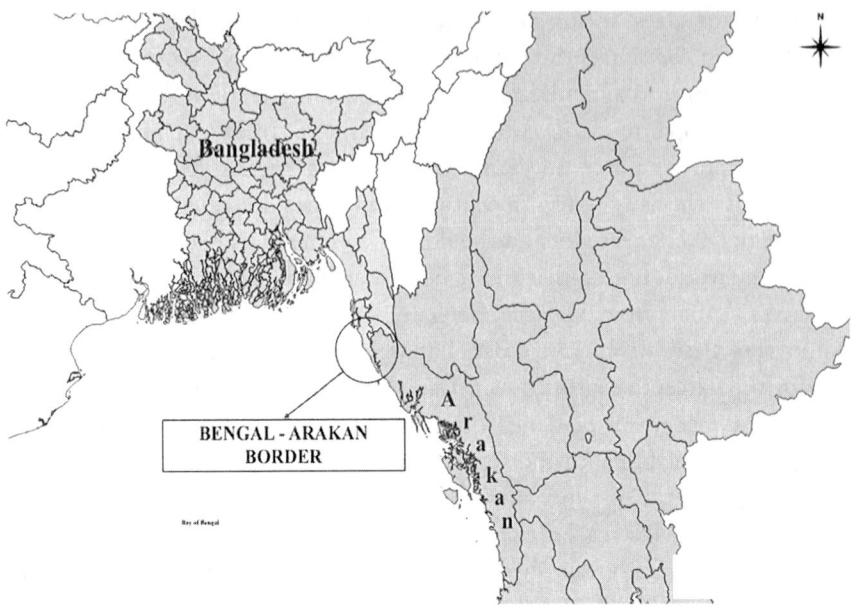

Map P.4 The border of Bengal–Arakan

Source: Adapted by Gazi Mizanur Rahman from Google Maps.

Note: Map not to scale and does not represent authentic international boundaries.

The Dutch employed them as domestic servants or agricultural labourers in their colonies.[60]

With the establishment of the British imperial administration and transregional networks in the 1830s, Bengali mobility into the Malay world took a relatively stable form, and the story of this book starts there.

Thematic Scope and Structure

The diverse and interrelated aspects of Bengali transnational mobility covered by this book are reflected in the following chapters. Chapter 1 illustrates the routes and points of connections between Bengal and the Malay world.[61] The maritime Bay of Bengal and land routes were possible avenues of mutual communication, which became robust between 1830 and 1851. During this period, the Straits Settlements were administrated from Calcutta. In the following years, the Straits Settlements came under the direct control of the Governor-General of India, an arrangement that continued until it became a crown colony in 1867.[62] Moreover, the print media of the Straits Settlements offered 'soft' connectivity by either publishing the news of Bengal or reproducing the reports of Bengal newspapers.

A particular issue that this book has encountered relates to the question of how to identify the Bengali among other South Asian migrants. Colonial records refer to migrants from different parts of South Asia by the generic term 'Indian', 'native of India', 'eastern Indian' and, to some extent, 'aliens' and 'others'. The term 'Bengali' was bundled with the non-Bengalis, for instance, 'Sikh', 'Hindustani' or 'Punjabi'. Such terminological and categorical ambiguities about the Bengalis hinder the remaking of the history of Bengali migration. Through the critical exploration of various sources, Chapter 2 shows that it is possible to map a distinctive demographic, ethnic and cultural profile of the Bengalis within the Indian diasporic space in the Malay world.

The Bengalis provide examples of mobility as convicts, indentured or *kangany* labourers and 'free' migrations under British imperialism. Both colonial governments in Bengal and the Straits Settlements regulated Bengali migrations. Penal migrants or indentured labourers were brought to Malaya, whereas many Bengalis migrated voluntarily in order to pursue better opportunities for commercial purposes as well as in the capacity of government employees. This category of migrants represented 'free' migration. Chapter 3 explores the evolution of the governance of these various categories of Bengali migrants.

British Malaya was rich in tin, rubber, coffee, oil and other minerals, creating job opportunities and drawing a multiracial group of people from neighbouring areas, including China, India and Bengal. During the nineteenth and twentieth centuries, the Bengalis were involved in professional and non-professional jobs. For example, some were engaged as clerks, doctors, lawyers, bankers, shipping managers, architects, accountants, engineers and teachers. The non-professional employees included coolies, artisans, shopkeepers, boatmen, security guards, firefighters, vendors (bread-sellers) and *lascar*s. Chapter 4 draws on scattered statistical data in the census reports describing the world of Bengali professionals.

Bengal was located at the apex of the Bay of Bengal, which is an extended northern arm of the Indian Ocean. It has been an important centre of the Indian Ocean world economy since at least the fifteenth century.[63] Chapter 5 focuses on the British trade of Bengal commodities and the Bengali migrants who conducted business in British Malaya. The spread of British imperialism and capitalism created economic connectivity between South and Southeast Asia. Such connectivity facilitated migrations and market integrations between the two regions. After the settlement of the Bengalis in Malaya, a new wave of Bengali traders and business people emerged. Chapter 5 explores two significant aspects within this broader context: the history of the export and import trade between Bengal and the Malay world; and the emergence of a Bengali trading community that engaged in a range of businesses, including cattle trade, book shops, grocery, boarding business and other hereditary businesses.

In the bulk of migration studies, the quotidian life of migrants during the colonial period is hardly highlighted.[64] To reconstruct the history of Bengali migration, one has to understand how they gained their livelihoods and well-being. The life and times of the Bengali expatriates in the Malay world are full of stories of aspiration and struggle. Even the beginning of the migration process in Bengal and their journeys onboard the ships that bore them generated anecdotes that revealed tears and fears. Chapter 6 mainly examines two areas: migrant experiences before embarkation from Bengal and the life of migrants after arriving in Malaya. Through these experiences, it explores the socio-economic condition of the Bengali migrants.

A sizeable Bengali diaspora started to be visible in the Malay world during the late nineteenth century. It gradually created social and cultural space alongside other migrating communities, such as the Chinese, Tamils and Burmese. Chapter 7 demonstrates the various shapes of the Bengali diasporic space. Regarding political practices, the Bengali transnational community was engaged in the Second World War (WWII) and involved in anti-colonial activities. They shared the same political ground as the Malays. In the post-WWII years, the Bengalis, among other transnational communities, struggled to achieve independence and promote democratic values and constitutional development in Singapore. These developments are discussed in this chapter.

Transnational communities are migrant populations living in a country other than their origin. They are comprised of groups of migrants within host societies who share the same original territorial, religious or linguistic orientations. These migrants have ties to their country of origin by maintaining family, religious, cultural, social and economic links across national borders. Ultimately, the result is that they have multiple identities and links in several cultures. They form associations and are involved in associational activities.[65] Initially, they function narrowly and try to escape unnecessary contact with their host societies.[66] In the specific case of northern Indian labour migrants, Crispin Bates has shed useful light on these issues of identity formation within the temporal contingencies of the British Empire.[67] Chapter 8 of this book maps the historical construction of the civil society space of the Bengali transnational community. The long-term residence of Bengali migrants is often seen as concurrent, creating cultural and ethnic 'enclaves' in their destination countries, especially in the urban areas. These enabled forming their own cultural space to preserve tradition in a 'multicultural' environment. Michael Mann terms this process as the 'formation of their own traditions'.[68] By the turn of the twentieth century, the Bengali diaspora had formed different associations, mostly of social, religious and cultural orientations. The Bengalis were associated with diverse ethnic and racial organisations and were involved in many charitable and humanitarian services. The Bengali transnational community did not confine their activities to the local associations; they established connections and networks beyond the Malay and Bengal worlds.

Through the thematic concentrations of the eight chapters outlined earlier, this book seeks to restore the history of the emergence and growth of the Bengali transnational community in the Malay world. Although the Bengali community formed an essential part of public life in the Malay world, there remains a clear gap in the existing historical scholarship. This book attempts to retrieve a Bengali history of long lineage and outline their contribution to the Malay world's social, economic and cultural arena. I also hope that it will contribute to the growing field of transnational mobility and space-making from the perspective of the Bengali experience and further ameliorate the misconception prevalent in the Malay public space that the Bengalis are a transient migrant labour pool with few roots in the Malay world.

Connected histories and the making of transnational communities are two burgeoning areas in contemporary Asian studies, as the earlier discussion indicates. South Asian transnational communities were introduced into the Malay world in multiple historical phases, yet during the British imperial era, migrations and diasporic experiences were distinctive. Migrants from today's South Asia were grouped together under the umbrella term 'Indian' and deprived of their difference. Despite recent studies on specific South Asian communities and their life-worlds, there is no remarkable literature on Bengali historical migration and diasporic experiences in British Malaya. This book is a humble effort to contribute to the study of Bengali historical mobility and their diaspora in the Malay world and to engage with their multi-layered experience in colonial and early postcolonial time and space.

Notes

1. 'Banalata Sen', a poem written by Jibanananda Das and translated by Sugata Bose. See Sugata Bose, *A Hundred Horizons: The Indian Ocean in the Age of Global Empire* (Cambridge, MA: Harvard University Press, 2009), 16–17.

2. In this book, the Malay world represents the Malay-speaking territories, particularly Malaysia, Singapore and Brunei. Indonesia is not covered in the book. Details on the scope of regional coverage are explained later in this chapter.

3. In the 2010s, the number of Bangladeshi workers was approximately 707,339, 40,000 and 150,000 in Malaysia, Brunei and Singapore, respectively. For details, see *The Telegraph*, 21 July 2013; *Financial Express*, 16 May 2016; Rayhena Sarker, 'Migration and Employment: A Study of Bangladeshi Male Migrant Workers in Malaysia', in *International Migration in Southeast Asia: Continuities and Discontinuities*, ed. Kwen Fee Lian, Md Mizanur Rahman and Yabit bin Alas (Singapore: Springer, 2016), 128.

4. South Asians are the multi-ethnic people of the southern part of Asia. Currently, South Asia consists of eight nation states: Bangladesh, India, Pakistan, Nepal, Bhutan, Sri Lanka, Maldives and Afghanistan. Mainland South Asia, particularly India, Pakistan and Bangladesh, was under the direct rule of the British Raj and lasted from 1858 to 1947. Therefore, when scholars historicise South Asia, they sometimes refer to this area as British India or colonial India.

5. Henri Lefebvre, *The Production of Space*, trans. Donald Nicholson-Smith (Oxford: Basil Blackwell, 1991).

6. Lefebvre, *The Production of Space*, 38–39.

7. For an excellent study on the capitalist construction of space in modern India through the lens of Lefebvre, see Manu Goswami, *Producing India: From Colonial Economy to National Space* (Chicago: University of Chicago Press, 2004).

8. Frances Pine, 'Migration as Hope: Space, Time, and Imagining the Future', *Current Anthropology*, 'Crisis, Value, and Hope: Rethinking the Economy', 55, no. S9 (2014): S1–S154, https://doi.org/10.1086/676526, accessed 12 February 2023.

9. Akira Iriye, *Global and Transnational History: The Past, Present, and Future* (Basingstoke: Palgrave Macmillan, 2013); C. A. Bayly, Sven Beckert, Matthew Connelly, Isabel Hofmeyr, Wendy Kozol and Patricia Seed, 'AHR

Conversation: On Transnational History', *American Historical Review* 111, no. 5 (2006): 1441–1464.

10. Emmanuel Akyeampong, 'Slavery, Indentured Labor, and the Making of a Transnational World', in *A Companion to Diaspora and Transnationalism*, ed. Ato Quayson and Girish Daswani (West Sussex: Blackwell Publishing Ltd, 2013), 163–171.

11. One can be surprised not to see any sources from the West Bengal State Archives or the National Archives of India. I confess that I did not use any records from Indian archives. I do not think I really would have benefitted much from visiting the National Archives in New Delhi as they would merely contain official publications (to which I already have access) and extracts from the 'A' proceedings of the Government of the Straits Settlements on policy issues that concern the Government of India. They would not have provided details beyond what is available in the comprehensively indexed National Archives of Malaysia. I have not explored the Government of West Bengal archives, but I have been informed that they are poorly indexed and contain no specific series relating to emigration from the province. It is not very certain, therefore, that much could have been found that was not available in the Malaysian archives and to which I have referred in the manuscript.

12. Kenneth R. Hall, *A History of Early Southeast Asia: Maritime Trade and Societal Development, 100–1500* (Maryland: Rowman & Littlefield Publishers, 2011); Ranabir Chakravarti, 'Early Medieval Bengal and the Trade in Horses: A Note', *Journal of the Economic and Social History of the Orient* 42, no. 2 (1999): 194–211; Hermann Kulke, 'Rivalry and Competition in the Bay of Bengal in the Eleventh Century and Its Bearing on Indian Ocean Studies', in *Commerce and Culture in the Bay of Bengal*, ed. Om Prakash and Denys Lombard (New Delhi: Manohar, 1999), 17–35; Sanjay Subrahmanyam, 'Persianization and Mercantilism: Two Themes in Bay of Bengal History', in *Commerce and Culture in the Bay of Bengal, 1500–1800*, ed. Om Prakash and Denys Lombard (New Delhi: Monohar, 1999), 47–85.

13. Hugh Tinker, *A New System of Slavery: The Export of Indian Labour Overseas, 1830–1920* (London: Oxford University Press, 1974); Steven Vertovec, 'Indian Indentured Migration to the Caribbean', in *The Cambridge Survey of World Migration*, ed. Robin Cohen (Cambridge: Cambridge University Press, 1995), 57–63; Richard B. Allen, 'Asian Indentured Labor in the 19th and Early 20th Century Colonial Plantation World', *Oxford Research Encyclopedia of Asian History*, 29 March 2017, https://doi.org/10.1093/acrefore/9780190277727.013.33, accessed 14 April 2021; Carl Vadivella

Belle, *Tragic Orphans: Indians in Malaysia* (Singapore: ISEAS, 2015); David Chanderbali, *Indian Indenture in British Malaya: Policy and Practice in the Straits Settlements* (Leeds: Peepal Tree Press, 2008); David Sinjeet Chanderbali, 'Indian Indenture in the Straits Settlements, 1872–1910: Policy and Practice in Province Wellesley' (PhD dissertation, Australian National University, 1983); John Solomon, *A Subaltern History of the Indian Diaspora in Singapore: The Gradual Disappearance of Untouchability 1872–1965* (London; New York: Routledge, 2016).

14. Margaret Shennan, *Out in the Midday Sun: The British in Malaya 1880–1960* (London: John Murray, 2000); K. S. Sandhu, *Indians in Malaya: Some Aspects of Their Immigration and Settlement (1786–1957)* (Cambridge: Cambridge University Press, 1969); Latiffa Khan, 'Indians in Malaya, 1900–1945' (MA dissertation, University of Hong Kong, 1963); S. Nanjundan, *Indians in Malayan Economy* (Delhi: Manager Publications, 1950); Sinnappah Arasaratnam, *Indians in Malaysia and Singapore* (London; Kuala Lumpur: Oxford University Press, 1970); Kernial Singh Sandhu, 'Indian Migration and Population Change in Malaya, c. 100–1957 A.D.: A Historical Geography' (MA dissertation, University of British Columbia, 1961); Amarjit Kaur, *Wage Labour in Southeast Asia since 1840: Globalisation, the International Division of Labour and Labour Transformations* (New York: Palgrave Macmillan Ltd, 2004); Jayati Bhattacharya and Coonoor Kripalani (ed.), *Indian and Chinese Immigrant Communities: Comparative Perspectives* (Singapore: ISEAS-Anthem Press, 2015).

15. Rajesh Rai, *Indians in Singapore, 1819–1945: Diaspora in the Colonial Port City* (Delhi: Oxford University Press India, 2014).

16. Arunima Datta, *Fleeting Agencies: A Social History of Indian Coolie Women in British Malaya*, Global South Asians (Cambridge: Cambridge University Press, 2021).

17. John Solomon, 'Review of *Indians in Singapore, 1819–1945: Diaspora in the Colonial Port City*, by Rajesh Rai', *South Asia: Journal of South Asian Studies* 38, no. 3 (2015): 536–538.

18. Michael Mann, *South Asia's Modern History: Thematic Perspectives* (London: Routledge, 2015), 215.

19. Crispin Bates, 'Some Thoughts on the Representation and Misrepresentation of the Colonial South Asian Labour Diaspora', *South Asian Studies* 33, no. 1 (2017): 7.

20. Dipesh Chakrabarty, 'Postcoloniality and the Artifice of History: Who Speaks for "Indian" Pasts?', *Representations* 37, Special Issue: 'Imperial Fantasies

and Postcolonial Histories' (Winter 1992): 1, 5; Dipesh Chakrabarty, *Provincializing Europe: Postcolonial Thought and Historical Difference* (Princeton: Princeton University Press, 2000), 27.

21. Crispin Bates, 'The State and Subaltern Assertion in the Diaspora: Towards a Pan-South Asian Identity?', in *The Politics of Citizenship, Identity, and the State in South Asia*, ed. Harihar Bhattacharyya, Anja Kluge and Lion König (New Delhi: Samskriti, 2012), 256. See also Neilesh Bose (ed.), *South Asian Migrations in Global History Labor, Law, and Wayward Lives* (New Delhi: Bloomsbury, 2020).

22. Sunil Amrith, *Crossing the Bay of Bengal: The Furies of Nature and the Fortunes of Migrants* (Cambridge: Harvard University Press, 2013).

23. On Sikhs in British Malaya, see Arunajeet Kaur, *Sikhs in the Policing of British Malaya and Straits Settlements (1874–1957)* (Saarbrücken: V. D. M. Verlag Dr Müller, 2009); Gerard McCann, 'Sikhs and the City: Sikh History and Diasporic Practice in Singapore', *Modern Asian Studies* 45, no. 6 (2011): 1465–1498; Isabella Jackson, 'The Raj on Nanjing Road: Sikh Policemen in Treaty-Port Shanghai', *Modern Asian Studies* 46, no. 6 (2012): 1672–1704. Mustafa Izzuddin's forthcoming book is titled *The Dawoodi Bohras of Singapore: Migration, Mercantilism and Culture in the Indian Diaspora* (Singapore: NUS Press, forthcoming).

24. Caroline Adams, *Across Seven Seas and Thirteen Rivers: Life Stories of Pioneer Sylheti Settlers in Britain* (London: Thap, 1987); Claire Alexander, Shahzad Firoz and Naaz Rashid, 'The Bengali Diaspora in Britain: A Review of the Literature' (working paper, Bangla Stories, London, 2010); Katy Gardner, *Global Migrants, Local Lives: Migration and Transformation in Rural Bangladesh* (Oxford: Oxford University Press, 1995); Katy Gardner, *Narrative, Age and Migration: Life History and the Life Course amongst Bengali Elders in London* (Oxford: Berg, 2002); John Eade, 'Bangladeshi Community Organization and Leadership in Tower Hamlets, East London', in *South Asians Overseas: Migration and Ethnicity*, ed. Colin Clarke, Ceri Peach and Steven Vertovec (Cambridge: Cambridge University Press, 1990); Claire Alexander, Joya Chatterji and Annu Jalais, *The Bengal Diaspora: Rethinking Muslim Migration*, Routledge Contemporary South Asia Series (London; New York: Routledge, 2015).

25. Vivek Bald, *Bengali Harlem and the Lost Histories of South Asian America* (Cambridge; Massachusetts; London: Harvard University Press, 2013).

26. Ansu Datta, *From Bengal to the Cape: Bengali Slaves in South Africa from 17th to 19th Century* (Bloomington: Xlibris Corporation, 2013).

27. Titas Chakraborty, 'Work and Society in the East India Company Settlements in Bengal, 1650–1757' (PhD dissertation, University of Pittsburgh, 2016).

28. Samia Khatun, *Australianama: The South Asian Odyssey in Australia* (London: Hurst Publishers, 2018).

29. Devleena Ghosh, 'Under the Radar of Empire: Unregulated Travel in the Indian Ocean', *Journal of Social History* 45, no. 2 (2011): 502, 508.

30. Prabir Ranjan Sengupta explores the history of the Bengali doctors who served in Malaysia and Singapore during most of the twentieth century. Although Sengupta's book is mostly biographical, it narrates the life and time of many Bengali migrating doctors and thus provides valuable insights into the micro-history of migration. However, the indentured and convicted labourers and free migration of different professionals are inadequately described in his book. See P. R. Sengupta, *Malaysia and Bengali Doctors 1907–2012: A Personal Perspective* (Bloomington: Xlibris, 2013).

31. Md Mizanur Rahman, *Bangladeshi Migration to Singapore: A Process-oriented Approach* (Singapore: Springer, 2017); Tasneem Siddiqui, *International Labour Migration and Remittance Management in Bangladesh* (Dhaka: RMMRU, 2009); Md Omar Faruque, *International Instruments and Bangladeshi Migrant Workers' Rights* (Dhaka: RMMRU, 2006); Muinul Islam, 'Bangladeshi Migration: An Impact Study', in *The Cambridge Survey of World Migration*, ed. Robin Cohen (Cambridge: Cambridge University Press, 1995), 360–366.

32. Nayeem Sultana, 'The Bangladeshi Diaspora in Malaysia: Organizational Structure, Survival Strategies and Networks' (PhD dissertation, University of Bonn, 2008).

33. A. K. M. A. Ullah, *Rationalizing Migration Decisions: Labour Migrants in East and Southeast Asia* (London: Ashgate, 2010).

34. Eric Williams, *Capitalism and Slavery* (Chapel Hill: University of North Carolina Press, 1944), 126; David Northrup, *Indentured Labor in the Age of Imperialism 1834–1922*, Studies in Comparative World History (Cambridge: Cambridge University Press, 1995), 17–18, 131; Tinker, *A New System of Slavery*; K. A. Neelakandha Aiyar, *Indian Problems in Malaya: A Brief Survey in Relation to Emigration* (Kuala Lumpur: The India Office, 1938), 7.

35. 'Bengali-speaking South Asian', Joshua Project, https://joshuaproject.net/people_groups/10790/MP, accessed 12 February 2023.

36. 'General Assembly Hears Appeal for Bangla to Be Made an Official UN Language', General Assembly of the UN, New York, 27 September 2010,

https://news.un.org/en/story/2010/09/353662-general-assembly-hears-appeal-bangla-be-made-official-un-language, accessed 20 September 2017.

37. 'Bangladesh Population (2018), Worldometers', http://www.worldometers.info/world-population/bangladesh-population/, accessed 15 January 2018.

38. *Census of India 2011*, 'Distribution of the 22 Scheduled Languages'. http://censusindia.gov.in/Census_Data_2001/Census_Data_Online/Language/Statement3.htm, accessed 15 January 2018.

39. *Engagement of Non-resident Bangladeshis (NRBs) in National Development: Strategies, Challenges and Way Forward* (Dhaka: Economic Relations Division [ERD], Ministry of Finance, Government of Bangladesh, 2018), 9.

40. Lukman Thaib and Bharuddin Che Pa, 'Regional Cooperation: Malay World and the Formation of ASEAN Community', *Global Journal of Human Social Science* 13, no. 2 (2013): 9–10.

41. Nicholas Tarling, *Piracy and Politics in the Malay World* (Nendeln/Liechtenstein: KRAUS Reprint, 1978), 2.

42. For the definition of the Malay world from different perspectives, see Ooi Keat Gin, *Historical Dictionary of Malaysia* (Maryland; Toronto; Plymouth: The Scarecrow Press, Inc., 2009), 181; D. S. Farrer, *Shadows of the Prophet: Martial Arts and Sufi Mysticism* (Singapore: Springer, 2009), 26; Anthony Milner, *The Malays* (West Sussex: Wiley- Blackwell, 2008), 2, 5.

43. Chai Hon Chan, *The Development of British Malaya 1896–1909* (Kuala Lumpur; New York: Oxford University Press, 1964).

44. R. C. Majumder, *Ancient Indian Colonies in the Far East, Vol. 2, Suvarnadvipa, Part 1* (Dacca: Asoke Kumar Majumdar, 1937), 385, 397–398; P. C. Chakravarti, 'Economic Conditions', in *The History of Bengal, Vol. 1, Hindu Period*, ed. R. C. Majumder (Dacca: University of Dacca, 1943), 660–662; Adhir Chakrabarty, 'Bangla o Bahirbissho: Prag Uponibesik Kal' [Bengal and Overseas: Pre-colonial Era]', in *Itihas Onusshandhan No. 4*, ed. Gautam Chottopadhay (Calcutta: K. P. Bagchi and Co., 1989), 52, 55; Ashin Das Gupta, *Vanghap Sagar* [The Bay of Bengal] (Calcutta: Pritikxan Publication, 1989), 13, 20, 22; D. G. E. Hall, *A History of South East Asia*, 4th ed. (Hampshire; London: McMillan Education Ltd, 1981), 13.

45. David O. Morgan and Anthony Reid, *The Eastern Islamic World Eleventh to Eighteenth Centuries* (Cambridge: Cambridge University Press, 2010), 398–401; R. C. Majumder, 'The Palas', in *The History of Bengal. Vol. 1, Hindu Period*, ed. R. C. Majumder (Dacca: University of Dacca, 1943), 121–122; R. C. Majumder and D. C. Ganguly, 'Bengalis outside Bengal', in *The History*

of Bengal, Vol. 1, Hindu Period, ed. R. C. Majumder (Dacca: University of Dacca, 1943), 670–688.

46. Michael Pearson, *The Indian Ocean* (London; New York: Routledge, 2003), 94; Dirk Hoerder, 'Crossing the Waters: Historic Developments and Periodizations before the 1830s', in *Connecting Seas and Connected Ocean Rims: Indian, Atlantic, and Pacific Oceans and China Seas Migrations from the 1830s to the 1930s*, ed. Donna R. Gabaccia and Dirk Hoerder (Leiden; Boston: Brill, 2011), 20.

47. Richard Winstedt, *Malaya and Its History* (London: Hutchinson House, 1951), 20; M. R. Fernando, 'Continuity and Change in Maritime Trade in the Straits of Melaka in the Seventeenth and Eighteenth Centuries', in *Trade, Circulation, and Flow in the Indian Ocean World*, ed. Michael Pearson (Hampshire; New York: Palgrave Macmillan, 2015), 114.

48. Kernial Sing Sandhu, 'Indian Settlements in Melaka', in *Melaka: The Transformation of a Malay Capital c. 1400–1980, Vol. 2*, ed. Kernial Sing Sandhu and Paul Wheatley (Kuala Lumpur; Oxford; New York: Oxford University Press, 1983), 179.

49. Leonard Andaya, 'Massoi and Kain Timur in the Birdshead Peninsula of New Guinea, the Easternmost Corner of the Indian Ocean World', in *Trade, Circulation, and Flow in the Indian Ocean World*, ed. Michael Pearson (Hampshire; New York: Palgrave Macmillan, 2015), 98.

50. Armando Cortesao (trans. and ed.), *The Suma Oriental of the Tome Pires: An Account of the East, from the Red Sea to Japan, Written in Malacca, and India in 1512–1515*, vol. 1 (London: The Hakluyt Society, 1944), 88, 93.

51. Morgan and Reid, *The Eastern Islamic World*, 389, 398–399; C. M. Turnbull, *A Short History of Malaysia, Singapore and Brunei* (Singapore: Graham Brash, 1981), 20; Anthony Reid, *Southeast Asia in the Age of Commerce 1450–1680, Vol. 2, Expansion and Crisis* (New Haven; London: Yale University Press, 1993), 93.

52. Anil Das, 'Bengali Kobi o Bideshi Parjatok der Dristy te Bengalir Banijjo' [Bengali Trade through the Lens of Bengali Poets and Foreign Travellers], in *Itihas Onusshandhan No. 4*, ed. Gautam Chottopadhay (Calcutta: K. P. Bagchi and Co., 1989), 108–114.

53. Ingelise Lamont Lanman, 'The Fabric of Malay Nationalism on the Malay Peninsula: 1920–1940' (PhD dissertation, University of California, Los Angeles, 1988); Mariam Pirbhai, 'The Multiple Voices of Indenture History: The South Asian Diasporic Novel in English' (PhD dissertation, Universite de Montreal, 2003).

54. Michael G. Vann, 'When the World Came to Southeast Asia: Malacca and the Global Economy', *News Letter, Association for Asian Studies* 19, no. 2 (2014): 22; Victor Lieberman, *Strange Parallels: Southeast Asia in Global Context, c. 800–1830, Vol. 2, Mainland Mirrors: Europe, Japan, China, South Asia, and the Islands* (Cambridge: Cambridge University Press, 2009), 805.

55. Balthasar Bort, *Report of Governor Balthasar Bort on Malacca 1678*, trans. (from the Dutch) M. J. Bremner with an introduction and notes by C. O. Blagden, *Journal of the Malayan Branch of the Royal Asiatic Society* 5, no. 1 (1927): 109–157; Romesh Dutt, *The Economic History of India: Under Early British Rule (From the Rise of the British Power in 1757 to the Accession of Queen Victoria in 1837), Vol. 1* (Trench, Trubner: Kegan Paul, 1902), 39; W. W. Hunter, *A Statistical Account of Bengal*, Vol. 5 (London: Trubner and Co., 1875), 124.

56. Radhakumud Mookerji, *Indian Shipping: A History of the Sea-borne Trade and Maritime Activity of the Indians from the Earliest Times* (Calcutta; London; New York: Longmans, Green and Co., 1912), 234; Frank Swettenham, *British Malaya: An Account of the Origin and Progress of British Influence in Malaya* (London; New York: John Lane Company, 1907), 29; for pre-modern Bengali maritime trade, see Sanjay Subrahmanyam, 'Notes on the Sixteenth Century Bengal Trade', *Indian Economic Social History Review* 24, no. 3 (1987): 265–289; Richard M. Eaton, *The Rise of Islam and the Bengal Frontier, 1204–1760* (Los Angeles: University of California Press, 1993).

57. Fernando, 'Continuity and Change in Maritime Trade', 126; Morgan and Reid, *The Eastern Islamic World*, 468.

58. Hall, *A History of South East Asia*, 417.

59. Rik Van Welif, 'Slave Trading and Slavery in the Dutch Colonial Empire: A Global Comparison', *NWIG: New West Indian Guide/Nieuwe West-Indische Gids* 82, nos. 1/2 (2008): 72.

60. Richard M. Eaton, introduction to *Slavery and South Asian History*, ed. Indrani Chatterjee and Richard M. Eaton (Indiana: Indiana University Press, 2006), 12.

61. Mookerji, *Indian Shipping*, 149.

62. Habibul Haque Khondker, 'Bengali-Speaking Families in Singapore: Home, Nation and the World', *International Migration* 46, no. 4 (2008): 182.

63. Rila Mukherjee, *Strange Riches: Bengal in the Mercantile Map of South Asia* (New Delhi: Foundation Books, 2006).

64. Most migration studies ignore the quotidian life of migrants during the colonial period. Several works have been cited in the literature review part to

support this claim. Therefore, those discussions have not been repeated here, referring to those earlier discussions.

65. R. Kastoriano, 'Immigration, Transnational Communities and Citizenships', *Journal Revue Internationale des Sciences Sociales* 165 (2000): 353; P. Levitt, 'Migrants Participate across Borders: Towards an Understanding of Forms and Consequences', in *Immigration Research for a New Century*, ed. N. Foner and R. G. Rumbaut (New York: Russell Sage Foundation, 2000), 461.

66. H. Van Amersfoort and J. Doomernik, 'Emergent Diaspora or Immigrant Communities? Turkish Immigrants in the Netherlands', in *Communities across Borders: New Immigrants and Transnational Cultures*, ed. P Kennedy and V. Roudometof (London: Routledge, 2002), 56.

67. See, for example, Crispin Bates, 'Introduction: Community and Identity among South Asians in Diaspora', in *Community, Empire and Migration: South Asians in Diaspora*, ed. Crispin Bates (New York: Palgrave Publishers Ltd, 2001), 1–45.

68. Mann, *South Asia's Modern History*, 214.

1

Contexts, Routes and Nodal Points

The two worlds of Bengal and Malaya were connected through language, religion, maritime trade and colonial administration. In addition to being a trade route, the Bay of Bengal carried flows of migrants, information, ideas, cultural practices, pilgrims and soldiers over the centuries. However, this tie between the two worlds became more direct and extensive as British bureaucratic control spread over the Malay Peninsula from Calcutta, creating opportunities in various capacities for the Bengalis. By exploring the cultural contexts of migration, and the routes and nodal points of bonding with the Malay world, this chapter examines the administrative web that cemented existing flows of people, commodities and cultural practices from Bengal.

Linguistic and Cultural Links

The linguistic connection between Bengal and Malaya dates back to the early Christian era. In the Malay Archipelago and mainland Southeast Asia, Austroasiatic languages are widely spoken, which are also used throughout some parts of India, Bangladesh, Nepal and the southern borders of China.[1] Hindu and Buddhist preachers from the Indian subcontinent, including Bengal, spread their beliefs in Southeast Asia in Sanskrit and Pali, leading to Indian linguistic influences in the region.[2] The influence of Bangla, in particular, can be seen through the use of a pre-Nāgarī script.[3] Srivijaya, a Buddhist thalassocratic empire based on the island of Sumatra, also had religious, cultural and trade links with the Buddhist Pala dynasty of Bengal.

The Malay language has borrowed many Sanskrit words.[4] The Bangla script and the Sanskrit language are found in the *Sejarah Melayu*[5] (Figure 1.1).

* অহো শূগুত পাহ্কা ভীমহারাত্রভীমত ভীদুভ
দ্রঘর্ণভূমি ভত্রপান বিক্রমাহ্ঙ্কনঙ্কু কর্ম্মুক্রা
রণমুথ থ্রিভবনস্পর্শশমিত্র বিহাতঙ্কু ধর্ম্মারথ
ভেশীকৃত সিংহাসন রনবিক্রম বাণরানত পনা
য়িত্রবনাথিক সদ্যার্দ্ধ হৃদয় দেবহৃদয় পরোদয়
কান মোনিমানমাণিকু র্দীর্ধর্ম্মরাত্রধিবাত্র পর
মেশ্বরী যাবত্রুবি°৷

* অহো দ্বস্তি পাহ্কা ব্রীমহারাত্রকা স্বরাহ্ গ্রা
সুগুত্রুন্ব অনাহ্ রণভূমিত্রবন বিক্রম্যা নংক্রনা
মুকুটরত্রু হথপিভবহ স্পর্শকৃথ্ৈ ৷   বিনাতঙ্কু°
ধর্ম্মবাহ্ যত্র সরন বিত্রন সিংহাসনবনবিক্রম্যা
বনার্ণবিনাবিক সদ্যানুদেববিহ্৷   পরবাদি
কান মুনমুনীমানিক ভীধর্ম্মরাত্রাত্রধিরাচ্ রাচ্পর
মেথরহ্৷

Figure 1.1   Bangla letters in *Sejarah Melayu*

Source: John Leyden (trans.), *Malay Annals* (London: Longman, Hust, Rees, Orme, and Brown, 1821), 24, 100.

Lanman suggests that Sanskrit influenced not only the Malay vocabulary but also ideas.[6] About 45 per cent of the total Bangla lexicon is composed of naturally modified Sanskrit words and corrupted forms of Sanskrit.[7] Similarly, there are many Sanskrit loanwords in the *Bahasa Melayu*.[8] Although Bangla belongs to the Indo-European languages family, while Malay belongs to the Malayo-Polynesian/Austronesian family, many common Sanskrit loanwords can be found in classic Malay and Bangla. Both languages have borrowed a good number of standard Arabic and Persian words (Tables 1.1 and 1.2).

One of the earliest references to Bengal in Malay texts is in Raja Culan's *Misa Melayu* (The Mass of Malay), dating back to the second half of the eighteenth century. It mentions that a British captain had come from Bengal. In *Hikayat Palembang* (The Tales of Palembang), the author wrote that 'raja Menggala' or 'jenderal Menggala' ordered the British troops to attack Palembang.[9] Bengal was variously termed as Benggala, Benggali, Menggala and Menggalah in Malay traditional texts. During the early nineteenth century, a Malay named Boreham[10] wrote a poem titled 'Syair Kisahnya Orang Wolenter Benggali' (Poem of the Bengali volunteers) narrating the events of New Year's Day, 1819. Syeikh Abdullah's *Cerita Siam* discussed British delegations from Bengal to Siam. The anonymous author of 'Syair Perang Inggeris di Betawi' (English war poems in Betawi) references Lord Minto and Bengal. As he informed *seri paduka raja* (his highness the king), *lor* Minto *yang maharajalela* (Lord Minto, the most powerful ruler) was *raja* Menggalah (the king of Bengal), and, in 1815, he noted that the British power was centred in Bengal. In his *Hikayat*, Munshi Abdullah described that Raffles came to Malaya from Bengal. Tuan Simi wrote a poem of thirty-eight verses, 'Syair potong gaji' (The poem of cuts in wages), in Singapore in the 1830s, which revealed that the rule of the Bengal government caused hardship for the workers.[11]

Table 1.1 List of some common Sanskrit loanwords in Malay and Bangla

Sanskrit Words	Usage in Malay	Usage in Bangla	Meaning in English
raja	*raja*	*raja*	king
rani	*rani*	*rani*	queen
sakti	*sakti*	*sakti*	power
sama	*sama*	*saman*	same/equal
samudra	*samudra*	*samudra*	ocean
koti	*kati*	*koti*	10 million
bhāṣā	*bahasa*	*bhasha*	language
bāhu	*bahu*	*bahu*	arm
topi	*topi*	*topi*	hat
duhkha	*duka*	*duhkha*	sorrow, sadness
dūta	*duta*	*duta*	envoy
dvi	*dwi*	*dvi*	two
dvi-bhāṣā	*dwibahasa*	*dvi-bhasha*	bilingual

Source: http://veda.wikidot.com/malay-words-sanskrit-origin, accessed 25 June 2019; *Bangla Academy Bayaboharik Bangla Abhidhan* [Bangla Academy Practical Bangla Language Dictionary] (Dhaka: Bangla Academy, 2015).

Table 1.2 List of some common Arabic loanwords in Malay and Bangla

Arabic Words	Usage in Malay	Usage in Bangla	Meaning in English
bāqī	*baki*	*baki*	remainder, leftover
dunyā/dünya	*dunia*	*dunia*	world
fitnah	*fitnah*	*fitnah*	slander
ḥalāl	*halal*	*halal*	permitted
ḥarām	*haram*	*haram*	forbidden
ḥisāb	*hisab*	*hisab*	counting/arithmetic
jawāb	*jawab*	*jawab*	to answer
qurbān	*korban*	*qurbani*	sacrifice
muʿāf	*maaf*	*maaf*	sorry
masjid	*masjid*	*masjid*	mosque
miskīn	*miskin*	*miskin*	poor
tārīkh	*tarikh*	*tarikh*	date
waqt	*waktu*	*waqt*	time

Source: Russell Jones (ed.), *Loan-Words In Indonesian and Malay* (Central Jakarta: Yayasan Pustaka Obor Indonesia, 2008); *Bangla Academy Bayaboharik Bangla Abhidhan* (Dhaka: Bangla Academy, 2015).

Ibrahim Kandu and Ahmad Rijaluddin visited Calcutta from Penang in the late 1810s. Both wrote about Bengal in the traditional Malay language and remarked on the profound mutual influence between Malaya and Bengal. Kandu was associated with translating the *Sejarah Melayu*. Rijaluddin wrote *Hikayat Perintah Negeri Benggala* (History of the Order of the State of Bengal) and was employed as a translator for European merchants, in particular, the Scott family of Penang.[12] Kandu described the governor's house, the atmosphere of his meeting, the British people and their customs in Bengal.[13] He wrote:

Such! Proud Bengala's King and court
Where chiefs and champions brave resort,
With ladies happy, gay, and free,
As fishes in Bengala's sea![14]

Kandu had a great travel experience in Bengal and held it in high esteem, noting, 'I must describe what I have seen, that Malays may no longer be ignorant of this great country, but be acquainted with all its wonders and all its beauties, so that their heart may be glad, and they may no longer be ignorant!'[15] He further stated, 'I write this history, that men [Malay] may not be ignorant of Bengal, and of the manners and customs of the Great Rajah of the English; and it is written at [*sic*] Bengal'.[16] Rijaluddin's book also discussed his experiences in Calcutta and its adjoining areas, including Barrackpore, Hugli, Chandannagar and Chinsurah. He wrote: '[M]y story is of a country to the north ... a country of great size called Bengal ... ' During the voyage of Ahmed Rijaluddin and Ibrahim Kandu, Bengal's fame had 'spread to the east and to the west, as far as Constantinople, Egypt, China, Mecca and Medinah'.[17]

Beyond the literary representations of mutual respect, Bengal and the Malay Peninsula share diverse economic, social and cultural traits. Both have tropical climates (Bengal being more humid), rice and fish are the staple food, betel-nut and betel-leaf chewing is common, and the *lungi* (sarong) is the main dress for men. There are also similarities in the way many tropical products, such as bamboo, are used.[18] A British civilian, who travelled from Bengal to Malaya, found the climate in the Straits Settlements suitable for those who had resided for a number of years in the damp environment of Bengal. Postcolonial Malaysia remains a paradise for food lovers, with a variety of cuisines and cooking styles[19] shaped by a multi-ethnic food culture during the colonial period. In the early twentieth century, Bengali food and dishes were well-known in Malaya. For example, M. A. Majid opened a *makan* house for Bengali *lascar*s and seamen at 94 Collyer Quay in Singapore, and Ramnath Biswas had dinner at a Sundarban Bengkalis house in Malacca, where he was served food and dishes that tasted like those of eastern Bengal cuisine. Anthony Kim had Bengali food at a nursing hostel on Young Road while he was working as a clerk at the British Military Headquarters in Kuala Lumpur.[20] When Bengali cuisine was cooked for commercial purposes, it was fused with Malay and other Indian cuisines in order to attract multi-ethnic consumers. When it came to the question of Bengali migration to Malaya, these cultural contexts provided considerable evidence. During the postcolonial period, the popularity of Bengali cuisines among other ethnic communities shows its boundary-crossing appetising aroma, but the sites of Bengali restaurants do reflect areas of ethnic 'enclaves' of Bengali migrants during the colonial period.

Maritime Connectivity

The eastward maritime highway of the Bay of Bengal stretched from Calcutta to the Burma ports of the Irrawaddy Delta, Thai ports on the isthmus of the Malay Peninsula, and the western shore of Sumatra.[21] It not only formed a maritime highway but also connected the emporia, polities and cultural networks of South and Southeast Asia, prompting Sunil Gupta to term it the 'Bay of Bengal Interaction Sphere'.[22] The history of transregional connectivity across the northern Bay of Bengal before European colonialism has been explored by Rila Mukherjee. She shows how the Bay of Bengal facilitated commodity and currency flows, the sharing of ideas and culture, and interactive networks between South and Southeast Asia before colonialism.[23] She further explores how the Portuguese made contact and trade during the sixteenth and seventeenth centuries from Sandwip (an island of Bangladesh) in the Bay of Bengal to Malacca and Macau of the Malay Sea.[24] Majumder and Ganguly have suggested that the Bengalis crossed the Bay of Bengal and promoted remarkable cultural associations for nearly 1,500 years between the diverse civilisations of Eastern and Southeastern Asia.[25]

Things began to change slowly with the arrival of the Europeans.[26] European merchant companies clashed over control of its ports, erected lighthouses and introduced different rules and regulations for crossing the bay. Although from the late sixteenth century, the Portuguese established control over the Bay of Bengal and the Malay Sea,[27] the arrival and growing dominance of the British in the region in the late eighteenth century left some visible political and economic marks. Warships of the British government frequently travelled from Calcutta to Singapore, Malacca, Penang and Hong Kong.[28] The logbook documenting the arrival and departure of British ships indicates that ships voyaged from Bengal, Bombay and Madras to China, Penang, Malacca and Borneo.[29] Rijaluddin depicted a panorama of the Calcutta port life in the era of sailing, writing: '[S]hips visit the capital without a break, there is no let-up day or night, thousands of ships arrive and depart and from the west to the east, from the north-west to the southeast.' The port streets were always noisy with 'sounds like the roaring of thunder'. The crowd consisted of different races, including Bengali, English, Portuguese, Dutch, Burmese, Chinese, Tamil and Malay.[30] Sailors from around the world enjoyed their leisure time at the Calcutta port. Most attractive was the 'winding lane near the shipyards' where 'the whores live, thousands of them Pathans, Indians, Mughals, and Bengalis'. Their customers were equally multiracial: English, Portuguese, French, Dutch, Chinese, Bengali, Burmese, Tamil and Malay.[31]

The British government regulated the routes and steamships and promulgated rules for passengers and freights. In 1837, the colonial administration proposed steamer services between Calcutta, the Straits Settlements, Java and China. The proposal recommended the purchase of a steamship suitable for carrying passengers and commodities. The service was expected to anchor at Penang and Malacca ports for a few hours and take upto ten days to journey from Calcutta to Singapore. After that, the ship would have five days to anchor in Singapore before making the return voyage to Calcutta, the round trip taking no more than a month.[32] According to the *Bengal Almanac*, ships needed twenty days on average to reach Malacca from Bengal.[33]

The British India Steam Navigation Co. conducted monthly and bimonthly steam services from and to Bengal, Burma and British Malaya ports. In 1863, monthly steam services were recorded from Calcutta to Rangoon, Moulmein (presently Mawlamyine), Penang, Malacca and Singapore, and bimonthly from Calcutta to Chittagong, Akyab, Rangoon and Moulmein.[34] The Bengal Marine department had five sea-going steamers in the 1870s. In contrast, it had about fifty-one water vehicles, namely pilot brigs, lightships, buoy vessels and river-going steamers,[35] perhaps for internal transportation.

In addition to Calcutta, Chittagong was a vital port facilitating human mobility and foreign trade. Until the eighteenth century, it remained the chief port of the northern bay and played a significant role in Indian Ocean trade.

However, it was superseded by the rise of Calcutta as the new capital of British India.[36] After constructing the Eastern Bengal Railway Company (EBR, 1857), Chittagong Port regained its importance. In 1873, the Conservator of Chittagong Port suggested that primary considerations should be care, safety, comfort and the general well-being of passengers on board a ship or steamer. He recommended that the sea-going vessels should be stronger and more powerful to survive a cyclone or strong seasonal wind. He added that during the southwest monsoon season, the vessels should not allow more than half a dozen deck passengers.[37] In the early twentieth century, the Chittagong Port was favoured as the terminus of the Assam–Bengal railway. It became the chief port of the new province of Eastern Bengal and Assam, although only briefly from 1905 to 1912. It was convenient for sea-going ships to reach the port through the Karnaphuli river. The sea-borne exports consisted chiefly of jute, tea, raw cotton and rice.[38]

When the steamer service began, the Bengal government had no specific rules for the passages. In 1828, the Governor-General of Bengal and the Marine Board implemented some rules and regulations related to *lascar*s, passengers, masters, officers and owners of ships, which came into effect at Bengal Presidency, Bombay, Malacca, Singapore and all other British ports.[39] These regulations recommended the appointment of an expert surgeon on board during the entire voyage. It also emphasised securing sufficient food, water, medical and surgical aids, medicine, clothes, bedding and proper accommodations for all sailors, *lascar*s and passengers. The owner of the ship would provide all facilities.[40] In 1833, passengers were asked to fill up an embarkation form, which would be submitted to the commander of the ship.[41] After assuming direct control of India in 1858, the British administration introduced Act XXV of 1859 to prevent overcrowding in vessels during the voyage.[42] This was modified in 1884, advising that steamships should not carry more than twelve commuter passengers between British India and other places unless the ship had a certificate of inspection. In contravention of this section, the owner and master of the steamship were subject to a fine of up to 1,000 rupees.[43]

The colonial administration erected many lighthouses from the southern limit of the Bay of Bengal to the Straits ports for convenience of navigation. As a result, the ships' captains could easily navigate the sea for 15–20 miles. Two new lighthouses were built on the Great Savage Rock at the entrance of the Arakan River and Cochin in 1844.[44] Another lighthouse was constructed at Kutubdia in 1846. In 1880, a further lighthouse was built on Pulau

Undan, on the summit of the island at Malacca.[45] Looking at the extent of government machinery and logistical support concerning maritime traffic, it may be suggested that the Bay of Bengal was high on the imperial agenda of connectivity between Bengal and Malaya.

Inland Connectivity

The EIC allowed only voyages across the Bay of Bengal during the fair-weather conditions. Therefore no wonder the then EIC looked for an alternate route for transportation during the monsoon season with its turbulent winds and storms. The location of Bengal at the eastern frontier of the subcontinent left it with a narrow land bridge with mainland Southeast Asia. Therefore, Bengal was considered a transit zone between the two regions, and attention was given to inland connectivity between Bengal and the Malay Peninsula.[46]

The British government considered that the rivers might be a means of communication between Bengal, Southeast Asia and southern China because the rivers and the sea formed unities between these regions while land formed the link between the bodies of water.[47] Though the Himalayas made barriers to access the territories of Assam, northern Burma, Yunnan and mainland Southeast Asia, there were many points of access via rivers and tributaries. The Tibetan-Himalayan rivers, including the Brahmaputra and Irrawaddy, played a crucial role in economic and transport links across southwestern China, Myanmar, Bengal and northeastern India. These regions are connected with the northern parts of mainland Southeast Asia. In these transitional spaces, Ludden shows how the people of the Brahmaputra-Meghan river basin made inland commercial connections over mountains into Burma and China at the end of the eighteenth century. This route is called the Southwestern Silk Road.[48] Three significant rivers, namely the lower Irrawaddy, Chao Phraya and the Mekong, crossed over mainland Southeast Asia.[49] The British surveyors and explorers experimented for decades to make connections between the Brahmaputra and Irrawaddy rivers in the province of Yunnan.[50] Major rivers of South and Southeast Asia linked the historic Sea Silk Route. These river networks have made the Bay of Bengal and the South China Sea 'visible participants' in the Indian Ocean's global space and formed part of the River Silk Route. Map 1.1 shows the Tibetan–Himalayan river basins. Dick and Rimmer have examined the economic and political development of the lower river valleys of the Irrawaddy, Chao Phraya and the Mekong since the 1850s by focusing on the changing nature of transport and

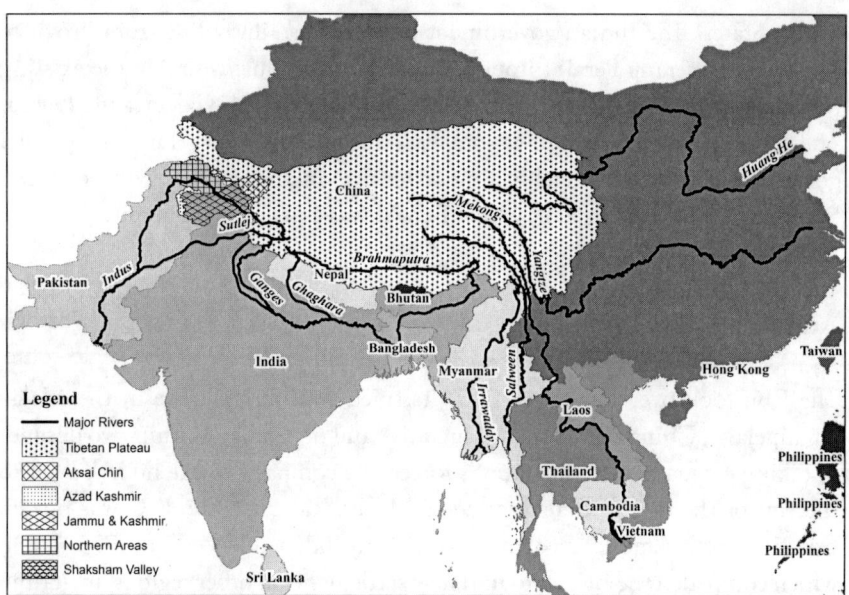

Map 1.1 Himalayan plateau and river basins

Source: Adapted by Gazi Mizanur Rahman from Google Maps.

Note: Map not to scale and does not represent authentic international boundaries.

communications patterns.[51] Clearly, a remarkable spell of ethnic mobility, trade and commercial activities took place in these river valleys.

In the context of pre-existing nodes and nodal points along land routes, the colonial administration often thought of establishing rail communication between Calcutta and southwestern China via Dacca and parts of the Malay Peninsula. In the 1870s, the Chittagong–Mandalay route was considered the 'shortest and [most] direct' for a possible connection between Bengal and China. In 1899, the Associated Chambers of Commerce recommended that Chittagong should be connected with Calcutta in the west and the Mandalay–Rangoon Railway in the east. Consequently, the British Indian government agreed to make several lines from Burma to China on behalf of the Consul-General in Yunnan by 1904. The Burmese government constructed a metallic road from Bhamo to Kulikha, and this road extended through the gorge of Taiping on the left bank of the Irrawaddy River opposite Manwaing.[52] In 1903, a meter gauge line was opened from Bangkok to Ban Pong, and the last stoppage was at Phetchaburi. Its purpose was to reach the border of British Burma and make an intersection with the railway system of the Federated

Malay States. The Indian government projected a railway line from Province Wellesley (Seberang Perai) through lower Siam and Burma to join the existing Mandalay and Pegu (Bago) railway and ultimately reach Calcutta via Dacca. They intended to connect Singapore with this railway line.[53] Thus, the colonial government proposed establishing extensive inland connectivity between South and Southeast Asia, in which Bengal was a major nodal point.

Administrative Linkages

The EIC took over Bengal in 1757. Its spice and opium trade in the Malay Archipelago, China and India was lucrative and profitable. Within two decades of taking over, a few considerations forced the company to extend its power to the rim of the Bay of Bengal and the Malay Sea. First, the EIC was ousted from its North American colonies (American Independence War, 1775–1783), which compelled the British to find new settlements in other regions, including Southeast Asia. Secondly, by 1771, Aceh was replaced by Kedah, one of the most important ports at the northern ends of the Malacca Strait; therefore, the EIC contemplated extending their opium and Coromandel cloth trade there. Third, the EIC needed to secure its trade and maritime highway from pirates and other European competitors in the Bay of Bengal and the South China Sea. Purchasing Penang Island from the Sultan of Kedah in 1786 reflected the EIC's security concern.[54] The island became a penal station not long after it was occupied.

From 1786 onwards, the Governor-General of Bengal presided over affairs in the Malay settlements. The Governor-General of Bengal assigned a resident to administer Penang until 1805. To fortify India's trade with China, the Governor-General of Bengal, Lord Minto (1803–1813), appointed Sir Stamford Raffles as the agent in the Malay states in 1810. Raffles launched an expedition against Java in 1811. During the Napoleonic wars (1803–1815), the EIC sought to consolidate its power in the entire Malay Peninsula. On behalf of the Governor-General of Bengal, Marquess of Hastings (1813–1823), Raffles and the *temenggung* (chief of public security) installed Husain Shah from Riau as sultan in Singapore in 1819, which was then a part of the Kingdom of Johor. Raffles built a British factory on the island on payment of 5,000 dollars per annum to Sultan Husain Shah.[55] From its founding until 1823, Singapore was a dependency of Bencoolen. From 1823 until the formation of the Straits Settlements, it was under the direct control of the Governor-General in India.

In 1824, the EIC permanently occupied Malacca from the Dutch in exchange for Bencoolen. In 1826, Penang, Malacca and Singapore formed the Colony of the Straits Settlements, and the subsequent endeavour was to obtain supremacy over the rest of the Malay Peninsula.[56]

The headquarters of the Straits Settlements remained in Penang. The EIC maintained its status as a 'fourth' presidency along with Bencoolen until 1830.[57] However, the status of 'presidency' was soon dropped, and it became a residency under the control of the Governor and Council of Bengal. When the income and expenditure of the Straits Settlements increased, its administration developed a sense of autonomy. Following Lord Dalhousie's (the Governor-General of India, 1848–1856) visit in 1850, the Straits Settlements were put under the direct authority of the Governor-General of India, with the power previously exercised by the Bengal Presidency being vested in the Governor of the Straits Settlements. However, as company rule ended in British India, the India Office replaced the authority of the Governor-General in India. The Act of 1866 put Singapore under the British government as a Crown Colony, effective from 1867. Though Singapore became a Crown Colony, the tie with British India and Bengal remained firm, underpinned by colonial trading networks and the mobility of workers towards Malaya.

During the period of direct governmental linkage, connectivity between Bengal and Malaya was organic. The Bengal government developed the Singapore port city and granted funds for education and public health.[58] In 1843, the Government of Bengal granted 5,000 dollars for establishing the Pauper Hospital in Singapore. In the same year, the Bengal government proposed to impose a tax to support people with low incomes and to contain public begging.[59] The colonial government in the Straits Settlements sometimes followed the policies of the Bengal government to run their administration. For instance, it was suggested that, like the Bengal government, the Penang administration should impose a monthly tax for cleaning roads during the northeast monsoon.[60] The Government of Bengal appointed administrators to the Straits Settlements as well as hired some expert officials from Bengal.[61] In 1837, an engineer, A. D. Radclyffe, was sent to deepen the harbours and waterways as well as to improve the condition of underwater mining of Singapore marina. Act XVI of 1839 was enacted to regulate the assessment and collection of the rents payable to the governments of Penang Island, Singapore and Malacca and for the foundation of a proper Survey Department.[62] Act III of 1847 authorised the appointment of constables and peace officers in the Straits Settlements, took away the power from the court and bestowed it on the Governors of Bengal and the Straits Settlements.[63] A prominent Bengali businessman, Annukul Chander, was made the first Bengali peace officer. Chander Road was named after him in Singapore.[64] Coleman designed the first church for Singapore, which was completed in 1837. The first chaplain, Reverend Edmund White, was appointed from Bengal.[65]

During the administration period from Bengal, some English-educated subordinate officers and clerical staff from Bengal were brought to develop and run the new administration in British Malaya. The practice continued until the Malay and Chinese could build their capacities. The British missionary introduced English education in Bengal earlier than the Straits Settlements. These missionary schools and the EIC government facilitated the creation of a clerical class in British India. The EIC initially brought clerical staff from British India until the local people could support the British administration on a large scale. This class of Bengali people was known as 'Baboo' or 'Babu'.[66] In his recollection, Mohinder Singh noted that most of the clerical staff working for the government were Bengalis.[67] 'Baboo Lane' in Singapore (Little India) took its name after them. It is assumed that due to the many Bengali clerical staff, the Straits Settlements government prioritised the Bangla language in the public sector. For instance, their recruitment advertisements asked for Bangla-speaking people in British Malaya. The Oriental Bank of Singapore also initiated issuing paper currency in Bangla.

British officials and administrators employed Bengali men and women as domestic servants in British Malaya as they did in Bengal.[68] Moreover, British Malaya was a penal colony for Indian convicts until 1873; therefore, the colonial authorities transported convict labourers from Bengal to Malaya and Singapore. They constructed many government buildings, churches and roads. Furthermore, an unidentified number of Bengalis migrated from Burma to Malacca and Singapore.[69] During the early twentieth century, many Bengali professionals, including doctors, came to British Malaya to meet demands in the medical sector—a topic which will be discussed in detail in Chapter 4.

Connectivity through the Press and Media

The printing press provided a new dimension of connectivity across the British Empire, allowing news and information to be extensively exchanged between Bengal and British Malaya. The Postage Act of 1840 extended newspaper circulation from one colony to another.[70] Public or private vessels transported letters and papers to the colonies. The British steamer *Lightning* brought the *Bengal Hurkaru*,[71] and the *Free Press* reproduced extracts of news from Bengal.[72]

As demonstrated in the printing press, Bengali Anglophones and urban elites evidently knew about the Malay nation during the early nineteenth century. For example, Raffles wrote about the Malay race and their culture in the *Journal of the Asiatic Society of Bengal* in 1809,[73] and after publishing *Abdullah's Story* (*Hikayat Abdullah*), the colonial government purchased twelve copies immediately and sent half of them to Bengal.[74] Meanwhile, the anti-British movement and revolutionary activities in Bengal became features in Malaya's newspapers.[75] The Straits Settlements' newspapers not only published the news of Bengal but also promoted the commercial products and academic institutions of Calcutta. For instance, an institution named the Montague Academy, located at Dharmatollah in Calcutta, advertised for boys and girls in Singapore to teach Greek, Latin, French, Urdu, English, Bangla, Mathematics, Railway and Revenue surveying.[76]

In 1872, the telegraph connected Bengal and the Straits Settlements, facilitating the almost instant news transition. Therefore, when Calcutta Radio started broadcasting, the daily programming schedule was reproduced in Malay newspapers. For instance, in 1936, the daily programme of Calcutta Radio was circulated in the Straits Settlements papers for the 'Malayan Listeners' Radio'. News bulletins, local news, Bengali folk music, commercial news, weather forecasting and the market price of Jute and Gunny cloths— all were produced in Bangla.[77] Such endeavours promoted goods and supplied information for Bengali communities as well as other expatriates from India.[78]

Conclusion

This chapter has outlined the historical connections between Bengal and the Malay world. The extensive use of Sanskrit and common loanwords in Malay and Bangla is a significant example of existing links between the two regions. With the consolidation of the British Empire, maritime highways, inland connections and authoritative linkage between the two places played a pivotal role in bringing them closer, which facilitated migration and space-making. By the late eighteenth century, the Bengal Presidency became the most crucial outpost in the British Empire in Asia. In addition, several states in the Malay Archipelago, including Penang, Malacca, Bencoolen, Amboina and Ternate, were subject to the Bengal government. This transregional administrative connectivity provided fertile ground for the mobility of people, culture, ideas and products from Bengal. In short, pre-modern cultural and commercial ties and spatial proximity between Bengal and Malaya provided a perfect context for the British colonial administration to forge deeper links between the two regions. Frustratingly, however, the stories of Bengali mobility in Malaya have remained mostly absent in historical studies, and the categorial ambiguity of 'Indians' frequently hides the Bengalis. The following chapter will explore these issues.

Notes

1. Hall, *A History of South East Asia*, 7.
2. G. Coedes, *The Indianized States of South-East Asia*, ed. W. F. Vella and trans. Susan Brown Cowing (Honolulu: University of Hawaii Press, 1968), 15, 14–65.
3. Coedes, *Indianized States of South-East Asia*, 30–31.
4. For a list of Malay words derived from Sanskrit, see http://veda.wikidot.com/malay-words-sanskrit-origin, accessed 25 June 2019.
5. *Sejarah Melayu* (the Malay Annals), an essential literary historical source about Malacca and the Malay world, was written sometime in the fifteenth or sixteenth century. It is a collection of stories focusing on the activities of the Malaccan Sultans, their courts, government officials and Malacca's foreign relations. It was edited by Abdullah bin Abdul Kadir Munshi (1797–1854) and published in the 1840s.
6. Lanman, 'The Fabric of Malay Nationalism'.
7. See https://www.britannica.com/topic/Bengali-language, accessed 25 June 2019.
8. The Malay language is spoken predominantly in the Malay world.
9. Benjamin Murtagh, 'The Portrayal of the British in Traditional Malay Literature' (PhD dissertation, University of London, 2005).
10. Benjamin Murtagh identified Boreham as Ibrahim.
11. Murtagh, 'The Portrayal of the British in Traditional Malay Literature'.
12. Rijaluddin wrote the book in 1811, and Ibrahim wrote his travel accounts in 1810. For details about them and their writings, see Maria Graham, *Journal of a Residence in India* (Edinburgh: George Ramsey & Co., 1813), 138–139, 201–207; C. Skinner, 'The Author of the Hikayat Perintah Negeri Benggala', *Bijdragen tot de Taal-, Land- en Volkenkunde* 132, nos. 2/3 (1976): 202; C. Skinner (trans. and ed.), *Ahmad Rijaluddin's Hikayat Perintah Negeri*

Benggala [A Narrative of the State of Bengal], Koninklijk Instituutvoor Taal-, Land- enVolkenkunde [Royal Netherlands Institute of Southeast Asian and Caribbean Studies] (The Hague: Martinus Nijhoff, 1982), 8, 27; Claudine Salmon, 'Bengal as Reflected in Two South-East Asian Travelogues from the Early Nineteenth Century', in *Commerce and Culture in the Bay of Bengal, 1500–1800*, ed. Om Prakash and Denys Lombard (New Delhi: Manohar, 1999), 383–402; P. Thankappan Nair (ed.), *Calcutta in the Nineteenth Century: Company's Days* (Calcutta: Firma K. L. M. Private Limited, n.d.), 101–107.

13. His travel account titled 'An Account of Bengal, and of a Visit to the Government House, by Ibrahim, the Son of Candu the Merchant' was compiled in Graham's *Journal of a Residence in India*, 201–207.

14. Graham, *Journal of a Residence in India*, 201–207.

15. Graham, *Journal of a Residence in India*, 201.

16. Graham, *Journal of a Residence in India*, 207.

17. Skinner, *Ahmad Rijaluddin's Hikayat*, 21.

18. A. M. Chowdury, 'Bengal and Southeast Asia: Trade and Cultural Contacts in Ancient Period', Paper presented at the conference for the the Integral Study of the Silk Roads: Roads of Dialogue, Bangkok, Thailand, 21–22 January 1991.

19. Gin, *Historical Dictionary of Malaysia*, 98.

20. National Archives of Singapore, Oral History Interview (hereinafter NAS, OHI), Anthony Kim Siong Bong, 18 February 1993, Acc. No. 001398.

21. David Joel Steinberg (ed.), *In Search of Southeast Asia: A Modern History* (Singapore; Hong Kong; Oxford; New York: Oxford University Press, 1985), 56; Sunil Gupta, 'The Bay of Bengal Interaction Sphere (1000 BC–AD 500)', *Bulletin of the Indo-Pacific Prehistory Association* 25, *The Taipei Papers (series 3), Proceedings of the 17th Congress of the Indo-Pacific Prehistory Association Taipei, Taiwan, 9 to 15 September 2002* (2005): 21.

22. Gupta, 'The Bay of Bengal Interaction Sphere (1000 BC–AD 500)'.

23. Rila Mukherjee (ed.), *Pelagic Passageways: The Northern Bay of Bengal before Colonialism* (Delhi: Primus Books, 2011); Rila Mukherjee, 'Ambivalent Engagements: The Bay of Bengal in the Indian Ocean World', *International Journal of Maritime History* 29, no. 1 (2017): 96–110.

24. Rila Mukherjee, 'The Struggle for the Bay: The Life and Times of Sandwip, an Almost Unknown Portuguese Port in the Bay of Bengal in the Sixteenth and Seventeenth Centuries', *Revista da Faculdade de Letras: Historia* 9 (2008): 67–88.

25. Majumder and Ganguly, 'Bengalis outside Bengal', 670–671; Majumder, *Ancient Indian Colonies in the Far East*, 82–83; Chowdury, 'Bengal and Southeast Asia'.

26. The term 'Europeans' refers to the imperial powers, trading companies (namely the British East India Company, the Dutch East India Company, the Portuguese East India Company and the French East India Company) and merchants of the sixteenth- and seventeenth-century Europe who established colonies across the world, particularly in South and Southeast Asia.

27. Om Prakash, *European Commercial Enterprise in Pre-colonial India* (Cambridge: Cambridge University Press, 1998), 58.

28. *Singapore Free Press and Mercantile Advertiser* (hereinafter *SFPMA*), 4 September 1856, 2.

29. *Singapore Chronicle and Commercial Register* (hereinafter *SCCR*), 20 January 1831, 3.

30. Skinner, *Ahmad Rijaluddin's Hikayat*, 75.

31. Skinner, *Ahmad Rijaluddin's Hikayat*, 131.

32. *SFPMA*, 30 November 1837, 2.

33. Samuel Smith and Co., *The Bengal Almanac for 1845 with a Companion and Appendix* (Calcutta: Bengal-Hurkaru and Chronicle Press, 1845), xlv.

34. Animesh Ray, *Maritime India: Ports and Shipping* (New Delhi: Munshiram Manoharlal Publishers Pvt. Ltd, 1993), 50.

35. *Report on the Administration of Bengal 1873–74* (Calcutta: Bengal Secretariat Press, 1875), 90; E. A. Gait, *Report on the Census of Bengal, 1901: Chapter I of Administrative Volume with Census Code* (Calcutta: Bengal Secretariat Press, 1902), xxxi.

36. Samuel Berthet, 'Boat Technology and Culture in Chittagong', *International Water History Association* 7, no. 2 (2015): 179–197, DOI: 10.1007/s12685-015-0133-y.

37. National Archives of Bangladesh (hereinafter NAB), Conservator of Chittagong Port to the Commissioner of the Chittagong Division, 25 September 1873, Proceedings of Governor of Bengal in Council, December 1873, General Department, Branch- Miscellaneous, 205.

38. Berthet, 'Boat Technology and Culture in Chittagong'.

39. Smith, *The Bengal Almanac for 1845*, 275–276.

40. Smith, *The Bengal Almanac for 1845*, 268–274.

41. Smith, *The Bengal Almanac for 1845*, 291.

42. *General Report on the Administration of the Several Presidencies and Provinces of British India During the Year 1859–60*, vol. 1 (Calcutta: Bengal Printing Company Limited, 1861), 9.

43. *The Indian Steam-Ships Act, 1884, as Modified up to the 1st July 1890, Office of the Superintendent* (Calcutta: Government Printing, 1890), 4–5.

44. Smith, *The Bengal Almanac for 1845*, 282–284.

45. *Straits Times Overland Journal* (hereinafter *STOJ*), 7 July 1881, 4.

46. *SCCR*, 3 September 1836; for a note on precolonial land connectivity between Bengal and mainland Southeast Asia, see Majumder and Ganguly, 'Bengalis outside Bengal', 670; overland connectivity between Bengal, mainland Southeast Asia and South China was familiar since the second century BCE, which was explored by many scholars, for instance, Chakravarti, 'Economic Conditions', 660–662; Chakrabarty, 'Bangla o Bahirbissho', 53–54; Hall, *A History of South East Asia*, 11; Chowdury, 'Bengal and Southeast Asia'; Sing Chew, 'The Southeast Asian Connection in the First Eurasian World Economy, 200 BCE–CE 500', in *Trade, Circulation, and Flow in the Indian Ocean World*, ed. Michael Pearson (Hampshire; New York: Palgrave Macmillan, 2015), 34.

47. Sunil Amrith, 'Islam in the Bay of Bengal: Between Tamil and Malay Worlds', public lecture, Tufts University, 14 November 2011, https://corpora.tufts.edu/catalog/tufts:MS165.002.001.00006?transcript, accessed 14 October 2017.

48. David Ludden, 'Cowry Country: Mobile Space and Imperial Territory', in *Asia Inside Out: Itinerant People*, ed. Eric Tagliacozzo, Helen F. Siu and Peter C. Perdue (Cambridge, MA: Harvard University Press, 2019), 75–100.

49. Iftekhar Iqbal, 'Reclaiming the Crossroads between India and China: A View from the River', *Economic and Political Weekly* 49, no. 51 (2014): 23; Howard Dick and Peter J. Rimmer, *Cities, Transport and Communications: The Integration of Southeast Asia since 1850* (New York: Palgrave Macmillan, 2003), 155.

50. Iftekhar Iqbal, 'The Space between Nation and Empire: The Making and Unmaking of Eastern Bengal and Assam Province, 1905–1911', *Journal of Asian Studies*, 74, no. 1 (2015): 71–73.

51. Dick and Rimmer, *Cities, Transport and Communications*, 155.

52. Iqbal, 'The Space between Nation and Empire', 74.

53. *Straits Times* (hereinafter *ST*), 3 May 1906.

54. *SFPMA*, 18 June 1857, 3; *New Nation* (hereinafter *NN*), 26 October 1972, 11; Horace St John, *The Indian Archipelago: Its History and Present State*, vol. 2 (London: Longman, 1853), 31–32; Asad-ul Iqbal Latif, *India in the Making of Singapore* (Singapore: Singapore Indian Association, 2008), 2; Malcolm M. Murfett et al., *Between Two Oceans: A Military History of Singapore from 1275 to 1971* (Singapore: Marshall Cavendish Editions, 2011), 36; Sandhu, 'Indian Settlements in Melaka', 194; Khoo Salma Nasution, *The Chulia in Penang:*

Patronage and Place-Making around the Kapitan Kling Mosque 1786–1957 (Penang: Areca Books, 2014), 39.

55. Virginia Matheson Hooker, *A Short History of Malaysia: Linking East and West* (Crows Nest, NSW: Allen & Unwin, 2003), 105.

56. Swettenham, *British Malaya*, 1–2; Charles Burton Buckley, *An Anecdotal History of Old Times in Singapore* (Kuala Lumpur: University of Malaya Press, 1965), 110; Gin, *Historical Dictionary of Malaysia*, 301; Walter Makepeace, Gilbert E. Brooke and Roland St J. Braddell (ed.), *One Hundred Years of Singapore: Being Some Account of the Capital of the Straits Settlements from Its Foundation by Sir Stamford Raffles on the 6th February 1819 to the 6th February 1919*, vol. 1 (London: John Murray, 1921), 20.

57. The other presidencies were Madras, Bengal and Bombay. In 1832, in recognition of the growing importance of Singapore, the Headquarters of the Straits Settlements was transferred there.

58. Colonel Butterworth, Governor of Prince Wales Island, Singapore and Malacca, wrote a letter to A. Turnbull, Under Secretary to the Government of Bengal, for granting some donations. See *SFPMA*, 8 February 1844, 5.

59. *SFPMA*, 8 February 1844, 5.

60. In February 1810, the editor of the *Prince of Wales Island Government Gazette* suggested following the policy of the Bengal government. Skinner, *Ahmad Rijaluddin's Hikayat*, 168.

61. *SFPMA*, 12 July 1838, 2.

62. Arnold Wright (ed.), *Twentieth Century Impressions of British Malaya: Its History, People, Commerce, Industries, and Resources* (London: Lloyd's Greater Britain Publishing Company Ltd, 1908), 318.

63. *SFPMA*, 4 September 1856, 2; *The Regulations and Laws Enacted by the Governor-General in Council, for the Civil Government of the Whole of the Territories under the Presidency of Fort William in Bengal*, vol. 7 (Calcutta: Baptist Mission Press, 1828).

64. Tommy Thong B. Koh, Timothy Auger, Jimmy Yap and Wei Chian Ng (ed.), *Singapore: The Encyclopedia* (Singapore: Didier Millet, 2006), 60.

65. J. F. A. McNair and W. D. Bayliss, *Prisoners Their Own Warders: A Record of the Convicts Prison at Singapore in the Straits Settlements Established 1825, Discontinued 1873, Together with a Cursory History of the Convict Establishments at Bencoolen, Penang, and Malacca from the Year 1797* (Westminster: Archibald Constable and Co., 1899), 45.

66. In Bangla, 'Baboo' is used as a suffix to a person's name to show respect while calling him by name. In addition, it was a title for Bengalis in the nineteenth

and twentieth centuries who obtained an English education and retained a close relationship with the colonial power. For a description of Bengali Baboos in Malaya, see Sengupta, *Malaysia and Bengali Doctors*, 33.

67. NAS, OHI, Mohinder Singh, 24 Jun 1985, Acc. No. 000546. He defined 'Baboo' as a clerk. Whosoever was doing a clerical job was known as 'Babu'.

68. Koh et al., *Singapore*, 248.

69. Sengupta, *Malaysia and Bengali Doctors*, 33.

70. Smith, *The Bengal Almanac for 1845*, 119.

71. *SFPMA*, 4 September 1856, 2.

72. *SFPMA*, 30 November 1837.

73. Anthony Reid, *Imperial Alchemy: Nationalism and Political Identity in Southeast Asia* (Cambridge: Cambridge University Press, 2010), 92.

74. Hooker, *A Short History of Malaysia*, 98.

75. *Straits Times Weekly Issue* (hereinafter *STWI*), 31 May 1883; *SFPMA*, 29 January 1930.

76. *ST*, 5 August 1856.

77. *Malaya Tribune* (hereinafter *MaT*), 29 February 1936; *ST*, 20 May 1936; *ST*, 12 May 1940; *ST*, 2 December 1936; *ST*, 15 December 1937; *ST*, 30 September 1936; *ST*, 15 October 1936; *SFPMA*, 5 January 1939.

78. Nalina Gopal, 'A Sea of Change, an Ocean of Memories: Migration and Identity', in *Singapore Indian Heritage*, ed. Rajesh Rai and A. Mani (Singapore: Indian Heritage Centre, 2017), 159.

2

The Bengali

Terminological Ambiguity and Demographic Profile

The terminological ambiguities surrounding Bengali hinder the reconstruction of Bengali migration and diaspora history in Southeast Asia. Colonial records commonly refer to migrants from different parts of South Asia using the generic terms 'Indian', 'native of India', 'eastern Indian' and the even less descriptive 'aliens' and 'others'. Existing secondary literature on South Asian historical migration uses the umbrella term 'Indian' continuously. Therefore, the specific category of Bengali often remains undefined and unclear. To add to the confusion, many non-Bengalis, who travelled from Calcutta to the Malaya ports, introduced themselves as Bengali. For retrieving a specific migrating community, it is essential to navigate such ambiguities. Bengali ethnic identity became distinct to the public in the early twentieth century. This chapter introduces alternative ways of restoring the diasporic identity and demographic profile of Bengalis in the Malay world.[1]

Rescuing the Bengali from the Indian

The term 'Indian' has been used in the colonial and postcolonial records of Malaysia, Singapore and Brunei to denote all people coming from what is today's South Asia because the region was under the jurisdiction of British India.[2] In the 1901 Census of India, Risley and Gait noted that the people of British India were catalogued under the head of Indian in the reports.[3] Crispin Bates has described some of the many ways in which the indentured labour migration across the Indian Ocean has been represented and misrepresented in the colonial records and how this has subsequently misinformed South Asian historiography.[4] The Registrar General of Statistics categorised the population as Indian in the Straits Settlements, the Federated Malay States and the Unfederated Malay States.[5] Reports under the Brunei government registered all South Asians as Indian.[6] Bengalis were also sometimes known as 'East Indians'. For instance, in a police report produced by the Commissioner of Police of the Prince of Wales Island in 1859, the whole population of Penang was segregated into Europeans and descendants, East Indians, Malays, Chinese and Indians proper.[7] Davis suggested that there was no sure way to figure out the exact number of 'East Indian' migrants from India,[8] and indeed, it remains problematic. In British Malaya, the people from India were undisputedly hugely diverse in region, religion, culture, language and ethnicity, a picture hidden by the attribution of umbrella terms to all South Asian migrants.

In the reports of the Straits Settlements, the Bengali was categorised under a few different heads, including 'Bengali and Other Natives of India', 'Other Natives of India' and 'Tamils and Other Natives of India'. By analysing the censuses of the Straits Settlements, the Federated Malay States and Malaysia published from 1871 to 1980, Charles Hirshman compiled all ethnic classifications in a table.[9] Initially, the Bengalis were counted under the heading of 'Bengalis and Other Natives of India'; however, the system of enumeration was changed to the 'Tamils and Other Natives of India' in 1891 because of the increase in the number of Tamil labourers arriving in Malaya. Map 2.1 illustrates the routes of Bengali migration to the Malay world.

Map 2.1   The routes of Bengali migration towards the Malay sea

Source: Adapted by Gazi Mizanur Rahman from Google Maps.

A huge number of 'Indian aliens' worked in Johor and Kedah.[10] Neelakandha noted that one-third of the labourers in rubber estates owned by the Europeans were Indian aliens.[11] Many immigrants in Brunei from different regions, including India, required registration on arrival and departure, and notification for changing of residence.[12] Some of them were registered as 'aliens' in census reports without specifying the region from which they had migrated (Figure 2.1). Brunei State Annual Reports estimated that 1,133 and 1,535 aliens were registered in 1923 and 1924, respectively.[13] This statistical 'other' was problematic because it was a reflection of the exclusion and marginalisation of a specific group of people—something very pronounced in the colonial Malay world.[14] The categorisation of the migrants as 'Indian aliens', 'aliens' and 'others' in the reports has made it difficult to estimate the exact number of Bengali migrants.

Colonisers identified and separated races and decided how different races would be categorised. In doing so, they decided who belonged to the register book and who did not. Though such categorisation led to the visibility of the dominant ethnic groups in governance protocol, it could not erase the history of diverse ethnic mobility. The government's policy did not exclude race or

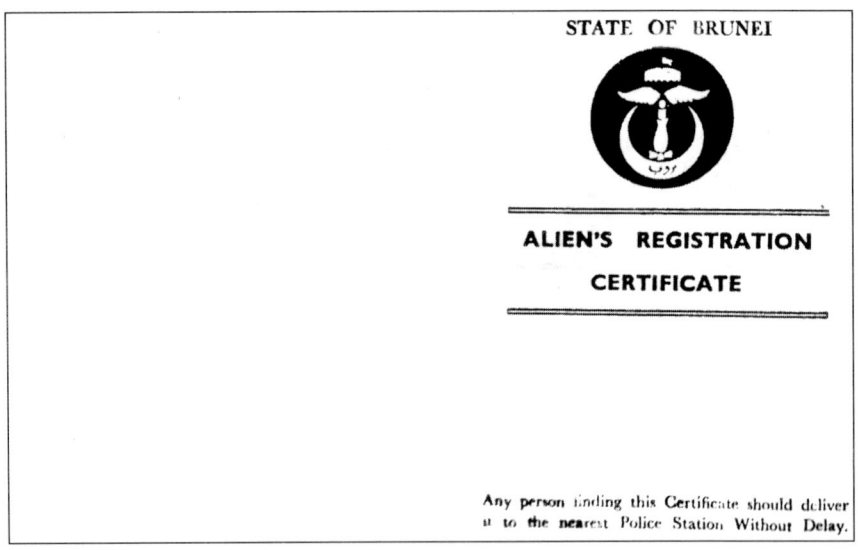

Figure 2.1   Cover page of the alien's registration certificate, Brunei

Source: Immigration and National Registration Department, Bandar Seri Begawan, Brunei Darussalam.

ethnicity in the early censuses. During the early colonial era, the government enumerated people based on regions such as Bengal and Hindustan. For example, the Singapore government showed the number of people from 1824 to 1836 from different regions of South Asia, including Bengal and Hindustan. However, during the late nineteenth century, the government began enumeration based on race, ethnicity and language. Charles Hirschman suggested that the word 'race' first appeared in the 1891 census, in an appendix containing instructions for the enumerators.[15] Therefore, the government was unaware of ethnic or racial identity initially. Even the government did not implement different rules or procedures for calculating convict and non-convict populations but was not unaware of them.

The colonial racial categorisation was powerful, but it had weaknesses. The perseverance of racial or ethnic exclusionary politics in the postcolonial nation state requires a historical perspective beyond focusing on the colonial state alone. Colonial administrators-cum-scholars hardly registered the dynamics of the creole and hybrid communities in their vision. Nation-bound thinking continues to exercise a strong influence in academic works and dominates journalism and popular perceptions in the countries of the Malay Peninsula.

Upon arrival in the Malay world, on many occasions, non-Bengali people—including Gujaratis, Pathans, Punjabis and Sikhs from different parts of India—either introduced themselves as Bengali or port clerks registered the new arrivals under such a generalisation.[16] This was because, as Metcalf argues, the people of northern India used to come to the Malay port cities via Calcutta.[17] The north Indians identified themselves as Bengali to non-Indian enumerators simply because they commonly understood this term.[18] Although such instances of generalisation were a known fact, they continued to persist for a considerable time.[19] Again, the task of locating Bengali migrants is complicated but not impossible.

Dealing with the Ambiguities

Despite the terminological ambiguities mentioned earlier, locating Bengalis within the South Asian diasporic community is still feasible. Bengalis were purportedly better positioned among other Indian ethnic groups to migrate to the Malay world, relatively speaking, making their presence inevitable. Re-reading population census reports, statistics of birthplace, language, and reviewing the historical information are viable ways of dealing with the ambiguities in the colonial records.

Re-reading Censuses and the Statistics of Birthplace

The most extensive inter-provincial mobility of the Bengalis was towards Burma, chiefly to Arakan State. More than two-thirds of the emigrants from Bengal, especially Chittagong, were immigrants to Akyab who travelled there during rice harvesting. However, many permanently settled on the wasteland in Upper Burma.[20] There were four categories of land in Burma: royal land, official land, wasteland and private land. Owing to the low demographic density in Upper Burma, particularly in Mandalay, Shan State, Kachin, Pegu and Hanthawady Basin, the Land and Agriculture Committee facilitated the settlement of cultivators in the wasteland.[21] Bengali seasonal migrants seized the opportunity to change their fortunes. Some Bengalis even went to Kachin State with British officials during the Burma–China Boundary Treaty in 1894 and settled there by marriage.[22]

The statistics regarding the birthplace of migrants could provide numerical information about Bengali migrants.[23] Lewis suggests that almost 77,771 and 79,263 individuals were recorded in Burma as having their birthplace in Bengal and Chittagong, respectively, in 1901.[24] The 1931 Indian census reported that some 257 persons of every 10,000 people spoke Bangla in Burma.[25] It is assumed that some of the Bengali people in Burma migrated further east to the Malay Peninsula by using Thailand as a corridor or overland via the Burma–Malaysia border.[26]

Colonial authorities mentioned in census reports that the birthplace of the Bengalis was in 'Adjacent Countries', 'Asiatic Countries', 'Asian Countries' and 'Outside India'. Adjacent Countries include the Straits Settlements, Malaya and present South Asian countries.[27] Asiatic or Asian Countries meant the territories of Asia, including the Straits Settlements, Borneo, China, Hong Kong, Java, Sumatra, the Philippines and Japan.[28] Outside India denotes Asian and European countries, including 'farther India' (Map 2.2), which supposedly covered Southeast Asia, including Burma, Malaya, Thailand and Indo-China.[29]

The sporadic references to the birthplaces of the Bengalis illustrate that their parent's mobility was spread across Asian territories, including British Malaya (Table 2.1). As per the census of 1911, the total population of Bengal and its princely states was 46,305,642.[30] Out of this number, about 117,374

Map 2.2   Farther India or adjacent countries

Source: J. G. Bartholomew, *Constable's Hand Atlas of India* (Westminster: Archibald Constable & Company, 1893), plate 58.

Table 2.1   The number of Bengalis as per birthplace

| Year of the Reports | Birthplaces of Bengalis | | | |
	Outside India	Adjacent Countries	Asiatic Countries	Asian Countries
1891	194,155	Not available		
1901	186,468	169,081	3,228	Not available
1911	Not available			117,374

Source: Risley and Gait, *Census of India, 1901, Vol. 1, Part 1*, 102–103; *Census of the British Empire 1901* (London: Darling & Sons, 1906), 106–107; Gait, *Census of India 1911, Vol. 1, India, Part II, Tables*, 134.

Notes: Birthplace is not the same as 'place of origin'. Some archival records mentioned 'place of origin', which cannot always be translated or assumed as the birthplace. I collected information from the archival records very cautiously; for example, 'where born' was written in the *Census of the British Empire 1901*, 'province or state in which born' was written in the *Census of India, 1901, Vol. I, India, Part I* and 'birthplace' was written in the *Census of India 1911, Vol. 1, India, Part II, Tables*. All these three sources referred to the birthplace instead of the 'place of origin'.

individuals from Bengal were shown to be born in 'Asiatic Countries', which definitely included Southeast Asia.[31]

As with the census reports of the Bengal government, the census reports of the Straits Settlements reveal that the birthplace of some Indians was outside of the Straits Settlements, but others were recorded in Singapore, Malacca and Penang. For example, as per the census report of 1911, the number of Indians born outside of the Straits Settlements was 21,840 in Singapore, 6,606 in Malacca, and 35,945 in Penang. In Singapore, the Indian residents who were born in Bengal and Madras represented 9.21 and 86.52 per cent of total Indian residents. About 2.14 per cent and 95.30 per cent of Indian migrants who were counted in Malacca were born in Bengal and Madras. The birthplace of Indian migrants who were enumerated in Penang, but born in Bengal and Madras, represented 3.18 per cent and 91.64 per cent of total Indian migrants. The report clearly shows that the second-highest number of Indians were recorded as born in Bengal, the highest concentration being born in Madras. The remaining number of Indian migrants who were registered in Singapore, Malacca and Penang were recorded as being born in Punjab, Central Province, Bombay, United Provinces, Burma and unspecified areas.[32] Most of the official figures covered only the British Indian ports of Bombay, Madras, Karachi and Calcutta, but this does not mean that all migrants sailed from those respective ports to the Malay world.[33] They could have migrated overland or disembarked from unregulated government ports.[34]

Revisiting Some Historical Literature

A reassessment of some historical interpretations reveals an alternative way of uncovering the specific identity and experiences of the Bengali migrants. As Blagden suggested, Chersonesus Aurea or the Malay Peninsula was primarily populated by the Siamese, Peguans (probably Mon ethnicity from Burma), Bengalis and fishers from neighbouring islands, who went there by boats when the Straits of Malacca had good weather.[35] When the Portuguese launched an expedition (1509) to Malacca, the local Malays considered them 'white Bengalis' or 'white-skinned Bengalis',[36] which denotes that the local Malay people were familiar with the Bengalis well before the arrival of the Europeans.

By the early sixteenth century, Malacca had around 40,000 of a polyglot population, of whom 1,000 were wealthy Gujaratis and 3,000 were other Indian merchants, including Parsees, Bengalis, Tamils and Malayalees.[37] With the British expansion into Bengal and Southeast Asia in the late eighteenth century, different individuals hailing from Bengal could be found in George Town in Penang and mentioned their occupations as traders, tailors, gunsmiths, woodmen, fishermen and *munshi*s (religious teachers).[38] In 1786,

Francis Light brought along some Bengali farmers from Calcutta to encourage agricultural enterprise in Penang.[39]

From 1830 to 1851, Malacca, Penang and Singapore were administered from Calcutta.[40] This administrative connectivity created opportunities for the Bengalis to be mobile in the Straits Settlements. Moreover, colonial authorities brought Bengali convicts to the Straits Settlements for public works.[41]

Some colonial records mentioned the Bengali population in the Straits Settlements without references to any specific number. For instance, a report of 1810 revealed that the number of Chulias and Bengalis was 5,604 in George Town.[42] In 1872, Charles Irving, the Straits Auditor-General, found a busy wood and *attap* (traditional housing found in the *kampong*s of Brunei, Indonesia, Malaysia and Singapore) township of about 3,000 people of many races, including Bengalis.[43]

The recruitment of Bangla-speaking employees at the Singapore Port Office indicates the constant flow of Bengali business people and commodities.[44] The Oriental Bank of Singapore took the first-ever initiative to issue paper currency in four local languages—Chinese, Malay, Bangla and Tamil—in 1849, in the denomination of 5 and 100 dollars (Figure 2.2).[45] However, further information regarding the issuing of paper currency cannot be tracked.

The demand for the Bangla language in public and academic institutions denotes the existence of a significant number of Bengali migrants. For example, the members of the school managing committee showed interest in establishing a Bengali school alongside other local language schools when Lord Bishop of

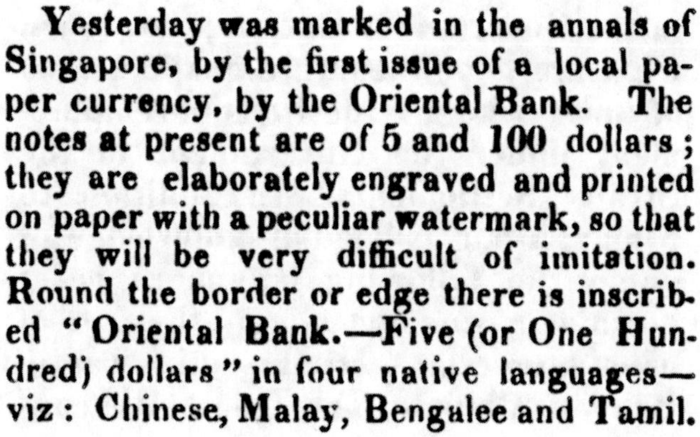

> **Yesterday was marked in the annals of Singapore, by the first issue of a local paper currency, by the Oriental Bank. The notes at present are of 5 and 100 dollars; they are elaborately engraved and printed on paper with a peculiar watermark, so that they will be very difficult of imitation. Round the border or edge there is inscribed "Oriental Bank.—Five (or One Hundred) dollars" in four native languages—viz: Chinese, Malay, Bengalee and Tamil.**

Figure 2.2 A news report on the Oriental Bank

Source: Singapore Free Press and Mercantile Advertiser, 10 May 1849, 2.

Calcutta Daniel Wilson (1778–1858) visited churches and newly established missionary schools in Malacca. Even St Anthony's Boys' School (presently St Anthony's Primary School, Singapore) advertised for the recruitment of teachers with linguistic skills, including the knowledge of Bangla.[46]

In public recruitment during the early stage of British colonial rule, after the Malay and Chinese languages,[47] South Asian languages, particularly Bangla, were given priority. In 1859, the government advised that the aspirants for some government jobs in the Straits Settlements should have proper colloquial knowledge of Hindustani, Tamil, Bengali and Chinese (Figure 2.3). Those languages had been set as the sine qua non.[48] However, when the number of Tamil labourers increased from the 1880s, their language was given preference among South Asian languages.[49]

Apart from this evidence, other government records show the significance of Bengali interpreters. In 1894, Kuala Lumpur Court asked for an interpreter who could read and write Bangla and English.[50] In 1895, the Federated Malay States, in particular, the Selangor Police, asked for a Bengali interpreter.[51] The demand for Bengali interpreters was extensive during the early twentieth century across the Unfederated Malay States, and chiefly at Kedah.[52]

In 1911, the Federated Malay States and Singapore categorised Indians by race and dialect. Nineteen Indian languages, including Tamil, Bangla,

QUALIFICATIONS FOR GOVERNMENT● APPOINTMENTS.—From a Notification in the Government Gazette, we earn what are to be the future qualifications of those who are desirous of employment, under the Government of the Straits Settlements. In addition to Malay, a fair colloquial knowledge of one of the following languages is set down as a *sine qua non* on the part of candidates viz.,—Hindustani. Tamil, Bengali, Chinese, Teloogoo. We can-

Figure 2.3   Government gazette on the qualifications of potential candidates
Source: *Straits Times*, 12 November 1859, 2.

Hindustani and Punjabi, were recorded in the Straits Settlements. Among those Indian languages, Bangla was spoken by 6 per cent, 1.8 per cent and 0.9 per cent in Singapore, Malacca and Penang, respectively. The percentages of Tamil-speaking people among Indians were the highest in those settlements, representing 76 per cent, 88.1 per cent and 81.09 per cent.[53]

The sustained presence of the Bengalis was reflected in the formation and growth of multi-ethnic organisations. For example, in 1916, a committee was formed in Singapore at 1 Jalan Besar to support the wounded British soldiers during the First World War. The 'Hindustani' and Bengali people identified themselves separately in that committee. The president, vice-president and treasurer were Bengali, and the remaining members originated from Punjab and the United Provinces (Uttar Pradesh).[54]

Not counting the offspring of Bengali inter-ethnic families is a technical shortcoming of the population census. Some Bengalis introduced themselves as Malay, and the offspring of Bengali–Malay parentage or Jawi Perkan[55] were not recorded as Bengali in census reports. Habibul Haque Khondker suggested that many Bangla-speaking Muslim migrants who hailed from East Bengal (now Bangladesh) identified themselves as Malay, learned the local language and assumed a Malay identity through marriage with the Malays.[56] Some were indifferent to the question of ethnic identity. For instance, the offspring of those Bengalis who came from East Bengal to Malaya in the early 1920s were registered as Pakistani in the 1950s because then Bengal was known as East Pakistan. Some of them still maintain their identity as 'Pakistani' on identification cards even following the independence of Bangladesh from Pakistan in 1971.[57] Some Bengalis opted for Malay ethnic identity and citizenship entitlement during the decolonising of British Malaya in the 1950s and 1960s. They had been settled there for a long time and married locally, so they adopted a Malay identity. That is why Kingsley Davis, when writing in the 1950s, did not rely on the official records and suggested that 'the official figures were not complete or uniform'.[58]

Many Bengalis came to Malaya from outside of Bengal. For instance, Dolly Sinha Davenport came from the United Provinces of India. She recalls that her father was a government electrical engineer transferred from Eastern Bengal to the United Provinces Municipal Board. Her parents came from Dhaka and Comilla, but she was educated and raised in the United Provinces. After her marriage, she came to Singapore in 1966. She further recounts that she met a few Bengali families in Singapore who migrated from the same province.[59]

The aforementioned records and explanations have made feasible the location of Bengalis among diverse Indian ethnic groups. Besides, the ethnic identity of the Bengalis became clear to the public during the early twentieth century. For instance, according to the Bengal census of 1911, the number of emigrants from Bengal to the Straits Settlements and the Federated Malay States was 3,300 and 3,059, respectively.[60] As the geographical categorisation, that is, Indian or Hindustani, was ambiguous, the census enumerators were instructed to register birthplace and ethnic identity during the census of 1921. With this system, the Malay enumerators could quickly record if any person, either Sikh or Punjabi from the United Provinces, described himself as a Bengali.[61] Thus, the British government officials and the public became aware of the issues of clarification of ethnic identification. Some interviewees of different ethnicities, such as Malayalee, Telugu, Tamil and Sikh, who were raised in Singapore in the early twentieth century, suggested that the Punjabis should not be mixed up with the Bengalis.[62]

Some Bengal-related streets and place names in Malaysia and Singapore testify to the Bengalis' earlier mobility. Anoma Pieris suggested that the Argyle Road was called Bangkali Kang (Bengali Road) in Singapore.[63] The Baboo Lane or Hindoo Road in the Serangoon area is closely related to the Bengali Hindu Baboo. A Bengali descendant remembers that the centuries-old area, Little India, particularly Norris Road, Lembu Road, Desker Road, Rowell Road, Kinta Road and Syed Alwi Road in Singapore are sometimes termed 'Bangla Town' or 'Bangla Bazaar'.[64] 'Bangla Town' or 'Bangla Bazaar' is also found in Malaysia.[65]

The British brought Bengali convicts from Bengkulu to Penang, Malacca and Singapore. Among other Indian convicts and indentured labourers, the Bengalis contributed to establishing religious institutions such as mosques or temples in the Straits Settlements. For example, the 'Benggali Mosque' (later renamed Bencoolen Mosque), established between 1825 and 1828 at Queen Street in Singapore,[66] took its name from the Bengali migrants who used to offer prayers over there. This was corroborated by a Bengali descendant, Anwarul Haque. As he remembers:

> There was a mosque at Queen Street. The *imam* of the mosque was Bengali. The mosque has been demolished now. It was known as [the] Bengali mosque. I can remember where the mosque was located. The Bengalis were concentrated at the mosque. In those days, the mosque was a meeting place of the Bengalis. Majority of the *Musulli* [pious persons] were Bengali.[67]

Apart from taking them to Singapore, the British transported Bengalis to Penang in the late eighteenth century and other places later. The Bengalis, among other Indians, were associated with the erecting of mosques at different places in George Town and Penang. The Bengali Mosque, presently called Qaryah Masjid Jamek Benggali in George Town, was built in 1801 on a piece of land donated by the EIC.[68] Another Bengali Mosque is located at Rajati Medu in Penang, which was established in 1855.[69]

Kampung Bengali and Jalan Kampung Bengali are located in present-day Penang, Perak and Pahang, which denotes the Bengali-concentrated areas. Archival records from between 1930 and 1980 reveal the construction work at Kampung Bengali.[70] Gabriel Lourdes remembered that his family lived at Kampung Bengali in Perak during the Japanese Occupation.[71]

Bengali miscegenation and interracial marriage are also significant in locating their migration during the colonial period. Some Bengali migrants de-territorialised their racial identity through miscegenation over time, particularly those who migrated in the early nineteenth century. This segment of the Bengali diaspora is ethnically categorised as Indian or is amalgamated with the Malays. Some examples are given here. A Bangla-speaking migrant, Ismail Ballah (c. 1843–1928), was born in Singapore to parents who had probably arrived in the 1830s. His eldest son, S. I. M. Ibrahim, became the President of the Bengal Muslim Association in Singapore, and his grandson, Ahmad bin Mohamed Ibrahim (1916–1999),[72] pursued a legal career and was Singapore's first Attorney-General. He played a significant role during the merger talks between Singapore and Malaysia in the 1960s, as well as being the legal advisor for the Singapore delegation, which went to London in 1963 for independence negotiations from British rule.[73] Ballah's family represented complete integration with mainstream Singapore society. However, this deeper integration often led to the misrecognition of the origin of such families. No wonder when Ballah died, a newspaper introduced him as an 'Arab'.[74]

Interracial marriage is a significant source of greater integration, inviting multiple language use and layered cultural practices. Nirmala Srirekam PuruShotam lamented about the loss of Bengali heritage within the hybrid of intermarriage between Bangla speakers with other language speakers such as Hindi or Chinese.[75] M. A. Majid, a towering figure among the Bengali diasporic community in the Malay world, who frequently appears in this book, migrated to Singapore in the 1920s and married a Chinese woman. He did not teach his offspring the Bangla language; instead, he communicated with them either in Malay or English. As a result, his children and grandchildren have been fully integrated into the Malay cultural world. Majid never returned to Bengal.[76] Another example is the family of Osman Ali, a Bengali migrant. Before his death, Ali requested that Majid adopt his youngest son, Akbar Ali. Majid fostered Akbar Ali and married him to a local woman in Singapore. Presently, a daughter of Akbar Ali, Balkis Bte Akbar Ali, runs the Balkis Family Clinic in Singapore,[77] but she has no connection with Bangladesh. Hena Sinha notes that her grandchildren rarely spoke Bangla.[78] The first or second generation of Bengali migrants who grew up in Malaya and Singapore did not speak fluent Bangla; therefore, they spoke in English or Malay.[79] Ronendra Karmakar recalled that he found that the third-generation of Bengali migrants, who intermarried with other races, were not interested in Bangla culture or associations and neither were their offspring.[80] There is no reason that they would be counted as Bengali in the government census.

Some Bengali migrants who settled in the Malay Peninsula were registered as Malay on their identity cards and adopted Malay or Chinese cultural practices. Ramnath Biswas met a Bengali who worked in a Chinese newspaper office in Kuala Lumpur and wore a Malay dress and Chinese wooden shoes. The Bengali migrant informed Ramnath Biswas in the Malay language that they were then 'Malay' because they had come to Malaya and settled here.[81]

These discussions have illustrated with various evidence that the ambiguous categorisation in the colonial records and the dynamics of the creole communities in British Malay were ignored by the colonial administrators-cum-scholars. Due to administrative and geographical reasons, Bengali migrants were tangled with other Indian ethnic groups. However, by using alternate ways, such as re-reading censuses and birthplace statistics and revisiting some historical literature, the book explores that many Bengalis were active in the Malay world, and some of their descendants have corroborated it. The following chapters, particularly Chapters 4 and 5, will explicitly show the Bengalis' diverse professional world. With the categorical confusion around the term 'Bengali' cleared, a related issue is the demographic profile of the Bengalis, which will be taken up in the next section.

Overcoming the Ambiguity

The population censuses of British Malaya were arranged according to administrative jurisdictions or units, such as the Straits Settlements,

Singapore, Malacca, Penang, the Federated Malay States and the Unfederated Malay States. By the time the Straits Settlements administration was in place, the Bengalis were already living in the region. Irregular publications of census reports prevented the formation of a complete demographic profile of the Bengalis. Between 1861 and 1901, the Bengali population increased by 69.01 per cent in the Straits Settlements,[82] with male migrants being higher in number.[83] Moreover, the documentation of the Bengali adolescent population in the census reports indirectly reveals that the Bengalis had settled with families in the Straits Settlements at least before 1861.[84]

As the Straits Settlements consisted of three major administrative units, Singapore, Malacca and Penang, the following discussion examines the Bengali population according to the administrative units.

Singapore

Singapore was the main British emporium in the Straits Settlements. The first census of Singapore was conducted in 1824, which revealed its population to be 10,683.[85] Census reports from 1824 to 1836 showed that the number of people from 'Hindustan and Bengal' had increased by 59.02 per cent in Singapore.[86] The primary reason for this increase was that the colonial government brought petty officers and clerks from Bengal. Second, Bengali convicts and 'free' labourers were transported to Singapore. Third, the victory over the First Anglo-Burmese War (1824–1826) allowed the British to take over northeastern India as well as Arakan and Tenasserim. As mentioned earlier, there was extensive Bengali movement towards Arakan. The Arakan and Tenasserim borders were directly connected with the Malay Peninsula during British colonialism. Therefore, this may have facilitated Bengali migration after the war. Fourth, the capital of the Straits Settlements was transferred from Penang to Singapore in 1832, leading to the increase of immigrants there. As per the report of 1833, there were 505 Bengalis out of 20,978 inhabitants in Singapore, making them the sixth-largest ethnic group among the fourteen ethnicities in Singapore.[87] However, this number would be higher if the unidentifiable Bengalis are considered, as discussed earlier. After making Singapore the capital city, the population was categorised as per the residential area. Census reports show that the number of Bengali migrants was higher in the municipality than in the suburbs.[88] Hence, it might be assumed that there was a considerable number of Bengalis in early colonial Singapore.

During the late nineteenth century, the number of Tamil immigrants increased in the plantation industries, as mentioned earlier. Consequently, the Tamil population was the highest among other South Asian migrants. Excluding the number of Tamils, the percentages of Bengali migrants, among other South Asians, were 27.60, 6.54 and 10.0 in 1921, 1931 and 1947, respectively.[89] It is intriguing why the Bengali population was almost three times larger in 1921 than in 1931 and 1947; perhaps the global economic depression and WWII might have been factors. As the census enumerators were instructed to register birthplace and ethnic identity during the enumeration of 1921, there is a low possibility that Bengali was blended with Punjabi or Hindustani, which might have led to an increase in the number of Bengali migrants recorded.

Penang and Malacca

Penang was the first British outpost in Malaya, occupied in 1786. The area of Penang covered Penang Island (formerly Prince of Wales Island), Seberang Perai (formerly Province Wellesley) and Manjung district (formerly Dindings). During the early nineteenth century, there were a noticeable number of Bengali migrants in Penang. The survey register of Penang recorded that the colonial authority occupied more than 2,000 acres at the end of September 1796, and the earliest occupants were brought from different regions, including China, southern India and Bengal.[90] In 1830, John Crawfurd reported that the population of Bengal was 4,624 in Penang.[91] In 1835, the number of Bengali migrants was 579 in Seberang Perai or Province Wellesley.[92] Their presence is reflected in their various activities. For example, in 1807, the 'Committee of Assessors' was formed to assist the colonial administration, and Syed Harun was made the representative of the Bengali community.[93] Besides, a gazette of the Prince of Wales Island issued a few names of property owners in the 1810s, which included Bengalis.

After relocating the capital of the Straits Settlements from Penang to Singapore, port operations declined, and consequently, the number of immigrants or labourers decreased in Penang. For example, the number of Bengali migrants shrank by 29.34 per cent between 1833 and 1859.[94] This negative trend continued until the early twentieth century, representing a decrease of 1.57 per cent between 1871 and 1901.[95] One more reason behind the decrease in Bengali migrants was the high mortality among the plantation labourers in Malacca and Penang. The Government of Bengal prohibited the supply of indentured labour in the deadly estates of the Straits Settlements and the Federated Malay States.[96] However, most of the Bengali migrants resided in urban areas. About 35 per cent of the total Bengalis lived in the Penang municipality in 1891, which increased to 59 per cent in 1901.[97] The Bengali population in Penang became proportionately low in three consecutive census reports in 1911, 1921 and 1931 due to the increasing number of Tamil migrants.[98]

Bengali merchants were familiar with Malacca before the Dutch Settlement but rarely settled there. During the British colonial period, the Bengali migrant population in Malacca increased by 144.44 per cent between 1829 and 1836,[99] only to rapidly decrease by 43.13 per cent of the total number of migrants between 1871 and 1901.[100] Most of them were male migrants whose age range was from 31 to 60.[101] The Bengali population in Malacca during the years of 1911, 1921 and 1931 was 124, 173 and 68, respectively.[102]

The Federated Malay States, the Unfederated Malay States and the Federation of Malaya

It was mentioned in the prelude that the colonial authority separated Malay states into two regional clusters in 1895—the Federated Malay States and the Unfederated Malay States. The Federated Malay States consisted of Selangor, Perak, Negeri Sembilan and Pahang and were governed centrally by an agent of the British government. Initially, the agent was called Resident-General, and later Chief Secretary. The Unfederated Malay States—comprised of Johor, Kedah, Kelantan, Perlis and Terengganu—were governed as British protectorates under indirect rule. The number of Bengali migrants was high in Perak and Selangor of the Federated Malay States because of the extensive rubber trade and production. Between 1891 and 1901, the Bengali population increased by 108.83 per cent in Perak and 141.37 per cent in Selangor. Though most were male migrants, the number of female migrants also steadily rose. In 1891, the Bengali female population was 171 in Perak and Selangor, whereas it was 435 in 1901, showing an increase of 154.38 per cent.[103]

Brunei Darussalam

Bengali migration took place on a small scale in Brunei before the discovery of oil. According to an official census, Bangla-speaking people were found in Brunei in 1932.[104] The oil economy flourished steadily from the 1930s onward, and concurrently, different ethnic groups from South Asia migrated to Brunei. By the mid-twentieth century, the need for labourers to work in the Seria oilfields was acutely felt.[105] This may have factored in the arrival of more Bengalis in the British North Borneo state. As mentioned earlier, Bengali was listed under the category of 'Indian' in Brunei. Such categorisation is still in practice in Brunei, Malaysia and Singapore. The census of 1981 reported that the birthplaces of the Indian population were in India, Pakistan, Bangladesh and Sri Lanka.[106] The Indian male and female population gradually grew between 1911 and 1981 in Brunei. In 1981, the total Indian population was 5,919, of which the percentage of male and female migrants was 70.11 and 29.89, respectively.[107]

The population census of the Brunei government reported the number of new and returned migrants. Though most Indian and Pakistani migrants returned to their homeland, a significant number remained as net immigrants, as shown in Graph 2.1. Some of them obtained citizenship or permanent residence from the Brunei government.[108] As Bangladesh was officially known as Pakistan during the census years 1946–1969, undoubtedly there were Bengalis among the 'Pakistani' immigrants.

By providing a sporadic demographic profile of the Bengali migrants in the Straits Settlements, Singapore, Malacca, Penang, the Federated Malay States and the Unfederated Malay States, the earlier discussions have cleared the categorical confusion and ambiguity around the term 'Bengali' during the colonial period. The Bengali migration continued in the postcolonial era, which will be discussed in the next section.

The Postcolonial Era: A New Wave of Bengali Migration

In 1947, Bengal was partitioned along communal lines. The Hindu-dominated West Bengal became part of India, and the Muslim-majority East Bengal became part of Pakistan. From then on, the people of East Bengal were identified as either East Pakistani or Pakistani until the creation of Bangladesh in 1971. The Bengalis from West Bengal came to be known as Indians. In 1957, the number of Indians was 696,000 in the Federation of Malaya and 124,000 in Singapore, of whom the majority of Pakistanis were Punjabi and Bengali Muslims.[109] The migrants from post-independence Bangladesh, particularly in the 1980s, identified themselves as Bangladeshi. However, the people of West Bengal retained their ethnic identity as Bengali. Bangladeshi identity

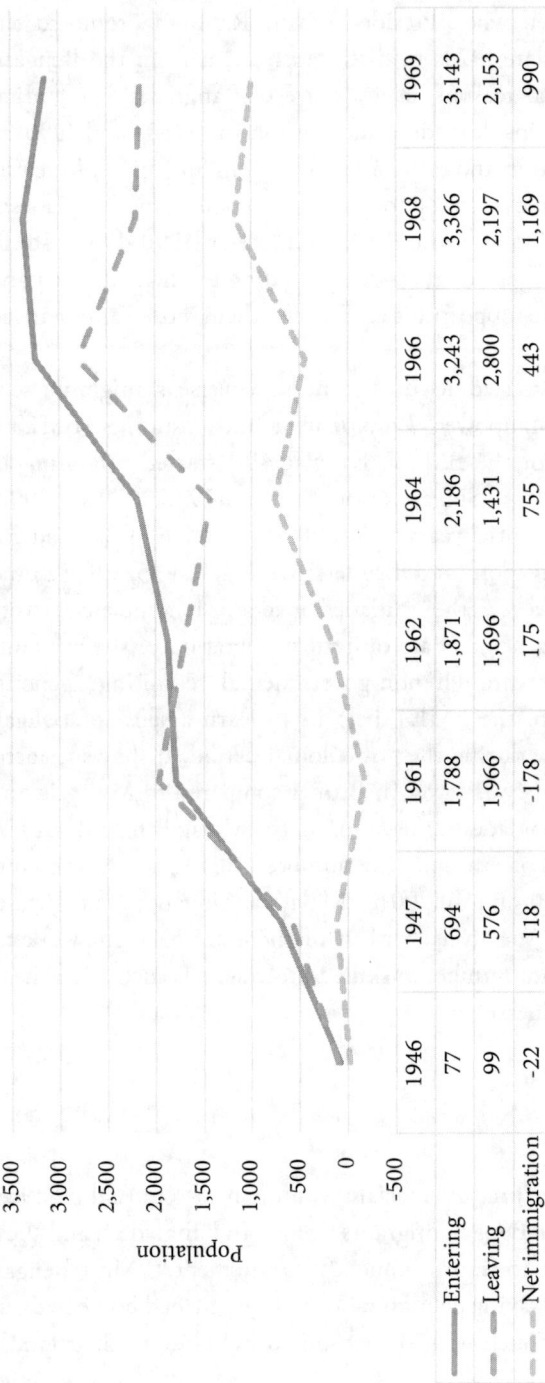

	1946	1947	1961	1962	1964	1966	1968	1969
Entering	77	694	1,788	1,871	2,186	3,243	3,366	3,143
Leaving	99	576	1,966	1,696	1,431	2,800	2,197	2,153
Net immigration	-22	118	-178	175	755	443	1,169	990

Graph 2.1   Net immigration from India and Pakistan in Brunei, 1946–1969

Sources: Report on the State of Brunei for the Year 1946 (Kuala Lumpur: Malayan Union Government Press, 1948), 12; *Report on the State of Brunei for the Year 1947* (Singapore: Malaya Publishing House, 1948), 6; *Report on the State of Brunei for the Year 1961–1962* (Kuala Belait: Brunei Press Limited,1964), 12; *Report on the State of Brunei for the Year 1964* (State of Brunei: Government Printing Press, 1966), 15; *Report on the State of Brunei for the Year 1966* (State of Brunei: Government Printing Press, 1968), 15; *Report on the State of Brunei for the Year 1968* (State of Brunei: Government Printing Press, 1969), 15; *Report on the State of Brunei for the Year 1969* (State of Brunei: Government Printing Press, 1970), 18.

was particularly emphasised when President Ziaur Rahman promoted the term 'Bangladeshi' in the late 1970s to distinguish them from the Bengalis of West Bengal. For several reasons, a new wave of Bangladeshi migration occurred in the Malay Peninsula and Brunei during the 1980s and 1990s.[110] First, the massive construction and development work in Singapore, Malaysia and Brunei led to more employment opportunities. Second, some Bangladeshi migrants moved to the region after the Persian Gulf War (1990–1991). Third, the growing Bangladeshi professional classes, including teachers, doctors and engineers, migrated for better opportunities. Some of them settled and married local women.

In 1976, Bangladesh started to document the overseas migrants sent through the Bureau of Manpower, Employment and Training (BMET). According to the records of the BMET, Bangladeshis started migrating in significant numbers to Malaysia, Singapore and Brunei in 1978, 1979 and 1992, respectively. Between those initial years and 2000, the number of Bangladeshi migrants to Malaysia, Singapore and Brunei rose to 252,733, 86,598 and 9,505, respectively.[111] However, the statistics give an incomplete picture because the records do not include data on return migration or the migrants who travelled privately or through non-governmental recruiting agencies. Nevertheless, the records of the BMET help us to learn a sense of Bengali (from Bangladesh) mobility during the postcolonial period. It shows that the number of Bengali migrants was lower in Brunei compared to Malaysia and Singapore. The trend of Bangladeshi migration in the Malay Peninsula can be found in recent statistics. For example, the number of Bangladeshi migrants was about 707,339, 150,000 and 40,000 in Malaysia, Singapore and Brunei in 2014, 2013 and 2016, respectively.[112] Most of them are itinerant workers, though there are a significant number of skilled professionals such as teachers, engineers, doctors and businessmen.

Return Migration

Ancestral homes (*desher bari*) have a special meaning in the cultural practices of the Bengali diaspora. The Bengali migrants from both Bangladesh and West Bengal had a strong desire to return home after retirement.[113] Most Bengali migrants were young; after saving enough money, they returned home because they were keen to stay in touch with their roots to live close to their family and relatives.[114] Sengupta recalled that many Bengalis returned to Bengal from Malaya soon after the Japanese Occupation. Many worried that if they settled here, their children could lose their Bengali identity. For example, Kshitendra Chandra Sengupta left Malaya permanently in 1945 with his family for his birthplace at Brahmanbaria. Many doctors, including B. C. Majumder, K. N. Ghosh, N. K. Sen, Jyoti B. Ray and K. C. Sengupta, returned home after retirement.[115]

Conclusion

This chapter has discussed a few alternative ways to address the issues surrounding obscuring Bengali ethnic identity within the generic term 'Indian'. These included the reinterpretation of historical records and literature and exploring population estimates obtained from indirect evidence, such as birthplace statistics. I have not relied exclusively on government records because most official figures concerning Indian migrants cover British-regulated Indian seaports, excluding those who could have migrated overland (across the Burma–Thai border) and disembarked from other seaports, such as Rangoon Port.

By examining the sporadic Bengali demographic data, this chapter shows that there has been a continuous flow of Bengali migrants, although their number has fluctuated. Some Bengalis settled in urban centres and suburbs and developed a long-term relationship with the region through residency and everyday interactions. In the postcolonial period, particularly in the 1980s and 1990s, a new wave of Bangladeshi migration, mainly of unskilled workers, led to the widespread perception of the Bengali migrants as itinerant labourers and temporary workers. One can distinguish between colonial and postcolonial Bengali migrants by calling them 'old' and 'new' diasporas. After the 1990s, the number of Bengali transient labourers increased. This migration trend can be termed 'new' diasporas, and the Bengali migrants before 1990 might be considered 'old' diasporas.

As this chapter suggests, the Bengali presence and continued flourishing in the Malay world in the postcolonial times built upon their remarkable mobility and diasporic engagement in the colonial period. Following this assessment of the identity and demography of the Bengali migrants and diaspora, the next chapter will discuss the governance of the Bengali migration process and their settlement in Malaya.

Notes

1. For an exploration of the limitations of colonial records and challenges in recovering the history of Bengali migrations, see Gazi Mizanur Rahman, 'Transnational History and Colonial Records: Locating Bengali Mobility in the British Malaya', *Journal of Maritime Studies and National Integration* 3, no. 2 (2019): 97–112.

2. Thomas R. Metcalf, *Imperial Connections: India in the Indian Ocean Arena, 1860–1920* (Berkeley; Los Angeles; London: University of California Press, 2007), xii.

3. H. H. Risley and E. A. Gait, *Census of India, 1901, Vol. I, India, Part I, Report* (Calcutta: Office of the Superintendent of Government Printing, 1903), 91.

4. Bates, 'Some Thoughts on the Representation', 7.

5. Aiyar, *Indian Problems in Malaya*, 116.

6. *Report on the State of Brunei 1911* (Singapore: Government Printing Press, 1912), 11.

7. *ST*, 2 July 1859.

8. Kingsley Davis, *The Population of India and Pakistan* (Princeton: Princeton University Press, 1951), 101.

9. Charles Hirschman, 'The Meaning and Measurement of Ethnicity in Malaysia: An Analysis of Census Classifications', *Journal of Asian Studies* 46, no. 3 (1987): 571–578; Faridah Abdul Rashid, *Research on the Early Malay Doctors 1900–1957 Malaya and Singapore* (Bloomington: Xlibris Corporation, 2012), 67.

10. Aiyar, *Indian Problems in Malaya*, 44.

11. Aiyar, *Indian Problems in Malaya*, 56.

12. Ibrahim bin Mohamed Dohfar, *State of Brunei Annual Report on the Social and Economic Progress of the People of Brunei for the Year 1941* (n.p., 1942), 13.

13. The largest 'alien' race was the Chinese. Another 'alien' ethnic group was the Indians who worked as shopkeepers and labourers in the oilfields. See *Report on the State of Brunei for the Year 1923* (Singapore: Government Printing Press, 1924), 8; *Report on the State of Brunei for the Year 1924* (Singapore: Government Printing Press, 1925), 8; *Report on the State of Brunei for the Year 1947* (Singapore: Government Printing Press, 1948), 1.

14. Petra Dannecker, 'Bangladeshi Migrant Workers in Malaysia: The Construction of the "Others" in a Multi-Ethnic Context', *Asian Journal of Social Science* 33, no. 2 (2005): 246–267; Petra Dannecker, 'Transnational

Migration and the Transformation of Gender Relations: The Case of Bangladeshi Labour Migrants', *Current Sociology* 53, no. 4 (2005): 655–674; Norena Abdul Karim Zamri and Adam Abdul Karim Zamri, 'In Lens of the Odd: Constructing the Otherness in Malaysian History, the Role of Financial Development and Manufacturing Sector Expansion on Emission Reduction for Sustainable Economic Development in the World's Biggest Emitter Asia', *International Journal of Advanced Science and Technology* 29, no. 10s (2020): 8208.

15. Hirschman, 'The Meaning and Measurement of Ethnicity in Malaysia', 561.
16. Roland Braddell, *The Lights of Singapore* (London: Methuen, 1934), 44; Hirschman, 'The Meaning and Measurement of Ethnicity in Malaysia', 564; McCann, 'Sikhs and the City', 1477.
17. Metcalf, *Imperial Connections*, 52, 111.
18. Rajesh Rai, 'Sepoys, Convicts and the "Bazaar" Contingent: The Emergence and Exclusion of "Hindustani" Pioneers at the Singapore Frontier', *Journal of Southeast Asian Studies* 35, no. 1 (2004): 5, 16; Winstedt, *Malaya and Its History*, 21; Sandhu, 'Indian Migration and Population Change in Malaya'.
19. *MaT*, 27 June 1916, 8.
20. For details of Bengali mobility across Myanmar, see Risley and Gait, *Census of India, 1901, Vol. 1, Part 1*, 90–91; E. A. Gait, *Census of India 1911, Vol. 1, India, Part II, Tables* (Calcutta: Superintendent Government Printing, 1913), 131, 136; Amarjit Kaur, 'Indian Ocean Crossings: Indian Labor Migration and Settlement in Southeast Asia, 1870 to 1940', in *Connecting Seas and Connected Ocean Rims: Indian, Atlantic, and Pacific Oceans and China Seas Migrations from the 1830s to the 1930s*, ed. Donna R. Gabaccia and Dirk Hoerder (Leiden; Boston: Brill, 2011), 137; Thet Lwin, 'Indians in Myanmar', in *Rising India and Indian Communities in East Asia*, ed. K Kesavapany, A. Mani and P. Ramasamy (Singapore: Institute of Southeast Asian Studies, 2008), 492.
21. Cheng Siok Hwa, 'Land Tenure Problems in Burma, 1852 to 1940', *Journal of the Malaysian Branch of the Royal Asiatic Society* 38, no. 1 (207) (1965): 106, 110, 120, 124.
22. Ganendra Mohun Das, *Banger Bahire Bangali* [Bengalis Outside Bengal], part III (Calcutta: Indian Publishing House, 1931), 424–425.
23. Davis, *Population of India and Pakistan*, 98.
24. C. C. Lowis, *Census of India 1901, Vol. XIIA, Burma, Part II, Imperial Tables.* (Rangoon: Office of the Superintendent of Government Printing, 1902), 182, 194.

25. J. H. Hutton, *Census of India, 1931. Vol. 1, India, Part 1, Report* (Delhi: Manager of Publications, 1933), 374.

26. This border was strategically crucial for the Japanese armies during World War II, prompting them to build the Thai–Burma Railway in 1942–1943 in order to facilitate transportation and communication during the war.

27. *Census of the British Empire 1901* (London: Darling & Sons, 1906), 106.

28. *Census of the British Empire 1901*, 106–107; Gait, *Census of India 1911, Vol. 1, India, Part II, Tables*, 134.

29. For details, see Hugh Clifford, *Further India: Burma, Malaya, Siam, and Indo-China* (London: Lawrence and Bullen Ltd, 1904); Risley and Gait, *Census of India 1901*, 106.

30. The information has been extracted from Gait, *Census of India 1911, Vol. 1, India, Part II, Tables*, 122–124.

31. Gait, *Census of India 1911, Vol. 1, India, Part II, Tables*, 127–128, 134.

32. H. Marriott, *Report on the Census of the Straits Settlements, Taken on the 10th March 1911* (Singapore: Government Print Office, 1911), 72–75.

33. Davis, *Population of India and Pakistan*, 98.

34. Mrs Hena Sinha was born and brought up in Burma. After her marriage, A. C. Sinha and Mrs Sinha, with her mother-in-law, disembarked from the Rangoon Port for Singapore. The discussion of Hena Sinha's involvement in societal and public spaces is illustrated in Chapters 7 and 8. Dr Sengupta informed us about some Bengali doctors and other professionals who came to British Malaya from Burma.

35. Bort, *Report of Governor Balthasar Bort on Malacca 1678*, 9.

36. Leyden, *Malay Annals*, 324; Wright, *Twentieth Century Impressions of British Malaya*, 86; Ian Lloyd and Wendy Moore, *Malacca* (Singapore: Time Edition, 1986), 28; Sarnia Hayes Hoyt, *Old Malacca* (Kuala Lumpur; Oxford; Singapore; New York: Oxford University Press, 1993), 30.

37. Anoma Pieris, *Hidden Hands and Divided Landscapes: A Penal History of Singapore's Plural Society* (Honolulu: University of Hawai'i Press, 2009), 41.

38. Nasution, *Chulia in Penang*, 49, 56.

39. *Star Online* (hereinafter *SO*), 6 March 2007.

40. *Annals of Indian Administration 1856* (Serampore: Printed by Marshall D'cruz, 1856), 289.

41. Windsor Earl, *The Eastern Seas, or Voyages and Adventures in the Indian Archipelago in 1832–33–34* (London: W. H. Allen, 1837), 353. Windsor Earl visited Java, Singapore, Borneo and Malaysia during 1832–1834, and sometimes he termed Bengal as 'Eastern India'.

42. Nasution, *Chulia in Penang*, 49, 56. In 1844, almost 50,000 inhabitants, including Bengalis, lived in the Province of Wellesley. See *SFPMA*, 25 April 1844.

43. Emily Sadka, *The Protected Malay States 1874–1895* (Kuala Lumpur: University of Malaya Press, 1968), 28.

44. *SCCR*, 13 February 1834, 3.

45. *SFPMA*, 10 May 1849, 2; Arnold Wright, *Twentieth Century Impressions of Siam: Its History, People, Commerce, Industries, and Resources* (London: Lloyd's Greater Britain Publishing Company, Ltd, 1908), 244.

46. *SCCR*, 30 October 1834, 2; *Mid-Day Herald and Daily* (hereinafter *MdHD*), 23 September 1897.

47. The Malay language was given importance in every sphere in the 1870s, followed by the Chinese language. See T. N. Harper, 'Globalism and the Pursuit of Authenticity: The Making of a Diasporic Public Sphere in Singapore', *Sojourn: Journal of Social Issues in Southeast Asia, Southeast Asian Diasporas* 12, no. 2 (1997): 268.

48. *ST*, 12 November 1859.

49. Bengalis were enumerated under the head of 'Tamils and Other Natives of India' in 1891, as mentioned earlier.

50. *ST*, 13 March 1894.

51. National Archives of Malaysia, Kuala Lumpur (hereinafter NAM), Public Records and Archives, State Records (hereinafter PRA), 'Application from Mr. Gheewala, Bengali Interpreter of Courts for the Post of Munshi to Selangor Police Force', file no. 1957/0054480W, 17 January 1895.

52. A range of archival records on the Bengali interpreter was found in the NAM; see Chapter 4.

53. Marriott, *Report on the Census of the Straits Settlements*, 66–68.

54. *SFPMA*, 16 September 1916. The following committee leaders were Bengali: President K. Kader Daud bin Abul Odud; Vice-President K. C. Sinha; Secretary Munshi Muhammad Ally; Treasurer Dr S. N. Bardhan; Member Kobad Ally. The rest were from other regions: Syed Gulabshad (Punjabi); Elahi Bux (United Provinces); Tunda Singh (United Provinces); Hoosen Ally (United Provinces); Ramananda Tewary (United Provinces); Mangal Singh (United Provinces); Mauluvi Singh (United Provinces).

55. The offspring of Indians and Chinese married local Malay women in British Malaya were called Jawi Pekan or Jawi Peranakan. In 1858, J. D. Vaughan noted that Jawi Pekan referred to the children of Malay mothers and Chinese, Kling or Bengali fathers. Both the terms 'Jawi Pekan' and 'Jawi Peranakan'

might be used interchangeably; however, upper-class people preferred to use Jawi Peranakan rather than Jawi Pekan. The term 'Jawi Pekan' applies to the people who came from the working class. See Kernial Singh Sandhu, 'Indian Immigration and Settlement in Singapore', in *Indian Communities in Southeast Asia*, ed. K. S. Sandhu and A. Mani (Singapore: Institute of Southeast Asian Studies, 1993), 787; *myMetro*, 24 April 2015; Nasution, *Chulia in Penang*, 8, 121, 125; C. M. Turnbull, *A History of Singapore 1819–1988* (Singapore: Oxford University Press, 1989), 37; Rashid, *Research on the Early Malay Doctors 1900–1957*, 67.

56. Khondker, 'Bengali-Speaking Families in Singapore', 183–185.

57. Anwarul Haque's father migrated from Sylhet to British Malaya, but 'Pakistani' is still written on his identification card. Interview with Anwarul Haque, 25 July 2018, Guild House, NUS, Singapore.

58. Davis, *Population of India and Pakistan*, 98.

59. Interview with Dolly Sinha Davenport, 23 July 2018, at her house in Singapore.

60. L. S. S. O'Malley, *Census of India, 1911, Vol. V, Bengal, Bihar and Orissa and Sikkim, Part 1: Report* (Calcutta: Bengal Secretariat Book Depot, 1913), 174.

61. C. A. Vlieland, *British Malaya (The Colony of the Straits Settlements and the Malay States under British Protection, Namely the Federated States of Perak, Selangor, Negeri Sembilan and Pahang and the States of Johore, Kedah, Kelantan, Trengganu, Perlis and Brunei: A Report on the 1931 Census and on Certain Problems of Vital Statistics)* (London: Crown Agents for the Colonies, 1932), 83, 84.

62. NAS, OHI, Sukumara Ittamuittil Menon, 9 May 1985, Acc. No. 000557; Natesan Palanivelu, 10 October 1985, Acc. No. 000588; Soundara Rajan, 25 November 1987, Acc. No. 000845; Seva Singh, 11 April 1984, Acc. No. 000418; Mohinder Singh, 24 June 1985, Acc. No. 000546.

63. Pieris, *Hidden Hands and Divided Landscapes*, 161.

64. Interview with Noorul Islam, 7 July 2018, ANA Book Store, Far East Plaza, Singapore; Interview with A. K. M. Mohsin, 16 July 2018, Rowell Road, Singapore. Mohsin came to Singapore in 1990 and obtained citizenship in 2005.

65. Nayeem Sultana, 'The Dynamics of a Multi-cultural Society along the Straits of Malacca: Networking and Integration of Migrant Bangladeshis in Malaysia', in *The Straits of Malacca: Knowledge and Diversity*, ed. Solvay Gerke, Hans-Dieter Evers and Anna-Katharina Hornidge (LIT Verlag: ZEF Development Studies, 2008), 149.

66. Rajesh Rai, 'Nestled in a Faraway Land: Early Indian Settlements in Singapore', in *Singapore Indian Heritage*, ed. Rajesh Rai and A. Mani (Singapore: Indian Heritage Centre, 2017), 293, 298; Rai and Mani, *Singapore Indian Heritage*, 293, 298; *ST*, 14 May 2019.

67. Interview with Haque.

68. Lynn Hollen Lees, *Planting Empire, Cultivating Subjects* (Singapore: Cambridge University Press, 2017), 244; see also Osman Abdullah Chuah, Abdul Salam M. Shukri and Mohd Syukri Yeoh, 'Indian Muslims in Malaysia: A Sociological Analysis of a Minority Ethnic Group', *Journal of Muslim Minority Affairs* 31, no. 2 (2011): 223–225; Nasution, *Chulia in Penang*, 131–132; *SO*, 6 March 2007. Later, the mosque was renovated, see NAM, PRA, 'Bengali Mosque Leth Street, Penang, 1958', file no. 2007/0034044W, 31 December 1958.

69. Nasution, *Chulia in Penang*, xxviii–xxix.

70. NAM, PRA, 'Debiting to Town Improvements Vote $7,000 Being the Estimated Cost of Relief Work at Kampong Bengali', file no. 1957/0269544W, 11 February 1931; NAM, PRA, 'Culvert at Jalan Padang Bengali at Telok Ayer Tawar, Province Wellesley (N)', file no. 1987/0001642P, 20 May 1963; NAM, PRA, 'JKK 48/81 Mengambil Alih Untuk Penyelenggaraan Jalan-Jalan dan Parit di atas lot-lot 1113, Jalan KG Bengali, Butterworth', file no. 1987/0003005P, 24 November 1981.

71. NAS, OHI, Gabriel Lourdes, 20 November 1984, Acc. No. 000509. He was born in Kuala Lumpur in 1925. He lived in Kampong Benggali during the Japanese Occupation. His parents migrated to Taiping in the 1890s and finally moved to Singapore in 1932.

72. It should be noted here that Mohamed Ibrahim was very familiar with M. A. Majid, a Bengali migrant. See Haja Maideen, *The Nadra Tragedy: The Maria Hertogh Controversy* (Malaysia: Pelanduk Publications Sdn Bhd, 1989), 68.

73. Vernon Cornelius-Takahama, 'Tan Sri Datuk Professor Ahmad Ibrahim', SingaporeInfopedia, National Library Board, Singapore, https://eresources.nlb.gov.sg/infopedia/articles/SIP_529_2005-01-07.html, accessed 7 July 2020; Khoo Kay Kim, 'Malay Attitudes towards Indians', in *Indian Communities in Southeast Asia*, ed. K. S. Sandhu and A. Mani (Singapore: Times Academic Press and ISEAS, 1993), 266–287, 282–283.

74. *ST*, 25 July 1928, 10.

75. Nirmala Srirekam PuruShotam, *Negotiation Language, Constructing Race: Disciplining Difference in Singapore* (Berlin: Mouton de Gruyter, 1998), 150.

76. Interview with Shafiya Khatoon, the eldest daughter of Mirza Abdul Majid, 1 August 2018, UBD, Brunei. The involvement of M. A. Majid in trade unionism, and sociopolitical and other activities has been discussed in Chapters 4, 7 and 8.

77. Balkis Bte Akbar Ali, Balkis Family Clinic, Blk 631, Bedok Reservoir Rd #01-968, Singapore.

78. NAS, OHI, Hena Sinha, 21 October 1983, Acc. No. 000354.

79. *Telegraph*, 21 July 2013; Khondker, 'Bengali-Speaking Families in Singapore', 184.

80. NAS, OHI, Ronendra Karmakar, 18 October 1983, Acc. No. 000343.

81. Ramnath Biswas, *Malaysia Vromon* [Travel to Malaysia] (Calcutta: Prokasok Sattonarayan Bhattacharjo, 1949), 133.

82. One of the earliest population censuses was conducted by the police department in 1860. The percentage has been calculated from different census reports: *Annals of Indian Administration in the Year 1859–60* (Serampore: Marshall D'cruz, 1860), 369; *Straits Settlements Blue Books 1871* (Singapore: Straits Settlements, 1872), Raffles Museum and Library, Accession no. I F/2, Microfilm No. NL2931, 6; *Blue Book for the Year 1888* (Singapore: Government Printing Office, 1889), 4, 18–19, 42; E. M. Merewether, *Report on the Census of the Straits Settlements, 1891* (Singapore: Government Printing Office, 1892), 43, 46; *Blue Book for the Year 1904* (Singapore: Government Printing Office, 1905), 9, 13, 45–47, 97.

83. For the Bengali male and female migrants in the Straits Settlements from 1861 to 1901, see *Annals of Indian Administration in the Year 1859–60*, 369; *Straits Settlements Blue Books 1871*, 6; *Blue Book for the Year 1888*, 4, 18–19, 42; Merewether, *Report on the Census of the Straits Settlements, 1891*, 43, 46; *Blue Book for the Year 1904*, 9, 13, 45–47, 97.

84. *Blue Book for the Year 1888*, 10, 11, 27–30, 46–47; *Blue Book for the Year 1904*, 42, 72, 84, 94, 115.

85. T. J. Newbold, *Political and Statistical Account of the British Settlements in the States of Malacca, Pinang, and Singapore with a History of the Malayan States on the Peninsula of Malacca*, vol. 1 (London: John Murray, 1839), 282.

86. The percentage has been calculated from Newbold, *Political and Statistical Account*, 283; John Crawfurd, *Journal of an Embassy from the Governor-General of India to the Court of Siam and Cochin China: Exhibiting a View of the Actual State of Those Kingdoms*, vol. 1 (London: Henry Colburn and Richard Bentley, 1830), 379.

87. Newbold, *Political and Statistical Account*, 283.

88. *Blue Book for the Year 1888*, 12, 31, 48; Merewether, *Census of the Straits Settlements*, 49, 52–68, 70–79, 86; *Blue Book for the Year 1904*, 14–15, 18.

89. J. E. Nathan, *The Census of British Malaya, 1921* (London: Dunstable & Watford, 1922), 191; Vlieland, *British Malaya*, 194–195; M. V. del Tufo, *Malaya, Comprising the Federation of Malaya and the Colony of Singapore: A Report on the 1947 Census of Population* (London: Crown Agents for the Colonies, 1949), 78, 296–299.

90. F. G. Stevens, 'A Contribution to the Early History of Prince of Wales' Island', *Journal of the Malayan Branch of the Royal Asiatic Society* 7, no. 3 (108) (1929): 393.

91. Crawfurd, *Journal of an Embassy from the Governor-General of India to the Court of Siam and Cochin China*, 31.

92. James Low, *The British Settlement of Penang*, with an introduction by James Jackson (Singapore: Oxford University Press, 1972), 125.

93. Nasution, *Chulia in Penang*, 78n14.

94. Newbold, *Political and Statistical Account*, 54–55; Low, *British Settlement of Penang*, 125–126.

95. *Straits Settlements Blue Books 1871*, 6; *Blue Book for the Year 1888*, 4, 18–19, 42; Merewether, *Report on the Census of the Straits Settlements, 1891*, 43, 46.

96. NAB, Proceedings A, Dept.: General, Br.: Emigration, January 1912, Government of Bengal, vol. 13.

97. Merewether, *Report on the Census of the Straits Settlements, 1891*, 104, 105–109, 110–111, 112, 114, 116, 118; *Blue Book for the Year 1904*, 54, 65–66, 77, 79, 81.

98. The number of Bengalis was 423, 470 and 205 in 1911, 1921 and 1931, respectively. See Marriott, *Reports on the Census of Straits Settlements*, 66; Nathan, *The Census of British Malaya, 1921*, 191; Vlieland, *British Malaya*, 193.

99. Newbold, *Political and Statistical Account*, 136, 137; Crawfurd, *Journal of an Embassy from the Governor-General of India to the Court of Siam and Cochin China*, 379.

100. *Straits Settlements Blue Books 1871*, 6; *Blue Book for the Year 1888*, 4, 18–19, 42; Merewether, *Report on the Census of the Straits Settlements, 1891*, 43, 46; *Blue Book for the Year 1904*, 9, 13, 45–47, 97.

101. *Straits Settlements Blue Books 1871*, 6; *Blue Book for the Year 1888*, 4, 10, 11, 18–19, 27–30, 42, 46, 47; Merewether, *Report on the Census of the Straits Settlements*, 43, 46; *Blue Book for the Year 1904*, 9, 13, 42, 45–47, 72, 84, 94, 97, 115.

102. Marriott, *Reports on the Census of Straits Settlements*, 66; Nathan, *The Census of British Malaya, 1921*, 191; Vlieland, *British Malaya*, 193.

103. Merewether, *Report on the Census of the Straits Settlements, 1891*, 156; *Blue Book for the Year 1904*, 120–123; *Census of the British Empire 1901*, 129.

104. Vlieland, *British Malaya*, 192.

105. *Report on the State of Brunei for the Year 1959* (Kuala Belait: Brunei Press Limited, 1961), 7.

106. *Report on the Census of Population, 1971* (Bandar Seri Begawan: Star Press, 1972), 55; *Summary Tables of the Brunei Population Census of 1981* (Negara Brunei Darussalam: Ministry of Finance and Economy, 1981), 50–51.

107. *Summary Tables of the Brunei Population Census of 1981*, 31.

108. *Report on the Census of Population, 1971*, 55; *Summary Tables of the Brunei Population Census of 1981*, 50–51.

109. T. E. Smith, 'Immigration and Permanent Settlement of Chinese and Indians in Malaya: And the Future Growth of the Malay and Chinese Communities', in *South East Asia: Colonial History, Vol. III, High Imperialism (1890s–1930s)*, ed. Paul H. Kratoska (London; New York: Routledge, 2001), 263; Sandhu, 'Indian Migration and Population Change in Malaya'.

110. Khondker, 'Bengali-Speaking Families in Singapore', 183–184.

111. Bureau of Manpower, Employment and Training (BMET), Statistical Reports, Ministry of Expatriates' Welfare and Overseas Employment, Government of the People's Republic of Bangladesh, http://www.old.bmet.gov.bd/BMET/stattisticalDataAction#, accessed 22 October 2016.

112. Sarker, 'Migration and Employment', 128; *The Telegraph*, India, 21 July 2013; *Financial Express*, Bangladesh, 16 May 2016.

113. Khondker, 'Bengali-Speaking Families in Singapore', 189–190.

114. Turnbull, *A History of Singapore 1819–1988*, 37; 'Learn Bangla in Singapore', *Telegraph*, 21 July 2013.

115. Sengupta, *Malaysia and Bengali Doctors*, 26, 39, 42–48, 64.

3

Governance of Migration and Diaspora

Bengalis migrated to British Malaya through an evolving system regulated from both the sending and receiving ends. The system underwent sporadic changes, revisions and additions, often in response to public criticism or the need for efficiency. However, the flow of emigration and demand for labourers remained largely unaltered. In the early 1920s, a fundamental alteration occurred in migration history with the introduction of passports. This system led to stricter control of mobility, and with the fashioning of a new administration in Malaya and India in the 1940s, migration became even more controlled. The Straits Settlements were dissolved in 1946; Singapore became a separate crown colony, and the Malayan Union was formed with the Unfederated and Federated Malay States. In India, British decolonisation left the subcontinent divided into India and Pakistan, which each devised specific sets of migration rules and regulations. These changes in the sending and receiving regions left marks on migration governance.

Types of Bengali Migrants

Before dealing with the theme in detail, it may be pertinent to note that, based on its characteristics and governing systems, Bengali migration can be divided broadly into bondage or systematic migration and 'free' migration. Convicts, indentured and *kangany* labourers can be placed under the first category. Non-government as well as government agencies transported such labourers through stringent systems. Those being transported like this had no choice or very little legal freedom of movement. The Bengalis who migrated willingly from the early colonial period for better opportunities in commercial ventures and the government sector can be termed 'free' migrants.[1] Though they are termed 'free', the choices of these labourers were still quite limited at home and overseas. These migrants also had only a little freedom of movement. There was another kind of migrant—those who had to leave India or Bengal due to political persecution. Many Bengali revolutionaries moved to Malaya during the anti-British and nationalist movements in Bengal.

Convicts

From the late eighteenth century, the EIC transported convicts from British India to the Malay Archipelago.[2] Regulation XVII of 1817 categorised the convicts as those accused of robbery, burglary, theft or any other form of open violence, who were liable to be whipped, imprisoned and transported for life.[3] The decline of the agricultural sector due to the extractive revenue policy known as the Permanent Settlement of 1793 and the destruction of the textile industry in Bengal led to property-related crimes, including burglary, banditry or dacoity, and housebreaking. Table 3.1 lists the types of offences that were committed. Early deportation of Bengali convicts took place in Bencoolen following the Calcutta Supreme Court's order in 1787.[4]

In 1817, Stamford Raffles was appointed as the Governor-General of Bencoolen, and he provided helpful information regarding the management and treatment of the convicts from Bengal and Madras. At the time of his reporting, there were about 500 of them. In 1823, the number increased to about 900.[5] Raffles favoured freeing these convicts following the completion of their punishment and permitting them to reside in the penal colony. He

Table 3.1   Classification of crimes committed by Bengali convicts, 1851

Crimes	Number of convicts
Murder	18
Burglary	5
Robbery with violence	63
Piracy	1
Forgery	1
Arson	4
Treason	12
Returning from transportation and escape	1

Source: Anoma Pieris, *Hidden Hands and Divided Landscapes: A Penal History of Singapore's Plural Society* (Honolulu: University of Hawai'i Press, 2009), 239.

proposed to divide these convicts into three classes. The first class was to enjoy most civil liberties and be permitted to settle on land granted to them and their children, provided that they had been in residence in Bencoolen for three years. The second class was to be employed in ordinary labour. The third class, men with records including the most notorious crimes, were to perform more arduous labour and be confined at night.[6]

The British brought South Asian offenders, including murderers, frauds, forgers and revolutionaries, to their newly occupied lands[7] in the Malay Peninsula from the 1820s to the 1870s. Aiyar, comparing overseas destinations of European convicts, suggests that Malacca, Penang and Singapore were the 'Sydney of India' till 1873.[8]

The Bengal government issued a few regulations for transporting convicts in the 1840s. In 1844, the Sudder Courts of Calcutta, Bombay and Agra passed an act for the transportation or imprisonment of offenders beyond sea for life.[9] However, deportation was not applicable to offenders who were physically unfit for transportation.[10] Many convicts vehemently opposed transportation for life beyond the seas as they compared crossing the *kala pani* (a taboo referring to ill fate because of crossing an ocean) as bad as *jeta junaza* (a living tomb).[11] For instance, the three judges of the Provincial Courts of Appeal in Calcutta reported that transportation was 'considered by many [convicts] as more severe punishment than death'. The same observation was echoed in the following statement of one Bakarganj judge: '[N]atives in general dread it [deportation overseas] more than hanging; and persons under that sentence have repeatedly requested me to get their sentences changed to death in preference.'[12]

The question is, why did the Bengal government issue such socially unacceptable transportation acts? It appears that the administration opted for colonising the penal body and minimising the labour cost in the zones of deportation. The British occupied new lands on the Indian Ocean rim during the early nineteenth century. They needed many labourers to produce export crops in Mauritius, South and East Africa, the Caribbean and other colonies. Meanwhile, the slavery system was abolished. Therefore, penal labour was profitable as a new mode of colonial extraction—as Foucault theorised.[13]

As a newly occupied outpost, the Straits Settlements needed more labourers. For this reason, Penang and Singapore turned into convict stations, and the convicts built the city's infrastructure.[14] Previously, the convicts were confined to the British Settlement in Bencoolen. Following the terms of the Anglo-Dutch Treaty, the Bengali convicts were transferred from Bencoolen to Singapore and Penang in 1824.[15] When the EIC ceded Bencoolen to the

Dutch, the 'Free Bengalis' also moved from Bencoolen.[16] Some of the 'Free Bengalis' were the Bengali convicts who had already completed their period of labour. The most significant number of convicts was in Penang; some 998 out of 1,469 came from Bengal in 1824. The remaining convicts were brought from Madras, Bombay and Sri Lanka.[17]

It is difficult to provide an exact figure for the Bengali convicts who were transported to the Straits Settlements. However, sporadic data suggests that the Bengali convicts were deported almost every year until the mid-nineteenth century. For example, about 122 convicts were sent from Bengal in 1837. They worked in different places in Singapore.[18] In 1851, the ship *Krishna* brought fifty-six convicts and fifteen guards from Calcutta to Singapore.[19] Around that year, the number of Bengali convicts was 113 in Chinatown, 408 in Kampung Gelam and 10 in the Country Districts.[20] A significant number of Bengali convicts were in Singapore Jail from 1825 to 1857 (Table 3.2).

To easily identify a convict's crime, jail clerks inscribed letters on their foreheads in their vernacular languages, including Bangla. The tattooing or stamping on the penal body was called *godna/godena* or *ulki* in Bangla.[21] With few exceptions, tattooed convicts either came from the districts of eastern Bengal or Burma.[22] In 1817, some thirteen Bengali convicts, marked on the forehead in Bangla script, charged with violent robbery in Rangpur district, Bengal, were transported to Penang.[23] The Bengal government abolished the *godna* or tattoo system in 1849.

Table 3.2   Number of Bengali convicts in Singapore, 1825–1858

Year	Number of convicts
1825	122
1826	23
1850–1851	540
1852	595
1855–1856	1845
1857–1858	890

Source: Interpolated from different sources: J. F. A. McNair and W. D. Bayliss, *Prisoners Their Own Warders: A Record of the Convicts Prison at Singapore in the Straits Settlements Established 1825, Discontinued 1873, Together with a Cursory History of the Convict Establishments at Bencoolen, Penang, and Malacca from the Year 1797* (Westminster: Archibald Constable and Co., 1899), 39, 41; Pieris, *Hidden Hands and Divided Landscapes*, 238, 240; *SFPMA*, 18 and 25 June 1857.

When convicts disembarked at a penal station in Malaya, they did so under the supervision of an executive engineer who was assisted by several workers, including a warder and an overseer of artificers and roads. All petty officers were raised from amongst the convicts and consisted of *duffadars* (non-commissioned officers in the former Indian army or police; presently, this rank is found in village policing at a union council level in Bangladesh), *tindals* (petty officers), peons and orderlies.[24] Therefore, some convicts were recruited to manage fellow convicts. For instance, in 1825, when the convicts disembarked in Singapore, they were initially placed in a godown under the supervision of four petty officers of Chittagong origin.[25] The length of deportation depended on the court sentences. If the conviction were for a lifetime (up to twenty years), the convict's deportation would be for sixteen years. If the court sentence was for seventeen years, the deportation period was twelve years. If the conviction was for seven years, transportation was for six years. For female convicts, whatever length of punishment was meted out, they were transported for three to five years.[26]

According to their respective punishments, all transported convicts were categorised into six classes (Table 3.3). The First Class consisted of trustworthy convicts who were eligible to be hired as workers while receiving a 'Ticket of Leave'[27] (TOL). In 1861, F. J. Mouat, the Inspector General of Jails in the Lower Bengal Province, visited the Straits Settlements and remarked that the TOL system was in full and effective operation.[28] The Second Class consisted of convicted petty officers, including peons, *jomadars* (collectors), orderlies, *punkah* (large cloth fan) pullers and servants, as well as those who worked unchained in hospitals and public offices. Third-Class convicts were those who completed probationary periods and worked with one leg chained on roads and public works. The Fourth Class consisted of fresh arrivals and those who were excluded from other classes. For eighteen months, this class worked in construction areas, including roads, bridges and culverts, with heavy leg chains. If their conduct improved, their chains were taken off after the expiration of an eight-month period, and they were promoted to the Second Class. The Fifth Class consisted of the most dreadful criminals, such as murderers, thugs, dacoits and deserters. The colonial government provided special instructions regarding them and forced them to do hard labour with chains. The Sixth Class consisted of aged people or superannuated convicts who were engaged in light work without iron chains.[29]

The afterlife of conviction sheds interesting light on the convicts' social integration and everyday life. For example, in 1857, after serving sixteen years

Table 3.3 Classification of Bengali convicts in the Straits Settlements, 1856

Classes	Penang		Malacca		Singapore	
	Male	Female	Male	Female	Male	Female
First	45	21	23	00	61	00
Second	11	00	11	00	09	00
Third	32	00	142	00	381	00
Fourth	142	00	17	00	38	00
Fifth	03	00	36	00	09	00
Six	75	08	16	00	33	59

Source: Pieris, *Hidden Hands and Divided Landscapes*, 241 (Appendix G).

Table 3.4 List of some Bengali convicts who stayed back in Singapore, 1855–1859

Name of Convicts	Type of Offences	When Expired	Class of Convicts
Dullah	Stabbing	1855	3
Anunda Pursaud	Robbery	1855	3
Juddonath Day	Murder	1857	5
Ducktburee (female)	Murder	1859	NA

Source: *SFPMA*, 16 February 1860, 3.

in the Straits Settlements and showing good behaviour, 551 convicts gained TOL, and several of them were allowed to marry.[30] The following list shows the convicts who, after completing the conviction period, stayed back in Singapore in 1859 (Table 3.4).[31]

In general, the residents of Singapore opposed accommodating the convicts into their society. Such anti-convict sentiment grew stronger following the Sepoy Revolt of 1857–1858, which triggered a significant increase in the migration of convicts. Some European merchants wrote to the Governor of the Straits Settlements that

> … commercial settlements like Penang and Singapore and especially the latter, should no longer be used as penal stations. So [as] long as these settlements were in their infancy, a body of convicts proved beneficial in the formation of roads, digging canals, &c., but now … a large commercial city such as Singapore … with a trade of ten millions [*sic*]

sterling, a harbor crowded with shipping, and large population earnestly engaged in mercantile and tradal [trade] pursuits, is no longer a proper place for the reception of criminals of India and most especially for that of the late sepoys of the Bengal army, men whose hands have been imbrued in the blood of women and children and whose hearts are full of hatred and revenge.[32]

A civilian committee was formed to submit a petition to the government requesting no more convicts, including mutineers from India. The Government of India appointed a committee in 1857 under F. J. Mouat, who recommended the establishment of a penal colony in the Andaman Islands or convicts' transportation to the West Indies as labourers. The government accepted these recommendations.[33] However, following the separation of the Straits Settlements in 1867, the Governor of the Straits Settlements allowed the petty offenders to merge unconditionally with the mainstream people by using the power of pardon.[34] Aiyar and Mahajani suggested that the convicts were integrated with the local population, especially in Penang.[35]

Not many records reveal the number of Bengali convicts who took the opportunity of pardon and stayed back in the Straits Settlements. Siddique and Shotam interviewed a descendant of a convict migrant who recalled that her great-grandfather was a convict transported to Singapore in the 1820s. After completing his punishment, he brought his family. The interviewee remembered that her grandfather was born in Singapore but went back to Kalighat (presently in Kolkata) to marry a Bengali woman. After that, the newlyweds returned to Singapore, and their offspring, including the interviewee's mother, was born in Singapore.[36]

It appears that a portion of convict migrants stayed back in Malaya in three specific ways: after the expiry of conviction, by receiving a Ticket of Leave and by taking a special pardon from the government. In addition, they were involved in different professions and married local men or women. Thus, some Bengali convicts integrated gradually with mainstream society.

Indenture and the Kangany System

The indenture system emerged in response to the need for labourers after the abolition of slavery. The system was introduced in Singapore and Malacca in the early 1830s. The indentured labourers were employed at plantation estates in Malaya, mainly from China and British India.[37] The EIC in India regulated indentured emigration to overseas colonies through its authorised seaports, including Calcutta. The Governor-General of India enacted Act XIV of 1839 for the emigration of labourers, which stated that persons accused of either recruiting or assisting the employment of labourers outside of EIC territories would be fined up to 200 rupees or given three months' imprisonment.[38] The emigrant acts protected Indian indentured labourers from maltreatment, fraud and misrepresentation and secured their proper medical care at emigration depots and during the passage. The recruiting agencies and brokers quite often violated the contracts of indentured labourers. Therefore, 'watchful care' was given to the labourers in the Straits Settlements until comprehensive protective measures were introduced. In 1876, a labour ordinance was issued incorporating such protective measures. It provided a variety of social amenities to the labourers. The Government of the Straits Settlements formed an Indian immigration protectorate in the colony and appointed magistrates to adjudicate labour grievances.[39]

Initially, the contract period for indentured labourers was three years, but it was extended to five years in 1882. After the termination of the contract, labourers were allowed to re-indenture or return to India.[40] Such contract papers were frequently written in dual languages (such as English and Bangla) so that indentured workers could fully understand their rights and responsibilities. If the labourers wished to return home, the recruiting agency or employer was supposed to provide them with a return fare; otherwise, the agency was fined. For instance, when a Dutch emigration agent failed to offer a sufficient return fare to a labourer, the Government of Bengal Presidency lodged complaints against the agent, who was compelled to pay the total repatriation cost of the labourer.[41]

Migration from British India to the Straits Settlements was interrupted by the Indian Emigration Act XIII of 1864 for a few years. The act made it illegal to employ Indians in the Straits Settlements for an unidentified period. It fined the responsible company up to 500 rupees in case of violation.[42] It recommended the cancellation of shipping licenses of the ship owners if they had shipped labourers under the name of ordinary passengers bound for the Straits Settlements. Article 4 of the act allowed the migration of Indian labourers to the British Colonies of Mauritius, Jamaica, British Guiana, Trinidad, St Lucia, Grenada, St Vincent, Natal, St Kitts, Seychelles and the Danish Colony of St Croix. However, it strictly forbade labour traffic to the Straits Settlements.[43] The government never provided any explanation as to the reasons for excluding its own dependencies and disallowing labourers from British India, but these can be speculated: the relationship between the governments of the Straits Settlements, Bengal and India was unstable during the 1850s and 1860s—mainly because the governing power of the Straits Settlements was changed twice within a decade. In 1851, the controlling power of the Straits Settlements was taken over by the Governor-General of India from the Governor and Council of Bengal, and this power was shifted to the Colonial Office from the Governor-General of India in 1867. After taking charge of the Straits Settlements, the Colonial Office induced the Government of India to permit labour immigration.[44] Consequently, the Indian government legalised labour migration to the Straits with Act XIV of 1872, which came into effect after four years, leading to the rapid recruitment and management of indentured labourers.[45] This formed part of the global distribution of Bengali indentured migrants, including to the Caribbean Islands.[46]

Despite the regulations of the Government of India, planters often treated the indentured labourers brutally and unjustly. Consequently, by the early nineteenth century, criticisms of the system surfaced in Calcutta and other places, and there were public demands to ban the system. In 1893, the ninth meeting of the Indian National Congress, the first political party in the Indian subcontinent, called upon the Indian government to stop 'forced' labour supplies.[47] The 'Indentured Coolie Protection Society' or 'Anti-Indentured Emigration League' was established in Calcutta in 1915. Some educated Indians, wealthy Marwaris and missionaries were members of the society.[48] Even some European planters expected 'free migrant labourers' from British India. The delegation of the Penang and Province Wellesley Planters Association appealed to the governor for free emigrants from India. European estate managers wanted cheap, abundant and tractable Indian labourers for the rubber plantations.[49] The demand for Indian labourers, combined with massive pressure from civil society to stop the indenture system, led the Indian authorities to recommend the Malay states to institute 'protectors' for Indian immigrants and to deploy a legal body to supervise the conditions of new arrivals.[50] Consequently, the Immigration Committee was created in 1907, and the official policy for the ending of the indenture system was made in 1910.[51] However, the practice of the indenture system continued until it was suspended during WWI, and it was only completely ended in 1920.[52]

After abolishing the indenture system, the Bengal government needed more clarity about sending free labourers to British Malaya because there were no proper regulations controlling it. The protector of emigrants recommended four aspects to consider for new labour migration. First, the wages of post-indenture labourers must be higher than those of indentured labourers. Second, special health care facilities for labourers were recommended. Third, migration was allowed from Bengal on the condition that the labour demands of Bengal be met first. Fourth, employers must ensure the provision of return fares.[53]

Several intermediary systems were developed to aid recruitment, including the *sardar* (or *sirdar*) and *kangany* systems. The role of intermediaries, particularly *sirdar*s, in the colonial labour migration has been explored.[54] *Kanganies* were mostly former labourers who were sent back 'home' and hired to recruit co-villagers under a system which was known as *kangany*, and it was introduced in British Malaya in the 1920s.[55] The *kangany* system was more liberal than the indentured system, but it could not make labourers completely free. In the system, employers or recruiting agencies hire a recruiter or *kangany*, providing them with advance money for expenses and the passage from India.[56] These loans would be written and legally enforceable by the *kangany* if the labourer stopped work and ceased to pay. Unfortunately, for many of these *kanganies*, workers would sometimes flee back to other colonies where the writs for debt recovery were unenforceable. The *kangany* occasionally received a fixed salary for special services. As he used to recruit his friends, neighbours and relatives from his home district, there was a chance to bring his whole family or eligible workers from his own neighbourhood.[57] These 'subaltern networks', as Bates has called them, are also known as chain migration.[58]

Kangany labourers, who worked in Ceylon, Burma and British Malaya, often did not sign a contract with the plantation owners. The most significant numbers used a thumbprint and were recruited by *kanganies*. *Kangany* labourers were mainly unskilled, especially those from rural southern India in the Tamil-majority area and poverty stricken. These labourers also hailed from the United Provinces (Bihar and Uttar Pradesh) and Bengal and were recruited into different industries, including plantation work and coal mining. For example, in 1916, a coal mine manager obtained permission from the Federated Malay States authorities to recruit miners from Bengal through the *kangany* system.[59]

Although Bengal and the Straits Settlements were under British colonial power, these regional administrations regulated migration in their own respective ways. The Bengal provincial government regulated recruitment and dispatched unskilled and skilled labourers and their dependents outside of British India using the Bengal Emigration Rules, 1923.[60] Some rules were modified, especially with regard to the emigration agents or *kangany*'s functions and their remuneration. For instance, *kanganies* must be from the labouring class, and on arrival, the *kangany* should show his licence to the emigration commissioner.[61] However, the *kangany* system could not improve the condition of labourers. The *kanganies* increased in number and developed a hierarchy in the system over time. A head *kangany* controlled a group of sub-*kanganies*. The *kangany* system contracted labourers to enter into credit bondage, which could lead to the unlawful deduction of their wages. As a result, labourers suffered from ill health and unjust treatment. Therefore, the Sastri report of 1936 recommended abolishing the *kangany* system, leading to its complete abolition in 1938.[62] Meanwhile, non-*kangany* or voluntary immigrants formed an increasing proportion of the Indian labourers in Malaya.

'Free' Migration

The Government of Bengal regulated 'inland' and 'colonial' emigrations separately. 'Inland emigration' meant migration to internal labour-demanding areas such as Assam, Sylhet, Cachar and Chittagong, where there was a demand for coolies in the tea industry. The term 'colonial emigration' meant migration to British or Foreign Colonies.[63] The colonial free migrants were independent wage earners, as opposed to indentured or *kangany* labourers. They migrated based on their capabilities, willingness and better opportunities. For colonial migration, labourers under the Government of the EIC needed to show an embarkation certificate bought with a small fee from the emigration agent of Indian ports with a counter-signature from the protector of emigrants. It was illegal for the master of any ship to allow on board any labourers without the certificate.[64]

The Government of Bengal took the necessary initiatives to prevent illegal recruitment. For example, sometimes illegal intermediaries or subordinates collected labourers for licensed recruiters, which was considered illegal. Therefore, the lieutenant governor of Bengal employed sub-agents by contract to remove 'irresponsible subordinates'. By the amendment of Act VII of 1871, those sub-agents were considered licensed recruiters. Furthermore, all recruiting agencies, namely sub-agents, recruiters and *mofussil* depots, underwent surveillance to prevent illegal recruitment. Thus, the entire mechanism was associated with securing emigrants brought under the government's strict control.

The Government of the Straits Settlements took some initiatives to stop illegal migration. Thailand was a regional hub for unlawful South Asian migration to China, Cambodia and Vietnam. People could quickly move from Bangkok to British Malaya or Singapore. The Bangkok Consul and Colonial Secretary of the Straits Settlements were concerned about this route.[65] In 1917, the Straits Settlements government stopped allowing Indian immigrants into Singapore without a passport.[66] This substantially discouraged illegal emigration from India to the Straits Settlements.

In the context of changing migration and labour relations, the Indian government passed the Act of 1886.[67] This new act was more liberal than the old one. The changes carried out in the new law were primarily technical. It secured the comfort of the emigrants in terms of their housing, food and general treatment at their workplaces. It also stated that unlawful recruiting was punishable with a heavy fine, and it ensured that the emigrant was moving to a foreign country of his own free will. There had been a steady increase in the popularity of emigration from the Lower Provinces of Bengal.[68] The Act of 1886 was amended in 1904 to incorporate provisions to prevent the spread of tuberculosis among migrants during voyages.[69]

The Indian Emigration Act of 1922 consolidated previous regulations and secured some social amenities for labourers, including a standard wage, compulsory education of their children, the payment of maternity allowances to female workers from the Government of British Malaya, regulated *kangany* recruiting and abolished the penal sanctions for breaches of contract.[70] The act distinguished between skilled and unskilled labourers, whose migration to the Malay states was subject to certain conditions of the act.[71] The Government of the Straits Settlements notified that if the contract period of unskilled labourers hired under the *kangany* system expired, their work permit would be renewed based on the advice of the Standing Emigration Advisory Committee, under the Indian Emigration Act VII of 1922.[72] Unlike unskilled labourers, each recruiter of skilled labourers was required to provide information on their destination and the number of dependents with them; accommodation; insurance for their health and well-being during the period of engagement; provision for repatriation at the end of the work period; and the terms of the employment.[73] The *Indian Emigration (Bengal) Manual 1926* came with some further minor amendments.[74]

The Indian Passport Act of 1920 recommended using passports. It established control over the foreign travel of Indians and foreigners who would travel to and within the presidencies and provinces of British India. The passport was issued to the British subject[75] (a passport of a British subject of 1940 is attached in Appendices 1.1 and 1.2) of the British Indian Empire, which covered present-day Aden, Ceylon, Pakistan, Bangladesh, Burma and non-French and Portuguese India to assure their national status as well as a foreign travel document. As per the Indian Passport Act of 1920, passports recorded their holder's name, profession, place and date of birth and identification marks alongside a photograph of the bearer.[76] The Government of India decided in 1921 that passports should not ordinarily be issued to the following four classes of people: the physically disabled, seditious individuals or revolutionaries, those suffering from contagious diseases, and people with criminal records.[77] In 1923, the Government of India decided that Indians should obtain a visa from the consul of their destination colony before leaving India.[78]

The Bengal government published a notification in 1943 to oversee migrants further. As per the notification, the additional district magistrate of Chittagong and the sub-divisional officer of Cox's Bazaar acted as the protector of emigrants for the port of Chittagong. However, the immigration of Indians was restricted to Malaya in the 1950s for political and social factors.[79] From the period of the re-occupation of Malaya in 1945, the authorities of British Malaya controlled immigration through the passport system.[80]

Conclusion

Among other South Asians, Bengalis migrated either under duress or willingly to the Malay world. Bengal was a province under the British Raj, so colonial authority in Bengal mostly followed the emigration act of the central government. The British Raj introduced different rules and regulations for the migrants' well-being and safety. Several intercessors emerged like the present-day migration agents. Though such intermediary systems were primarily concerned with the transatlantic and trans-Pacific migration of South Indians, people from other regions, including Bengalis, also migrated under those systems. Sometimes, the Bengal authority modified rules and regulations. From the mid-twentieth century, a remarkable shift occurred in migration history with the introduction of the passport and visa system. This new surveillance of human mobility took effect intensively after the independence of Malaya and British India. After the decolonisation of the British Raj, Bengal was partitioned into East Bengal and West Bengal as part of Pakistan and India, respectively— its emigration policies being governed by the two new states since then.

As the influence of the Labour Party grew in Britain in the first half of the twentieth century, colonial labour relations, including for those migrating transregionally across the British Empire, took a turn for the better. Despite many remaining difficulties, the diverse South Asian population, including the Bengalis who migrated to British Malaya, enjoyed more scope in pursuing different occupations and settling down, which is reflected in their visible diasporic presence throughout various professions. These will be the subject of the next chapter.

Notes

1. Apart from migration, the word 'free' also has been used in this book to denote those convicts who had already completed their punishment and received freedom.
2. For the detailed history of convict transportation from South Asia to Southeast Asia, see Gazi Mizanur Rahman, 'Colonising the Penal Capital: Locating the Bengali Convicts in Cosmopolitan British Malaya', *Asian Studies, The Twelfth International Convention of Asia Scholars (ICAS 12), ICAS Conference Proceedings*, vol. 1 (June (2022): 569–582, https://doi.org/10.5117/9789048557820/ICAS.2022.066, accessed 18 June 2022; Anand A. Yang, *Empire of Convicts: Indian Penal Labor in Colonial Southeast Asia* (California: University of California Press, 2021); Ronit Ricci (ed.), *Exile in Colonial Asia: Kings, Convicts, Commemoration* (Honolulu: University of Hawai'i Press, 2016); Clare Anderson, 'The Bel Ombre Rebellion: Indian Convicts in Mauritius, 1815–53', in *Abolition and Its Aftermath in Indian Ocean Africa and Asia*, ed. Gwyn Campbell (London; New York: Routledge, 2005), 50–65; C. M. Turnbull, 'Convicts in the Straits Settlements 1826–1867', *Journal of the Malaysian Branch of the Royal Asiatic Society* 43, no. 1 (217) (1970): 87–103; Kernial Singh Sandhu, 'Tamil and Other Indian Convicts in the Straits Settlements, A.D. 1790–1873', *Proceedings of the First International Conference Seminar of Tamil Studies, Kuala Lumpur, International Association for Tamil Research* 1 (1966): 197–208.
3. John R. Mclane, *Land and Local Kingship in Eighteenth-Century Bengal* (Cambridge: Cambridge University Press, 1993), 75–76.
4. Anand A. Yang, 'Indian Convict Workers in Southeast Asia in the Late Eighteenth and Early Nineteenth Centuries', *Journal of World History* 14, no. 2 (2003): 191.
5. McNair and Bayliss, *Prisoners Their Own Warders*, vii, 7.
6. Quoted in McNair and Bayliss, *Prisoners Their Own Warders*, 3–6.

7. The area covered British penal colonies, particularly Bencoolen, Malacca, Penang, Singapore and the Andaman Islands. McNair and Bayliss, *Prisoners Their Own Warders*, 11; Yang, 'Indian Convict Workers', 197; Pieris, *Hidden Hands and Divided Landscapes*, 69, 270.

8. Aiyar, *Indian Problems in Malaya*, 4.

9. *The Acts of the Supreme Government, Part I, 1834 and 1835, in Continuation of the Regulations of Supreme Government from 1793 to 1834* (Calcutta: Baptist Mission Press, 1836).

10. Smith, *The Bengal Almanac for 1845*, 159.

11. McNair and Bayliss, *Prisoners Their Own Warders*, 9.

12. Yang, 'Indian Convict Workers', 188.

13. Michel Foucault, *Power/Knowledge: Selected Interviews and Other Writings 1972–1977* (Brighton: Harvester Press, 1980).

14. In Singapore, slavery was abolished in 1823; therefore, the government needed labourers to run the colonial economy and infrastructural development.

15. John F. Riddick, *The History of British India: A Chronology* (Westport: Praeger, 2006), 35; Kim, 'Malay Attitudes towards Indians', 267.

16. British Library, India Office Records and Private Papers, 'Correspondence of the Bengal Government with the Penang Government and the Government of the Dutch East Indies Regarding the Removal from Bencoolen of Certain Free Bengalis, Emancipated Caffrees and Convicts', IOR/F/4/1184/30747: September 1826–March 1829; see also Amrith, *Crossing the Bay*, 76.

17. Yang, 'Indian Convict Workers', 197–198.

18. Yang, 'Indian Convict Workers', 198.

19. *SFPMA*, 25 July 1851, 2.

20. Pieris, *Hidden Hands and Divided Landscapes*, 238.

21. Clare Anderson, *Legible Bodies: Race, Criminality and Colonialism in South Asia* (Oxford; New York: Berg, 2004), 1–2, 15–18, 19–24, 39–43, 82, 104.

22. Anderson, *Legible Bodies*, 82.

23. Anderson, *Legible Bodies*, 34.

24. McNair and Bayliss, *Prisoners Their Own Warders*, 89.

25. McNair and Bayliss, *Prisoners Their Own Warders*, 39.

26. McNair and Bayliss, *Prisoners Their Own Warders*, 85.

27. The ticket of leave was a certificate of permission or a document that allowed convicts to earn their livelihood and reside on their own before the expiration of their sentences. When the convicts had shown trustworthy and good behaviour after spending a certain period of punishment, they obtained the certificate, which gave them freedom. Initially, the ticket was issued in

Britain and later introduced in the British Empires, including the United States, Canada, Australia and Southeast Asia.

28. McNair and Bayliss, *Prisoners Their Own Warders*, 10–11.

29. *Annals of Indian Administration 1856*, 291; *SFPMA*, 25 June 1857, 3; McNair and Bayliss, *Prisoners Their Own Warders*, 84–85; Nasution, *Chulia in Penang*, 167.

30. *SFPMA*, 25 June 1857, 3.

31. *SFPMA*, 16 February 1860, 3.

32. Quoted in Yang, 'Indian Convict Workers', 206.

33. McNair and Bayliss, *Prisoners Their Own Warders*, 143.

34. McNair and Bayliss, *Prisoners Their Own Warders*, 76, 143–144.

35. Aiyar, *Indian Problems in Malaya*, 4; Usha Mahajani, *The Role of the Indian Minorities in Burma and Malaya* (Bombay: Vora & Co., Publishers Private Ltd, 1960), 95–96.

36. Sharon Siddique and Nirmala Puru Shotam, *Singapore's Little India: Past, Present, and Future* (Singapore: Institute of Southeast Asian Studies, 1990), 10.

37. Kingsley Davis, *Population of India and Pakistan* (Princeton: Princeton University Press, 1951), 102; Kaur, *Wage Labour in Southeast Asia since 1840*, 3–4.

38. *The Bengal and Agra Annual Guide and Gazetteer for 1841, Vol. 1* (Calcutta: William Rushton and Co., 1841), 103.

39. Chanderbali, 'Indian Indenture in the Straits Settlements, 1872–1910'.

40. G. A. Grierson, *The Administration of the Lower Provinces of Bengal from 1882–83 to 1886–87* (Calcutta: Bengal Secretariat Press, 1887), 14; Stanley L. Engerman, 'Contract Labor, Sugar, and Technology in the Nineteenth Century', *Journal of Economic History* 43, no. 3 (1983): 645; Davis, *Population of India and Pakistan*, 103.

41. P. C. Emmer, 'The Meek Hindu: The Recruitment of Indian Labourers for Service Overseas, 1870–1916', in *Colonialism and Migration: Indentured Labour Before and After Slavery*, ed. P. C. Emmer (Dordrecht, The Netherlands: Martinus Nijhoff Publishers, 1986), 207.

42. Nagendiram Rajendra, 'The Straits Settlements 1867–1874' (MA thesis, Australian National University, 1976).

43. Chanderbali, 'Indian Indenture in the Straits Settlements, 1872–1910'.

44. Mahajani, *The Role of the Indian Minorities*, 96.

45. Chanderbali, 'Indian Indenture in the Straits Settlements, 1872–1910'.

46. Chanderbali, 'Indian Indenture in the Straits Settlements, 1872–1910'.

47. *Daily Advertiser*, 1 February 1894, 2.
48. NAB, Proceedings A, Dept.: Finance, Br.: Emigration (Calcutta: Bengal Government Press, 1915).
49. Carl A. Trocki, 'Political Structures in the Nineteenth and Early Twentieth Centuries', in *The Cambridge History of Southeast Asia, Vol. 2, The Nineteenth and Twentieth Centuries*, ed. Nicholas Tarling (Cambridge: Cambridge University Press, 1992), 113.
50. Trocki, 'Political Structures in the Nineteenth and Early Twentieth Centuries', 113.
51. Virginia Thompson, *Postmortem on Malaya* (New York: The Macmillan Company, 1943), 122; *ST*, 6 April 1912, 9; Northrup, *Indentured Labor*, 131.
52. Davis, *Population of India and Pakistan*, 104.
53. NAB, Proceedings A, Dept.: General, Br.: Emigration, Government of Bengal, vol. 13, January 1912. Protector of Emigrants to Secretary to Government of Bengal.
54. Crispin Bates and Marina Carter, 'Sirdars as Intermediaries in Nineteenth-century Indian Ocean Indentured Labour Migration', *Modern Asian Studies* 51, no. 2 (2017): 463.
55. Davis, *Population of India and Pakistan*, 103–104; Aiyar, *Indian Problems in Malaya*, 7. The indentured system was introduced in 1826 and ended in 1920, whereas the *kangany* system was arguably introduced in India and Ceylon in 1910. The indentured and *kangany* recruiting systems seemed to work in parallel from 1910 to 1920.
56. Mahajani, *The Role of Indian Minorities*, 97.
57. Davis, *Population of India and Pakistan*, 104.
58. Crispin Bates and Marina Carter, 'Enslaved Lives, Enslaving Labels: A New Approach to the Colonial Indian Labor Diaspora', in *New Routes for Diaspora Studies*, ed. Sukanya Banerjee, Aims McGuinness and Steven C. McKay (Indiana: Indiana University Press, 2012), 67–94.
59. Amarjit Kaur, 'Hewers and Haulers: A History of Coal Miners and Coal Mining in Malaya', *Modern Asian Studies* 24, no. 1 (1990): 90.
60. *Indian Emigration (Bengal) Manual 1926* (Calcutta: Bengal Government Press, 1926), 52.
61. *Indian Emigration (Bengal) Manual 1926*, 73–74.
62. Norton Ginsburg and Chester F. Roberts Jr, *Malaya* (Seattle: University of Washington Press, 1958), 322; Thompson, *Postmortem on Malaya*, 123.
63. Grierson, *The Administration of the Lower Provinces of Bengal*, 13.

64. The Emigration of Natives Act, 1844 charged 1 rupee for the embarkation certificate for Jamaica, British Guiana and Trinidad. See Smith, *The Bengal Almanac for 1845*, 165.

65. NAB, Proceedings A, Dept.: Finance, Br.: Emigration, January 1914. Colonial administrators in Calcutta, Bangkok and Singapore discussed illegal migration in 1913.

66. *Blue Book for the Year 1888*, 14. In the mid-nineteenth century, the Government of Straits Settlements started issuing a passport to British subjects.

67. Grierson, *The Administration of the Lower Provinces of Bengal*, 16; *Report on the Administration of Bengal 1884–85* (Calcutta: Bengal Secretariat Press, 1886), 296.

68. Grierson, *The Administration of the Lower Provinces of Bengal*, 18.

69. *Report on the Administration of Bengal 1904–1905* (Calcutta: Bengal Secretariat Book Depot, 1906), 125.

70. Thompson, *Postmortem on Malaya*, 122.

71. *Indian Emigration (Bengal) Manual 1926*, 88.

72. *Indian Emigration (Bengal) Manual 1926*, 99.

73. Davis, *Population of India and Pakistan*, 106.

74. For templates and amendments of different contract forms of various professions, including artisans, shop assistants and clerks, see *Indian Emigration (Bengal) Manual 1926*, 69, 71; NAB, Bundle 3, Proceedings B, List 95, Dept & Br.: Emigration, 1936–38.

75. British subjects were identified by birth or naturalisation in British India as well as a British-protected person or the spouse or widow of such a person. The usage of passports as a British subject was discontinued when the British colonies became independent. In 1947, the new Dominions of Ceylon, India and Pakistan came into being. Bearers in the Dominions of Pakistan and India were entitled to opt for Indian, Pakistani or British nationality. The emergence of passports, visa schemes and bureaucracy relating to migration and citizenship in India has been discussed by Haimanti Roy, 'Paper Rights: The Emergence of Documentary Identities in Post-Colonial India, 1950–67', *Journal of South Asian Studies* 39, no. 2 (2016): 329–349; see also Radhika Mongia, *Indian Migration and Empire: A Colonial Genealogy of the Modern State* (Durham: Duke University Press, 2018).

76. Gopal, 'A Sea of Change, an Ocean of Memories', 168.

77. *Indian Emigration (Bengal) Manual 1926*, 79.

78. *Indian Emigration (Bengal) Manual 1926*, 79.

79. In the context of post-war counterinsurgency and the declaration of an emergency in Malaya, the government launched a 'hearts and minds' programme to contain communism. Due to security concerns, the government reinforced migration control. The deteriorating economic condition of Malaya was also a potential factor for imposing restrictions on migration. See Amrith, *Crossing the Bay*, 220; Horace Stone, *From Malacca to Malaysia, 1400–1965* (London: Harrap and Co. Ltd, 1966), 176.

80. Ginsburg and Roberts Jr, *Malaya*, 322.

4

Professionals and the Working Class

Most early colonial Bengali migrants travelled and worked under contract and experienced poor health, insecurity and desperation. Nevertheless, with the end of the indenture system, the government gradually introduced regulations to secure migrants' welfare and interests. British Malaya offered new and extensive work opportunities in different plantations and mines, including rubber and tin mines. Though most workers were Chinese and Tamils, many came from northern India and Bengal. The ethnic identity of Bengali professionals and workers was often conflated with that of non-Bengalis, and their vocations were not officially recorded. However, piecemeal sources can help us to locate many Bengali professionals. This chapter examines various formal and informal occupations that Bengalis engaged in, shedding light on their vibrant presence in colonial and postcolonial Malaya.

At the Construction Site and Cattle Farm

The term 'coolie' is widespread in British colonial history in Asia. It broadly refers to hardworking labourers who performed menial jobs; however, the definition of coolie differs according to different perspectives and circumstances. I had used this term consciously and in a non-diminishing manner to reflect the professional category of labourers in colonial registers when they migrated as workers to British Malaya and other colonies. South Asian and Chinese coolies worked in construction sites and rubber estates in the Straits Settlements. Most South Asian coolies were Tamils, and most female coolies were 'passive victims' in the migration process and lived in the plantations.[1] Alongside other South Asians, Bengali coolies worked in different sectors, including roads and railways, harbours and cattle farms. The

Singapore Governor fully implemented the Indian Immigrants' Protection Act in order to protect the well-being of labourers, in particular those who came from India and Bengal.[2] L. H. Clayton, the Chairman of the Immigration Committee in Malaya, made provisions for social amenities for labourers and coolies. He showed a keen interest in employing Bengali coolies. However, he noted that the recruitment of Bengali coolies rested on the cooperation of the Indian government.[3] I. R. Belilios (1846–1910),[4] a cattle trader, recruited mostly Bengali[5] clerks and coolies for his farm business, and their number significantly increased in the 1890s. Aristarchus Moses, an Armenian Jewish merchant, migrated from Calcutta to Singapore in 1820 and established a trading farm in 1840. Like Belilios, Moses employed Bengalis as stevedores and keepers at his house and warehouses.[6]

In the Plantation and Mining Sectors

British colonialists and capitalists needed labourers to support their flourishing economy in Malaya. However, in the British view, the Malay people were 'lazy and useless' and did not have the stomach for prosperity; they only worked for their needs.[7] Syed Hussein Alatas critically analysed the colonial construction of the myth of 'lazy natives' with reference to Malay, Filipino and Javanese labourers for the period between the sixteenth and twentieth centuries. He showed the origins and functions of the myth and explained colonial capitalism and its attitude towards labour.[8] However, this colonialist view was one of the major reasons for bringing South Asians to the Malay Peninsula. It was also reflected in the application of the European capitalists. In the 1880s, two European estate managers sought permission from the colonial government to bring Indian unindentured labourers to the rubber plantations of the Malay states because they were cheap, abundant and tractable.[9]

The Malay Peninsula was rich in mineral resources. However, the local people rarely worked in the rubber plantations, leading to a remarkable flow of immigrant labourers in British Malaya.[10] In 1915, the Government of India informed the public that the Federated Malay States were interested in employing skilled and unskilled Indian labourers in the police or military forces, as watchmen and guards in tin mines, as coachmen in plantation estates or in similar capacities.[11] After that, different mines and plantations recruited Bengali labourers. For example, the Simpang Estate in Perak covered 640 acres, and its human resources comprised Tamils, Chinese, Malays and

Bengalis.[12] In 1925, the Scudai Pulai Rubber Estate earned its highest profit with a labour force consisting of different ethnicities, including the Bengalis.[13] Salil Kumar Chakravarti recalled that many Bengali plantation labourers, including his father, had worked in a rubber estate in Negeri Sembilan in the Federation of Malaya.[14]

Apart from the plantation sites, a good number of Bengali migrants worked in the tin industry and coal mines. For example, the Tambun Mine was located in Perak. Its workforce consisted of different ethnic groups, including 900 Bengali and Kling labourers, a Malay (as manager), Chinese workers and a European (as an assistant).[15] In the following extract, Mushahid Ali recalls the involvement of his family in tin mining, as they switched jobs from one sector to the other, where they met other Bengali workers:

> We came from Taltala Village under Balagonj police station in Sylhet. My father [Munshi Asmat Ali] and my uncle Muniruddin came to British Malaya in 1922. They worked in unskilled jobs down the west coast of Malaya; from Penang, they went to Batu Gajah in Perak to seek work in the tin mines as boilermen or engine drivers. Eventually, they went to Ampang, Selangor, where there were other people from East Bengal, particularly Sylhet. They worked for a while there before moving south to Johor. While Asmat Ali found work as a boilerman in Kota Tinggi [at Sungei Besi Tin Mine], Muniruddin went to Singapore in 1939 to seek work in the British military base and eventually settled over there. In those days, the British encouraged the people of Sylhet to come to Malaya.[16]

In Supporting Roles

British officials and merchants maintained social status by hiring Indian *ayah*s (domestic helpers). In British India, they employed other assistants, including tailors, gardeners, *chaprasi*s (attendants), barbers and *dhobi*s (washermen or washerwomen). Bengali *ayah*s were often found in British official bungalows, including that of Viceroy Lord Minto,[17] and many of them accompanied colonial officials to Malaya. One Bengali *ayah* assisted a British civilian family when they were travelling to British Malaya and Java during the mid-nineteenth century.[18] Chinese and Bengali domestic servants worked across British Malaya, including at the Governor's palace in Singapore.[19]

The Government of the Straits Settlements brought Bengali *baboo*s to support clerical workers.[20] Baboo Lane may have been named after them at Serangoon Road. Promoting the prevalence of Bengali clerks, the government recommended that apart from the Malay language, any aspirant for government employment in the Straits Settlements should have adequate knowledge of Hindustani, Tamil, Bangla, Chinese and Telugu.[21] Bangla was also reported to have been widely used in Penang.[22] An old Bengali, Imami, worked as *jamadar* under Benson Maxwell, the Recorder of Penang from 1855 to 1871. When Maxwell retired, Imami went to Bangkok, where he spent the rest of his life.[23]

A significant number of Bengali clerks worked at the British Resident Office at Taiping city in Perak. Some settled in the Malay Peninsula.[24] For example, Shaik Ismail bin Abdullah, alias Ismail Ballah (c. 1843–1928), was born in Singapore to a family who arrived there in the 1830s from Bengal. Ballah worked at the German Consulate in Singapore from 1893 to 1928.[25] He was mentioned several times in the files of the German Foreign Ministry on the administrative and financial matters of the German Consulate between 1892 and 1928. Ballah joined the consulate as an office assistant in February 1893. When the German Consulate in Singapore was closed from 1914 to 1926, he received—through the Swiss Consulate—a salary for the safekeeping of the consulate archives. His post there, in local terms, was 'First Tambi' (an office server).[26] He also used to keep a record of German exports and imports to and from Singapore. Angullia Mosque, or the Chander Road Mosque, where he was a popular and prominent community leader, was close to his home at Roberts Lane, and he usually prayed there.[27]

In the Legal Profession

The legal profession was very prestigious in Bengal during the British colonial period. Most political leaders in Bengal chose careers in the law profession. Bengali solicitors were found throughout British Malaya, some of them being well-known and respected among the Bengali and other diasporic communities.[28] Srish Chandra Goho (1891–1948) was one of those who came from Calcutta to Malacca in 1907 as a business partner of a Chinese businessman.[29] He practised law while continuing his business. He was involved with the mobile magistrate court. Other lawyers, including his brother-in-law, accompanied Goho from Bengal to Malacca. He became a member of the Singapore Bar, and his son continued his legacy, also practising law there until 1956. Other examples of Bengali legal professions can be easily found. M. A. Majid was not a trained solicitor, but he had knowledge of various legal issues and helped seamen and others in the court of Singapore. During the postcolonial period, Dolly Sinha was popular among Bangladeshi migrants. She completed Bar-at-Law in 1977 and practised at Singapore Court for nineteen years. She opened a law firm named Dolly Sinha Devanport and Co. She recalls that when she was practising law in the 1980s, people called her office 'Little Bangladesh High Commission' because most of the injured or maltreated Bengali workers used to come to her office for legal assistance.[30]

Police and Watchmen

During the colonial period, the Bengalis filled the subordinate ranks of many professions. Bengali police officers and security guards were relatively few compared to their other South Asian counterparts and often confused with Punjabis in documented evidence. However, some scholars have differentiated between Bengali and other Indian police officers. For example, the Perak Armed Force consisted of Malays and Indians, who were mostly Punjabis, Pathans, Jats and Bengalis.[31] The Singaporean Police Force also included Bengalis, among other ethnic groups, who were employed at thirty police stations in the 1890s.[32] The deputy superintendent of police, George Wahab, reported that the salary was unattractive. Therefore, most Bengali and other Indian police officers returned home after completing two or three years of service.[33] Even in the early postcolonial period, when nationality and race became a sensitive issue, a few Bengali migrants joined the police forces. For instance, after the Japanese Occupation, Kishore Bhattachary joined the Singapore Police Force at Orchard Road Division and served for twenty years. He was attached to the Gurkha Contingent and promoted to a corporal rank.[34]

Mechanics and Technicians

Different industries and companies flourished in British Malaya during the early twentieth century. The government and private companies recruited diverse people from South Asia, including Bengalis. The oil sector thrived in Malaya and on the western coast of Borneo following the successful drilling of the British Malayan Petroleum Company (BMPC) in the 1920s. In 1927, Burmah Oil Company and Royal Dutch-Shell jointly formed the Burmah-Shell Oil Storage and Distributing Company of British India.[35] In 1929, the Burmah-Shell Oil Storage and Distributing Company recruited some 'Indian' welders on behalf of the BMPC for its Sarawak oilfields.[36] Since Bangla-speaking people were found in Brunei as early as 1932,[37] it may be safely assumed that some Bengalis worked in the oil sector on the western coast of Borneo.

The Calcutta-based Aluminium Manufacturing Company recruited a few spinners, including Abdul Rahman, Samon Ali and Sree Kishan, on behalf of Diethein & Co., Singapore. The Aluminium Manufacturing Company deposited a sum of 100 rupees for every worker as security at the Office of the Protector of Emigrants and agreed to provide free accommodation, which was not mentioned in the formal job contract.[38]

In 1931, Thomas J. Bata opened an outlet for the Bata Shoe Company in Singapore. In 1936, a factory was built at Klang in Selangor to produce footwear for both the domestic and overseas markets.[39] Some Bengali skilled workers were employed at the Bata factory and outlet in Malaya.[40] For example, in 1940, a Bengali mechanic named Mubarak Khan was appointed at the Bata shoe factory at Klang. Sudhansu Ranjan Das Gupta, a Bengali engineer, worked at Texas Instruments (TI), an American technology company, for twenty-two years from its opening in Singapore in 1969.[41] Dolly Sinha remembers that she met some Bengali engineers, including Samir Datta, Roben Banarjee and his son Gautam Banarjee, who worked in Singapore during the 1980s.[42]

A Marine Workforce

The history of the Bengali sailor goes back a long way.[43] For their trading and military ships, European East Indian Companies employed Bengali *lascars*, who mainly were Muslims from the Sylhet and Noakhali regions. From the early seventeenth century, they made irregular voyages to many cosmopolitan port cities, including Alexandria, Naples, Tunis, London, Liverpool, Glasgow, Antwerp, Kobe, Shanghai, Singapore, Rangoon and Ceylon.[44] From the 1850s onwards, Bengali *lascars* were crucial for running British ships.[45]

Bengali firemen and seamen were found frequently in British Malaya. Bengali *lascars* were reported to be more virtuous and morally sound than their European counterparts. They were considered sober, hardworking and obedient; some spoke English. However, they did not escape colonial criticism;

Parkinson labelled Bengali *lascars* 'weak, cowardly, and unaccustomed to cold'.[46] It is estimated that more than 50 per cent of the Bengali skilled labourers and seamen worked in various steamship companies and departments, including the local British Steamship Co. (Coastal), HM Naval Base, the Royal Army Force (RAF), the War Department and the Public Works Dept. in British Malaya.[47] There were more than 3,000 Bengali *lascars* in Singapore during the First World War. However, this number decreased to less than 700 in 1925 due to a lack of employment, discrimination and corruption in the Master Attendants' Office.[48] Noorul Islam's father was a seaman whose parents had come from Sylhet to Singapore. Islam recalls that some Bengali seamen used to engage in new business during their time of unemployment, and his father started a bookshop in 1938.[49]

A number of Bengali *lascars* moved to Britain from Singapore, with many older *lascars* working on East Indian ships before arriving in Britain. Mohammed Rahman, whose transnational life started when his uncle took him to Singapore in 1909 to find work on the ships, described his life as a *sareng* (ship foreman). He moved to Britain before the Second World War. Another Bengali, Fazlu Miah, had been working in the Merchant Navy before jumping on a ship bound for Liverpool in 1952.[50]

Several Bengalis worked as firemen on coal-burning ships, a job that could be fraught with danger. About forty-two individuals, including ten Bengali firemen, were wounded when *SS Poh Hin Guan* was rescued in the Perak River in 1896.[51] In 1892, the *Pinang Gazette* reported the sinking of a steamer named *Rajah Kongsee Atjeh* near Muka Head (presently in Malaysia) and the death of two Bengali firemen.[52]

Interpreters and Miscellaneous Professions

The recruitment of Bengali interpreters reflected the need to know the Bangla language in the administration and other public spaces, including courts and police stations. James Low, the colonial administrator of Penang (who later became a planter), recommended the recruiting of interpreters of Asian languages such as Bangla in the Penang Court.[53] In 1894, the Kuala Lumpur Court advertised a vacancy for a Bengali interpreter with a salary of Straits Settlements 480 dollars per annum.[54] The demand for Bengali interpreters was extensive across the Federated Malay States as well.[55] In 1915, the Kedah Court asked the assistant corporal police to send a Bengali interpreter.[56] Salil Kumar

Chakravarti was one individual who worked in different professions, including as an interpreter at the Singapore High Court.[57] Apart from the courts or police stations, the Singapore Harbour Board and Marine Department also employed Bengali translators or interpreters.[58]

A Bangla-speaking police officer was even deployed to facilitate communication between the current Bangladeshi workers and law enforcement in Singapore, which can be traced back about 200 years. Nabel Al Masri is a Bengali and a special constable corporal (Cpl) in the National Service in the Singapore Police Force. He is a Singaporean citizen; his parents migrated to Singapore at the turn of the twenty-first century. His fluency in Bangla has made him popular among Bangladeshi workers; as a community engagement officer, he delivered a series of crime prevention talks in Bangla in the Bangladeshi workers' dormitories, with 500–3,000 workers attending each time.[59]

Some Bengalis found work as supervisors and accountants.[60] Ramnath Biswas (1894–1955) was born at Baniachang in Sylhet. He was a soldier of the Bengali Paltan in Mesopotamia, but he came to Malaya in 1915. He worked as a supervisor at Singapore Harbour for about fifteen years. Biswas can be considered a modern Bengali globetrotter and started travelling from Singapore in 1931.[61]

Other Bengali professionals worked as orderlies, sanitary officers and chefs. In his travel account, Biswas described that he had met a range of Bengalis in different positions: a Bengali office assistant who worked at a Chinese newspaper office in Kuala Lumpur, a Bengali sanitary officer at Kajang who was expecting to return home after saving a certain amount of money, and a new Bengali migrant in Kuala Lumpur. The last migrant informed Biswas that about 150 families had arrived in Malaya more than five years ago (around 1925). All of them had settled in Kuala Lumpur, Ipoh, Batu Gajah and Taiping. He further told Biswas that more Bengali families were waiting to migrate to Malaya. Among the new migrants, the following professions were recorded: tinsmith, ironsmith, electrician, compositor and overseer. According to Biswas, Bengali Muslims quickly acquired jobs as chefs and waiters at restaurants in Singapore.[62]

Physicians and Teachers in Medical Institutions

The arrival time of the earliest batch of Bengali medical practitioners in Malaya still needs to be discovered. However, modern medical education started in Bengal well before the Straits Settlements.[63] Consequently, many Bengalis received modern medical education at least a generation earlier than the Malays. The EIC established two medical colleges in Calcutta and Madras in 1835 to train local people. With the help of local philanthropists and nawabs, the Government of Bengal established two more medical colleges in Eastern Bengal, the Mitford Hospital (1858) and Sir Salimullah Medical College (1875). The graduates of these medical colleges were mainly upper-class Bengalis, Europeans and Anglo-Indians. They were employed in the army corps, serving in the military and public hospitals.

The graduates from these medical institutions served the health sectors in British Bengal and other colonies. The beginning of medical education in Bengal is reflected in the growth of Bengali medical specialists in the Straits Settlements. Apart from being employed by the government, Bengali practitioners may have migrated individually to British Malaya from the late nineteenth century. A regular medical school, the first in the Malay Peninsula, was founded in 1905 and named the Straits and Federated Malay States Government Medical School. It was renamed King Edward VII Medical School in 1913 and given the status of medical college in 1921.[64] The school was a milestone for modern medical education in Singapore and Malaysia.

Malaya had a massive demand for medical staff, and the colonial authority offered jobs immediately after those qualified physicians arrived in the Malay Peninsula. K. C. Sinha quipped, '[A]s I got down the steps of the ship, the job was waiting there'.[65] P. R. Sengupta suggested that two of the earliest Bengali doctors, namely Paresh Nath Sen from Dacca and Sarojininath Bardhan from Comilla, arrived in British Malaya in possibly 1907.[66] Dr Sengupta wrote a biographical book on the Bengali doctors and their contributions in Malaya throughout the twentieth century. He showed how the Bengali doctors and their descendants contributed to the public health service and the development of medical education in the Straits Settlements. In this chapter, his book has been used extensively to retrieve the history of Bengali doctors.

By the turn of the twentieth century, the Government of the Straits Settlements had introduced a series of healthcare services, including the Maternal and Child Health Service in 1907.[67] Therefore, the government appointed a considerable number of medical practitioners, including Paresh Nath Sen (1878–1948).[68] Sen was attached as an assistant surgeon to the District Hospital at Port Dickson in Negeri Sembilan in 1908. He worked at different hospitals, including Port Dickson Hospital (1908–1921), Kuala

Lumpur General Hospital (1921–1924), Kuala Lipis Hospital (1924–1931) and Tanglin Hospital (1931–1934).[69]

As mentioned earlier, the Government of the Straits Settlements established a medical school in 1905. Some Bengali practitioners, including Bardhan (1874–1927)[70] and Kali Charan Ghosh (1903–1963), served the new school. Dr Bardhan joined as a demonstrator in the Pathology Department. After completing a Diploma in Tropical Medicine and Hygiene (DTMH) and Diploma in Public Health (DPH) in London, he was appointed to the Malacca General Hospital in 1922. His contribution was invaluable in establishing the pathology service in Malacca. There is a cenotaph at Bukit Serindit, Malacca, dedicated to Dr Bardhan, with a bilingual inscription in Bangla and English.[71]

Dipendu Sarbadhikary and Sengupta worked in different health institutions during the advancement of medical education in Malaysia. Benoy Kumar Sen started his career in horsemanship in the Medicine and Surgery Department at the Malacca General Hospital in 1955.[72] Amar Chatterjee, a physiologist, joined the Universiti Sains Malaysia (USM). Sarbadhikary worked at the University of Malaya in Kuala Lumpur and the Department of Psychiatry at the USM.[73] Sengupta was one of the pioneering general surgeons who started a career in Malaysia in 1967. He successfully served in government and private institutions and became a general surgeon and professor of Surgery at the University of Malaysia Sarawak (UNIMAS).

Bengali specialists in obstetrics and gynaecology served with dedication in British Malaya. K. C. Sinha came to Singapore in 1912 and joined as a general practitioner at Kandang Kerbau Maternity Hospital. His son and grandson, A. C. Sinha and R. K. Sinha, were prominent obstetricians and gynaecologists in Singapore.[74] Members of the Sinha family served at the Kandang Kerbau Maternity Hospital for almost fifty years. Rajabali Jumabhoy recalled that A. C. Sinha gained popularity as a medical doctor, and his descendants carried out the same profession in Singapore.[75]

The mortality rate of coolies and labourers was high in rubber plantations and mining areas during the early twentieth century. The Government of the Federated Malay States recommended that estate owners hire qualified dressers in their estate hospitals.[76] Some Bengali doctors, including Kshitendra Chandra Sengupta (1891–1968) and Dwijendra Kumar Majumder (1898–1961), served in these facilities.[77] K. C. Sengupta was employed as a medical practitioner at the Bahau Estate in 1914, one of the biggest rubber plantations near Seremban owned by Dunlop Rubber Company. However, he later moved to a hospital under an oil palm estate run by the SCOFIN (Société Financiere de Caoutchouc) group in Labis, Johor.[78] Majumder was posted to the District Hospital at Port Dickson before serving as a medical officer in several rubber estates. During the Great Depression of 1929, the labourers suffered severely from privation, so he provided free treatment and served as a voluntary doctor at prisons, orphanages and convents. Dr Majumder's patients often could not pay their fees and met him instead with a few eggs or some home-grown vegetables.[79]

Some Bengali medical practitioners were experts in dermatology and tuberculosis. Madhuri Majumder began her career as a medical officer at Melaka General Hospital in 1961 and later founded the Dermatology Department at Ipoh General Hospital. She was the first female dermatologist in Malaysia.[80] Narayan Chandra Sengupta (1918–2010) worked at Seremban General Hospital from 1948 to 1950. In 1950, he joined the Singapore Anti-Tuberculosis Association (SATA) and became its director in 1958.[81]

The British occupied the highest ranks in the medical sectors, so when they left Malaya in the wake of independence in the 1950s, the health sector suffered from insufficient skilled medical practitioners. During this critical period, some Bengali doctors worked as chief medical & health officers (CM & HO) in different states. For example, S. K. Biswas in Kelantan and S. K. Mukherjee in Trengganu both became CM & HO; M. L. Gupta was the head of the Health Department in Pahang; H. K. Ray was the Director of General Hospital, Kuala Lumpur; Rabindar Nath Ray was the Chief of General Hospital in Sabah; and A. N. Ray was the CM & HO in Johor.[82] In their various capacities, these Bengali practitioners served public health as well as involved themselves in developing public health policies in Malaysia.

Several Bengali practitioners worked in the Armed Forces Medical Corps in Malaya. During the 1950s, the people of Malaya demonstrated for *merdeka* (independence of the Federation of Malaya), and political unrest was everywhere across the country. It was hazardous to work in the Defense Ministry in these chaotic circumstances. Nevertheless, some Bengali doctors worked in the Ministry of Defense, including Lt Col Kanak Sankar Dutta, Lt Col Gopal Chandra Dutta and Maj Amiya Kumar Bag. During the Indonesia–Malaysia confrontation in the 1960s, Dutta was sent to Sarawak and was attached to a unit in Bau in the First Division for one year.

Many Bengali doctors sacrificed their lives during the Second World War and the insurgency period (1948–1960) in Malaya. Dr Bimol Sinha was killed by the Japanese air attack in 1942. P. R. Sengupta notes that his professional experiences were beyond 'the imagination and comprehension' during the postwar confrontation between the communist insurgents and government forces in Malaya. In 1955, Dr Santosh Kumar Roy died in a tragic helicopter crash while attending an emergency call in the jungles of Negeri Sembilan.

Many Bengali doctors received awards for their great service in British Malaya during the colonial and postcolonial periods. For instance, the Governor of Singapore decorated Bardhan as *rai sahib* in 1919. Dr Madhuri Majumder was given the honorary title of *datuk* by the Sultan of Perak in 1989.[83] Dr S. K. Biswas (in Johor) and Dr P. R. Sengupta (in Sarawak) were also named *datoship*[84] by the state authorities. Dr Aleya Banerjee was awarded the Certificate of Appreciation by the Sultan of Malaysia on 31 August 1969 for her exemplary service during the communal riots of May 1969 in Kuala Lumpur. Some other Bengali doctors were bestowed with federal and/or state awards for their outstanding contributions over the years, namely M. N. G. Majumder, Sushil Kumar Biswas, K. S. Dutta, Anjan Sen Mazumder, Ajoy Chowdhury, Atindra Nath Ray, S. K. Mukherjee, G. C. Dutta, K. K. Mandal, R. N. Roy and Ranu Mukherjee.[85]

Changes in the Profession among Bengali Descendants

Some of the offspring of Bengali labourers or workers who had migrated to the Straits Settlements in the early nineteenth and twentieth centuries were educated and transitioned into high positions in government and non-government offices. Mushahid Ali (b. 1941), son of Munshi Asmat Ali (1893–1982), was born and grew up in Johor. He moved to Singapore in 1949 for a better education. After finishing college, he started working as a reporter in a newspaper and later worked at Radio Television Singapore from 1963 to 1966. He resumed studies at the University of Singapore in 1966 and graduated from there, eventually joining the Ministry of Foreign Affairs. He served as a diplomat in seven countries, including Malaysia, Saudi Arabia, Indonesia, England, Japan and Cambodia, and retired in 2001. Presently he is working as a senior fellow at the S. Rajaratnam School of International Studies (RSIS) of Nanyang Technological University. Of his three children, Yasmin Ali works as a counsellor with the permanent mission of the Republic of Singapore at the United Nations, New York. His younger son is a banker in the USA. Another son, Imran Ali, is working in Singapore as a journalist. Mashhur Ali (b. 1943), brother of Mushahid Ali, studied in Singapore and joined the civil service after graduating from the University of Singapore. After serving forty years, he retired as a senior officer. He has four children who are working and living in Singapore.[86]

Anwarul Haque (b. 1939), son of Muniruddin (1903–1980), was born and raised in Singapore. After graduating from the University of Singapore in 1964, he joined the government's Legal Service Department as a deputy director of legal aid. He served in different district courts from 1964 to 1973 as a deputy magistrate, Deputy Public Prosecutor (DPP) and district judge. In recognition of his public service, he was awarded the Bintang Bakti Masyarakat (BBM; Public Service Star) and the Pingat Bakti Masyarakat (PBM; Public Service Medal) by the government. He later left for England to gain further education in law. On his return to Singapore in 1982, he started a legal practice.[87]

Salil Kumar Chakravarti (b. 1928) was born in a rubber estate in the Negeri Sembilan, where his father worked. In 1949, Chakravarti started working as an immigration officer in the Immigration Department and held various positions for thirty-four years before retiring in 1983.[88]

Ronendra Karmakar's father, an engineer for Singapore Municipality, had migrated to Singapore in 1916. Ronendra Karmakar (1923–2006) was born at Belilious Lane and raised in Singapore. His first job was at the Penang Harbour Board in 1939. After that, he worked in various areas, including as an overseer for Malay Gammon at Singapore Harbour Board and as a checker and draughtsman for Singapore Municipality in 1941. Karmakar supervised transportation (lorries) and assisted in the fieldwork relating to the Stone Crushing Depot. When the British retook power over Singapore after the Second World War, he resigned and started a small shop, but he did not do well in business and eventually joined the British Army as a clerk. Interestingly, he turned to creative pursuits and became a successful cartoonist in 1947.

As a cartoonist, his career began at the Teachers' Training College (TTC), and he was able to become a full-time cartoonist from 1974 onwards, with work published in the *Straits Times* and the *New Nation*. He taught cartooning and contributed to developing this art in Singapore. Even after his retirement in 1978, he was re-employed as an education officer overseeing cartooning under the Ministry of Education (MOE). He retired from the ministry in 1983.[89]

These discussions on professional lives show that Bengali migrants were involved in almost every sector throughout the nineteenth and twentieth centuries. They have primarily been employed as skilled professionals rather than low-wage earners until the mid-twentieth century. With the passing of the 1980s and 1990s, the number of unskilled or labourer migrants noticeably increased. Three factors might be responsible for this upward trend in unskilled labour: the unstable political and economic situation in Bangladesh, the interruption of Bangladeshi migrations to the Middle East due to the Gulf War, and simultaneously, the demand for labourers and construction workers in Singapore and Malaysia. However, within a generation, descendants of this later wave of unskilled Bengali migrants again moved into new professions and up the social scale. Some of them obtained higher education and became government officials. On the other hand, the offspring of skilled migrants continued their parents' professions or opted to re-migrate to Europe, Australia and America.

Conclusion

The Straits of Malacca played a crucial role in connecting the Pacific Ocean and the Indian Ocean. It facilitated the movement of people, ideas and commodities in neighbouring areas and beyond. Anthony Medrano has termed this phenomenon the 'edible tide' in a different way. He indicated how diverse migrants met and fostered the industrial zone in Malacca from the late nineteenth to the mid-twentieth century.[90] We can extend the idea of the 'edible tide' into the colonial economy, which facilitated labour migration to the coastal colonies across the Pacific and Indian Oceans. After the disembarkation of diverse South Asian migrants in port cities, which marked the meeting place of two oceans, immigrants were involved in the flourishing of the plantation economy, as had occurred in the colonies on the Caribbean islands. Most South Asian labourers who supported the plantation economy came from southern India, namely Tamils.[91] However, a portion came from Bengal and the United Provinces as miners and plantation workers. These individuals also played a significant role in both skilled and semi-skilled professionals. For example, among other South Asians, Bengali doctors and Sikh police created a space in the professional world in British Malaya. Bengali doctors contributed to developing the institutions of medical education. Some were chief health administrators in several states of Malaysia, entrusted with implementing the government's medical policies. Professional trends among Bengali migrants were reversed in the postcolonial period in the Malay Peninsula; now, most Bangla-speaking migrants in Malaysia, Singapore and Brunei are manual labourers, whereas only a small number of them are working in skilled professions such as teachers, engineers and doctors, for example.[92] The high number of Bangla-speaking migrants is reflected in the advertisements and billboards of the two mobile operator companies of Singapore, which are written in Bangla (Appendices 1.3 and 1.4) to attract Bangladeshi transient workers.

After their migration, Bengalis formed associations and organisations that marked them out as Bengalis in any way. However, Bengali migrants did not make any professional body; instead, they created sociocultural organisations, such as the Malaysian Bengalee Association and Bengal Muslim Association, which have been discussed in Chapter 8.

During the colonial period, Bengali migrants were not all professionals or labourers. Many found success as petty traders. Their frequent multiple entrepreneurship, which allowed them to create a transnational commercial community in the Bengali diaspora and Malay public sphere, deserves detailed attention. Therefore, the next chapter focuses on this area.

Notes

1. Arunima Datta, '"Immorality", Nationalism and the Colonial State in British Malaya: Indian "Coolie" Women's Intimate Lives as Ideological Battleground', *Women's History Review* 25, no. 4 (2016): 584–601.
2. *ST*, 8 May 1875, 2.
3. *ST*, 29 October 1909, 7.
4. Isaac Raphael Belilios (popularly known as I. R. Belilios), a Venetian Jew, was born and brought up in Calcutta. In the mid-nineteenth century, he migrated to Singapore and started importing cattle and sheep in the Serangoon area, where a street was named after him.
5. The people who migrated from the Bengal Presidency were certainly not all Bengalis because its area covered present-day parts of north India, northeast India, West Bengal of India, and Bangladesh. It was the home of diverse cultural people. However, it presumes that as Belilios was born and brought up in Calcutta, he probably recruited mainly from the inhabitant of Calcutta. Besides, some employee names are seen as Bengali. For instance, Khorod Babu, Dobbier Uddin, Abdul Wodhud and Islam Babu. Such a list of employees was expanded in the 1890s to include Akhil Chandra Sarcar, Hare Das, Nazmul, Ram Lal Banerjee and Amrtto Lal Dattu. See Siddique and Puru Shotam, *Singapore's Little India*, 45, 60, 62; *Little India: Historic District* (Singapore: Urban Redevelopment Authority, 1995), 17.

6. *SFPMA*, 8 April 1899, 3; Ernest Chew, 'Pioneers of Early Colonial Singapore 1819–1850', http://www.sabrizain.org/malaya/library/rtc.pdf, accessed 15 July 2020; Margaret Sarkissian, 'Armenians in South-east Asia', *Crossroads: An Interdisciplinary Journal of Southeast Asian Studies* 3, nos. 2/3 (1987): 6; see also C. M. Turnbull, *A History of Modern Singapore, 1819–2005* (Singapore: National University of Singapore Press, 2009).

7. Swettenham, *British Malaya*, 169–170, 304–305; Metcalf, *Imperial Connections*, 49.

8. Syed Hussein Alatas, *The Myth of the Lazy Native: A Study of the Image of the Malays, Filipinos and Javanese from the 16th to the 20th Century and Its Function in the Ideology of Colonial Capitalism* (London: Frank Cass, 1977).

9. Trocki, 'Political Structures in the Nineteenth and Early Twentieth Centuries', 113.

10. Robert W. Hefner, introduction to *The Politics of Multiculturalism: Pluralism and Citizenship in Malaysia, Singapore, and Indonesia*, ed. Robert W Hefner (Honolulu: University of Hawai'i Press, 2001), 18; Aiyar, *Indian Problems in Malaya*, 5.

11. NAB, Proceedings A, Dept.: Finance, Br.: Emigration, Calcutta, November 1915 (Calcutta: Government of Bengal).

12. Some 35 Bengalis were working in the Simpang Estate. See Wright, *Twentieth Century Impressions of British Malaya*, 391.

13. *SFPMA*, 11 July 1925, 15.

14. NAS, OHI, Salil Kumar Chakravarti, 3 August 2007, Acc. No. 003209.

15. Wright, *Twentieth Century Impressions of British Malaya*, 514.

16. Interview with Mushahid Ali, 19 July 2018, Far East Plaza, Singapore.

17. Graham, *Journal of a Residence in India*, 204–205.

18. A Bengal Civilian, *De Zieke Reiziger, or Rambles in Java and the Straits in 1852* (London: Simpkin, Marshall and Co., 1853), 42.

19. Pieris, *Hidden Hands and Divided Landscapes*, 211.

20. The British introduced Western education in Bengal in the early nineteenth century, and English replaced Persian in 1835. They opened English schools and colleges in Bengal, for instance, the Hindu College (1817) and the Dacca College (1841). This policy further created an English-educated middle class, many of whom found clerical jobs in government administration. This class of people was known as *baboos* or *bhadralok* in Bengal. In his interview, Mohinder Singh recalled *baboos* from Bengal. See NAS, OHI, Mohinder Singh, 24 June 1985, Acc. No. 000546.

21. *ST*, 12 November 1859; *SFPMA*, 8 December 1859, 4.

22. For details on using the Bangla language, see *SCCR*, 26 August 1837, 2. A Chittagonian Hindu priest named Sarda Prosanno Bhattacharya worked in a Vishnu temple in Penang. See Das, *Banger Bahire Bangali*, 482.

23. J. W. Norton Kyshe, 'A Judicial History of the Straits Settlements 1786–1890', *Malaya Law Review*, 'Special Issue to Commemorate: The One Hundred and Fiftieth Anniversary of Singapore' 11, no. 1 (1969): 133.

24. Das, *Banger Bahire Bangali*, 478.

25. The German Consulate was opened in Singapore in 1892 at 22 Scotts Road near the present location of Goodwood Park Hotel. See Faridah Abdul Rashid, *Biography of the Early Malay Doctors 1900–1957 Malaya and Singapore* (Bloomington: Xlibris Corporation, 2012), 88.

26. Email of Gerhard Keiper (Political Archive of the Federal Foreign Office, Berlin) 13 May 2019. The location of the ancestral homeland of Ismail Ballah in Bengal is yet to be identified.

27. Cited in Rashid, *Biography of the Early Malay Doctors*, 608.

28. In his travelogue, Suniti Kumar Chattopadhyay wrote that many Bengali professionals, including lawyers, served their clients efficiently in Malaya. He visited British Malaya with Rabindranath Tagore and published a series of travel accounts in *Probashi* (a monthly Bangla magazine) in 1928. See Suniti Kumar Chattopadhyay, 'Jabodeeper Path e', *Probashi* 28, no. 1 (1335): 142–145, 266–273, 480–487, 594–602, 761–768; Suniti Kumar Chattopadhyay, 'Jabodeeper Path e', *Probashi* 28, no. 2 (1335): 270–278, 579–586, 867–888; see also Das, *Banger Bahire Bangali*, 477–482.

29. *ST*, 26 July 1948; NAS, OHI, Sivadas s/o Sankaran, 1 September 1995, Acc. No. 001681; see also Danny Chue, 'S. C. Goho and Wartime Singapore', Singapore Memory Project, Memory of Danny Chue, 2015.

30. Interview with Davenport.

31. Patrick Morrah, 'The History of the Malayan Police', *Journal of the Malayan Branch of the Royal Asiatic Society* 36, no. 2 (1963): 59.

32. Gretchen Liu, *Singapore: A Pictorial History 1819–2000* (London: Curzon, 2001), 109.

33. Ang Seow Leng, 'A History of the Singapore Police Force: Men in Blue', *BiblioAsia* 11, no. 3 (October–December 2015): 27.

34. NAS, OHI, Kishore Bhattachary, 8 March 2010, Acc. No. 003490.

35. J. H. Bamberg, *The History of the British Petroleum Company: The Iranian Years, 1928–1954*, vol. 2 (Cambridge: Cambridge University Press, 1994), 107.

36. NAB, Proceedings A, Br.: Emigration, Dept.: Revenue, September 1929 (Calcutta: Government of Bengal), vol. 143.

37. Vlieland, *British Malaya*, 192.

38. In February 1939, the Manager of Aluminium Manufacturing Company in Calcutta sought permission from the Government of Bengal to send some spinners to Singapore. NAB, Proceedings A, Br.: Emigration, Dept.: Revenue, March 1939 (Calcutta: Government of Bengal), vol. 199.

39. 'Bata Shoe (Singapore) Pte Ltd', *SingaporeInfopedia*, National Library Board, Singapore; http://eresources.nlb.gov.sg/infopedia/articles/SIP_892_2005-01-26.html, accessed 25 May 2019; see also https://batamsia.wordpress.com/about/, accessed 25 May 2019.

40. NAB, Proceedings A, Br.: Emigration, Dept.: Revenue, Calcutta, March 1940, (Calcutta: Government of Bengal), vol. 206.

41. NAS, OHI, Sudhansu Ranjan Das Gupta, Acc. No. 003928, 16 October 2014.

42. Interview with Davenport.

43. In the pre-colonial period, merchant and naval ships were built in Bengal, particularly Dhaka and Sylhet. Das, *Banger Bahire Bangali*, 22. Chittagong, Noakhali and Comilla were the home of some reputed sailors during the sixteenth century, and they worked in the sea-going ships. Therefore, the European steamer companies trained sailors of those districts to command first barges and steamers. See Berthet, 'Boat Technology and Culture in Chittagong'.

44. Bengali seamen worked in the Portuguese East India Company ships. See Pearson, *The Indian Ocean*, 186. For discussion on the Bengali *lascar*s on Britain-bound ships, see E. A. Gait, *Census of India 1901*, vol. VI, Bengal, Part-I, Report (Calcutta: Bengal Secretariat Press, 1902), 136; Adams, *Across Seven Seas*; Bald, *Bengali Harlem*, 137.

45. Claire Alexander et al., 'The Bengali Diaspora in Britain'.

46. C. Northcote Parkinson, *Trade in Eastern Seas 1793–1813* (Cambridge: Cambridge University Press, 1937), 215.

47. NAS, Straits Settlements Original Correspondence (hereinafter SSOC), Acc. No. 273/639/1-14 (CO), 1 January 1938–31 December 1938, image number: D2016050717 (hereinafter NAS, SSOC, 273/639/1-14 [CO]).

48. NAS, SSOC, 273/639/1-14 [CO]; see also Ashfaque Hossain, 'The World of the Sylheti Seamen in the Age of Empire, from the Late Eighteenth Century to 1947', *Journal of Global History* 9, no. 3 (2014): 440.

49. Interview with Noorul Islam. He was born in 1952 in Singapore.

50. Katy Gardner, *Age, Narrative and Migration: The Life Course and Life Histories of Bengali Elders in London* (Oxford; New York: Berg, 2002), 44, 91, 233.

51. *SFPMA*, 20 July 1896, 2; *MdHD*, 20 July 1896, 3.

52. *Daily Advertiser* (hereinafter *DA*), 7 November 1892, 3.

53. Nasution, *Chulia in Penang*, 165.

54. *ST*, 13 March 1894, 2.

55. Different offices of the Malayan government called for the recruitment of Bengali interpreters. See NAM, PRA, 'Request That a Bangalee [Bengali] Interpreter Be Appointed at Sungai Petani Court', file no. 1957/0361064W, 1 February 1915; NAM, PRA, 'Applies for the Post of Bengali Interpreter', file no.1957/0363247W, 25 November 1915.

56. NAM, PRA, file no. 1957/0361860W, 28 April 1915.

57. NAS, OHI, Chakravarti, Acc. No. 003209, 3 August 2007. Chakravarti was born on 24 July 1928 in a rubber estate in Negeri Sembilan, Federation of Malaya.

58. S. R. Nathan, *S. R. Nathan: 50 Stories from My Life* (Singapore: Editions Didier Millet, 2013), 94; S. R. Nathan, *An Unexpected Journey: Path to the Presidency* (Singapore: Editions Didier Millet, 2011), 183–184. S. R. Nathan (the sixth President of Singapore) was a seamen's welfare officer in the 1950s. He wrote a few autobiographies.

59. *ST*, 3 November 2017; *Today*, 3 November 2017.

60. A Chinese trader recruited one Bengali accountant. At the same time, another Bengali worked as an assistant to a revenue collector at Kedah, helping collect revenues from defaulters, among other jobs. See NAM, PRA, 'Lim Peng Hooi Ketua Pajak Chukai Chukai Baling Teriak Kata Bengali K. G. Laboomall Bawak Masuk Barang Perniagaan Dengan Parcel Itu Tiada Mau Bayar Chukai Kepada Nia', 1957/0361245W, 27 February 1915; *MaT*, 8 July 1922, 7.

61. Ramnath Biswas started his career as a manager at the Jatiya Bhandar Samity in Sylhet. He secretly maintained membership with the revolutionary organisation Anushilan Samity. He was sacked from his job when the employer discovered his revolutionary connection. During the First World War, he joined the Bengali Paltan as an officer in the Bengali Labour Core and went to Iraq. Soon after, he left the military job as he considered it 'enslavement in the name of discipline'. He migrated to Malaya to work as a miner and moved to Singapore as a supervisor at the Singapore Harbour.

62. Ramnath Biswas, *Bhavoghurer Bileth Jatra* [A Wanderer's Journey to Britain] (Calcutta: Dasgupta and Co. Ltd, n.d.), 43, 46.

63. Lim Kean Ghee, *The History of Medicine and Health in Malaysia* (Perak: Sin Boon Beng Printing Snd. Bhd, 2016), 16.

64. For details, see J. S. Cheah, 'Approaching 100 Years of Medical and University Education in Singapore', *Journal of the Singapore Medical Association* 44, no. 1 (2003): 1; J. S. Cheah, 'History of Medicine in Singapore', *Singapore Medical Journal* 38, no. 6 (1997): 273; Y. K. Lee, 'The Founding of the Medical School in Singapore in 1905', *Annals Academy of Medicine Singapore* 34, no. 6 (2005): 4, 7, 9; see also Muzaffar Desmond Tate Abdullah, Khoo Kay Kim and Selvamany Gabriel, *The History of Medicine in Malaysia: The Foundation Years* (Malaysia: Academy of Medicine of Malaysia, 2005).

65. NAS, OHI, Hena Sinha, 21 October 1983, Acc. No. 000354.

66. Sengupta, *Malaysia and Bengali Doctors*, 40–41, 111–112.

67. *ST*, 6 January 2015.

68. Dr Paresh Nath Sen (1878–1948) was born in Dacca and graduated from Calcutta Medical College in 1903 as a Licentiate of Medicine and Surgery (LMS).

69. Sengupta, *Malaysia and Bengali Doctors*, 40–41.

70. Sarojininath Bardhan (1874–1927) was born in Comilla of East Bengal; he obtained his BA from Dacca in 1902 and graduated with LMS from Calcutta Medical College in 1907.

71. Sengupta, *Malaysia and Bengali Doctors*, 31, 40, 80, 111–112; Das, *Banger Bahire Bangali*, 476.

72. Later, he joined as general surgeon at the Singapore General Hospital and apart from practising, he taught medical students until 1965.

73. Sengupta, *Malaysia and Bengali Doctors*, xii, 81.

74. Sengupta, *Malaysia and Bengali Doctors*, 48–49, 112–113, 117–118. Sri Devi (the wife of Dr Sushil Kumar Biswas) was one of the first woman gynaecologists in Malaysia.

75. NAS, OHI, Rajabali Jumabhoy, 9 September 1981, Acc. No. 000074.

76. Wright, *Twentieth Century Impressions of British Malaya*, 249.

77. Kshitendra Chandra Sengupta was born in Brahmanbaria, Bangladesh. He was brought up in Comilla and trained as a doctor at the Dacca Mitford Medical College. Dwijendra Kumar Majumder was born in Faridpur, Bangladesh, and graduated from the R. G. Kar Medical College of Calcutta University. See Sengupta, *Malaysia and Bengali Doctors*, 37.

78. Sengupta, *Malaysia and Bengali Doctors*, 42.

79. Tak Ming Ho, *Doctors Extraordinaire* (Perak: Perak Academy, 2006), 78–79.

80. S. Sundralingam, 'Datuk Dr Madhuri Majumder', *Ipoh Echo, Ipoh's Community Newspaper, Ipoh Food, Ipoh Media*, 16 March 2013, http://www.ipohecho.

com.my/v2/2013/03/16/datuk-dr-madhuri-majumder/, accessed 26 March 2018; *SO*, 26 April 2003.

81. Sengupta, *Malaysia and Bengali Doctors*, 58–59.

82. Sengupta, *Malaysia and Bengali Doctors*, 61–62, 185–186.

83. Sengupta, *Malaysia and Bengali Doctors*, 137–138.

84. *Datuk* or *dato* is a title given to a person upon being conferred with certain orders of honour in Brunei and Malaysia.

85. Sengupta, *Malaysia and Bengali Doctors*, 202–203.

86. Interview with Mushahid Ali; he is the vice-chairman of GESS School Advisory Committee.

87. Interview with Haque.

88. NAS, OHI, Chakravarti, 3 August 2007, Acc. No. 003209.

89. NAS, OHI, Karmakar, 10 October 1983, Acc. No. 000343.

90. Anthony D. Medrano, 'The Edible Tide: How Estuaries and Migrants Transformed the Straits of Melaka, 1870–1940', *Journal of Southeast Asian Studies* 51, no. 4 (2020): 579–596.

91. Sunil Amrith, 'Tamil Diasporas across the Bay of Bengal', *American Historical Review* 114, no. 3 (2009): 547–572.

92. Rahman, *Bangladeshi Migration to Singapore*.

5

In the World of Trade and Commerce

Exporting goods from Bengal into the Malay world took a new turn with British imperial expansion. The EIC established monopolistic maritime trade, which reshaped the commercial network for the circulation of Bengali commodities across the Indian Ocean world, particularly in the intra-Asian markets around the rim of the Bay of Bengal. They transported Bengali commodities to long-distance seaports, including Europe, Africa, the Americas and Australia. The movement of these goods steadily increased, which integrated the market and facilitated Bengali mobility within the British colonies. Most of the formal professions undertaken by the Bengalis in the Malay world have been discussed in the preceding chapter. This chapter explores two other aspects related to Bengali migrant employment: the flow of products from Bengal and the involvement of Bengali migrants in trade and commerce. It mainly focuses on Bengali petty traders who played an essential role in shaping a transnational commercial space from the late nineteenth century.

Bengal Commodities across the Indian Ocean World

Before the advent of colonialism, seaports in the Indian Ocean, particularly those located between the coast of Bengal and the Malay Archipelago, were integrated into local, intra-regional and inter-regional networks of merchant communities and zones of commodity exchange. In other words, these commercial zones were structured in micro-, meso- and macro-regions.[1] The increasing dominance of European, and especially EIC, shipping from the mid-eighteenth century did not change this spatial organisation of commercial activities around the seaports.[2] After getting hold of Bencoolen, Bengal and Penang by the end of the eighteenth century, the British controlled the trade network across the northeastern Indian Ocean. During the early nineteenth century, the British took over Malacca and Singapore and formed the Straits Settlements, which included three main seaports: Penang, Malacca and Singapore. These seaports were made duty free for all merchants and were clearinghouses of intra-Asian and long-distance trade.[3] A large quantity of Bengal commodities was transported from the Calcutta port to the ports of the Malay Peninsula, notably Malacca, Penang and Singapore. The EIC re-exported most of the commodities from these seaports to the eastern coast of the Indian Ocean, particularly Java, China, Thailand and Australia. Thus, the British created an exclusive commercial zone between South and Southeast Asia.

A wide variety of Bengal commodities were frequently advertised in the Straits' newspapers and were noted in the export–import reports of the Straits Settlements. Drawing from several reports of John Phipps, Superintendent of the Master Attendant's Office at Calcutta Port, and Straits' newspapers, this chapter provides a picture of the Bengal commodities which were exported to the Malay world.[4] These included various products of cotton and muslin, such as handkerchiefs, Bengal canvas, towels and chintz; jute products such as Bengal twine, gunnies, bags and rope; Bengal opium, rice, sugar, pulse, castor oil, safflower, saltpetre, wheat, cigars and coal. The latter was a significant source of fuel for the ships at Singapore port up until the early twentieth century.[5]

Initially, Penang was a hub of British commercial activities in the Malay Peninsula. In 1828–1829, the EIC exported goods from Bengal to Penang valued at 302,250 rupees.[6] Following the shifting of the capital from Penang to Singapore, the Singapore port became a major centre of commercial activities. It has played a significant role in the growth of intra-Asian and transcontinental trade since the early nineteenth century and was the nerve line of British trade among the three main seaports in the Straits Settlements. The supply of goods from Bengal to Singapore increased steadily (Table 5.1). The value of exported goods and treasure from Bengal to Singapore was 2,334,381 rupees and 2,340,430 rupees, amounting to 89.78 and 84.15 per cent of the total values of all goods transported to Singapore in 1834 and 1835, respectively.[7] From the Bengal side, though the Calcutta port was the main gateway for maritime trade in the colonial period, the Chittagong port played a significant role in the medieval and early modern periods. It played second fiddle to the Chittagong port, which gained the attention of foreign traders from the late nineteenth century.[8]

Most of the products that arrived in Singapore were re-exported into neighbouring areas, including China, Siam, Cambodia, the Dutch East Indies

Table 5.1   Prices of imported products to Singapore from Bengal and other places (in Rs)

Imported From	1827–1828	1828–1829	1829–1830	1830–1831	1832–1833	1833–1834
England	1,920,126	2,422,850	3,455,776	2,445,894	3,879,821	3,037,625
Calcutta	2,316,466	2,977,086	2,796,415	2,559,592	2,654,878	2,657,426
Madras	414,697	1,090,278	574,586	102,588	456,645	778,155
Bombay	370,889	382,249	278,393	222,341	549,440	279,485
Penang	883,015	842,888	000	000	000	5,410
Malacca	278,627	418,402	000	000	000	000
Java	2,284,637	1,449,140	1,781,427	2,389,223	2,164,054	1,939,251
China	1,792,674	5,622,135	7,184,407	6,015,048	4,123,703	3,772,831

Source: John Phipps, *A Practical Treatise on the China and Eastern Trade: Comprising the Commerce of Great Britain and India, Particularly Bengal and Singapore, with China and the Eastern Islands* (London: W. H. Allen, 1836), 271.

(Indonesia) and the Philippines.[9] Table 5.2 shows a list of Bengal products that were re-exported from Singapore to different destinations. There was a high demand for Bengal cotton in Java,[10] which the Dutch colonial government exploited by imposing an extra duty on Bengal goods there in 1831.[11]

The EIC established a monopoly over the Bengal opium trade, which helped to increase the government's revenue income. British policies from 1790 to 1816 shaped Bengal into an opium-producing centre of the world.[12] Initially, the EIC exported a small quantity of opium from Bengal to China in 1773 in exchange for tea.[13] This trade was vital to the colonial authority because it generated a huge profit, which helped to offset some of the financial burdens of the British administration in India. The first sale of Bengal opium was in 1828 in Penang.[14] In 1827, some 690 chests of opium were imported from Calcutta to Singapore.[15] This was increased by 756 per cent in 1840, which amounted to 5,913 chests.[16] Bengal opium was shipped from Singapore to its surrounding areas, including Bali, China and the Malay states.[17] In 1838–1839, some 2,263 chests of Bengal opium were shipped from Singapore to different places, and this was increased to 5,497 chests in 1839–1840.[18] The British merchants brought opium from Bengal, Patna and Benares to the Straits Settlements.[19] Along with the British merchants, some South Asian traders privately continued long-distance opium trade with Southeast Asia, often settled in Malaya, Singapore and as far away as Hong Kong.[20]

Table 5.2 Bengal commodities re-exported from Singapore to other regions

Products	Quantity	Volume/Unit	Re-exported To	Month	Year
Rice	1,390	Palletised Load System (PLS)	China	April	1833
Rice	700	PLS	Manila	April	1833
Bengal Piece Goods	62.50	corges	Batavia	April	1833
Handkfs	1,550	pieces	Batavia	December	1833
Chintz	60	corges	Bangkok	April	1833
Bengal Canvas	120	bolts	Cochin China	June	1837
Cotton	903	bales	Macao	August	1842

Source: *SCCR*, 18 April 1833, 4; *SCCR*, 25 April 1833, 4; *SCCR*, 12 December 1833, 4; *SFPMA*, 22 June 1837, 3; *SFPMA*, 25 August 1842, 1.

Table 5.3 Advertising Dacca products in Singapore

Agency and Dealers' Name	Advertised for Selling
Oilman's Stores	Dacca soap
Prime Allsop's and Bass' Ale	Dacca muslin for ladies' dress
John Little & Co.	Dacca muslin dresses
Mrs Nugent's Millinery Rooms	Dacca-worked dresses
Sayle & Co.	Dacca twist cottons

Source: Different newspapers advertised almost every day from the 1830s to the 1880s; for example, *ST*, 16 February 1848, 1; *SFPMA*, 7 May 1846, 1; *ST*, 4 November 1856, 3; *SFPMA*, 27 May 1847, 1; *ST*, 19 October 1883, 28.

Straits' newspapers regularly advertised commodities imported from Bengal. For instance, Crane, Brothers & Co. and M. C. Joakim advertised for selling fresh Bengal *dal* (pulse), biscuits, napkins, bathing towels and fine Bengal tablecloths in Singapore in 1840.[21] Some staple products, including soap, gram, cloths and cheese, were exported from Dacca to the Straits Settlements.[22] Importers of Dacca products (Table 5.3) advertised some items with the tag of 'Dacca' as a branding term. In 1883, Sayle & Co. advertised for Dacca cotton twists and sold them at 12 cents per yard.[23] The demand for Dhaka cotton remained unchanged in the postcolonial period. For instance, in 1960, one trader imported cotton sarees and Manipuri cotton from Dhaka.[24]

Table 5.4   Dacca soap re-exported from Singapore to Indonesia

Quantity	Volume/Unit	Re-exported To	Months/Frequency	Year
99	*catti*es	Batavia	January	1833
60	*maund*s	Batavia	18 April	1833
50	bags	Batavia	25 April	1833
25	bags	Batavia	May	1833
30	PLS	Batavia	December	1833
18.50	PLS	Batavia	February	1834
5.50	PLS	Batavia	March	1834
55	PLS	Batavia	May	1834
11.50	PLS	Batavia	June	1837
10.50	PLS	Batavia	September	1838
36	*picul*s	Java	August	1849

Source: Excerpted and calculated from different reports published in several newspapers; see *SCCR*, 17 January 1833, 4; *SCCR*, 25 April 1833, 4; *SCCR*, 18 April 1833, 4; *SCCR*, 30 May 1833, 4; *SCCR*, 12 December 1833, 4; *SCCR*, 6 February 1834, 4; *SCCR*, 13 March 1834, 4; *SCCR*, 15 May 1834, 4; *SFPMA*, 22 June 1837, 3; *SFPMA*, 13 September 1838, 3; *SFPMA*, 4 August 1849, 7.

It is difficult to provide exact figures for the variety and extent of trade of Dacca products in Singapore, as all products were blended with Bengal commodities in the custom house registry books. However, some newspaper reports shed light on the high demand for Dacca soap, which was re-exported from Singapore to Indonesia. In addition, the EIC or other merchants measured Bengal products with different types of scales, for instance, the Palletised Load System (PLS), maunds, bags and chests (Table 5.4).

The products of Bengal jute,[25] such as rope and hemp, were re-exported from Singapore to various destinations, including China and Portland (USA).[26] To meet the excessive demand for Bengal jute products, Borneo Company Limited set up the first integrated power spinning and weaving factory in Bengal in 1859.[27] Therefore, the export of Bengal jute products was increased in the Asian and global markets, and the revenue income of jute commodities contributed to developing the railroads and telegraph connections in Bengal.[28] A significant portion of Bengal jute was supplied from eastern Bengal.[29]

These discussions show that the Bengal-based merchant network facilitated the flow of Bengali commodities after settling in the Malay Peninsula. They imported Bengal commodities to the Straits Settlements and re-exported them from Singapore to other parts of Southeast Asia and the Asia Pacific. The circulation of these products in the British colonies led to increasing Bengali mobility. Combining these movements of people and products also encouraged Bengali engagement with small businesses in Malaya—a topic discussed in the next section.

Bengali Traders and Individual Entrepreneurs

The settlement of the Bengali mercantile community in British Malaya can be traced back to at least the early nineteenth century. In Penang and Singapore, Bengali traders were found among other Indian ethnic groups, including Tamils and Gujaratis.[30] They set up retail shops in almost every town in Malaya, particularly in Johor, Batu Pahat, Muar, Malacca and even in some smaller villages. The Bengali petty business community was reputed to have kept their shops open until midnight, especially in Singapore.[31] Bengali traders and shopkeepers included convicts as well as clerks.[32] What follows is an account of trade and commerce conducted by the Bengalis.

Cattle Traders and Milkmen

Some Eurasians, including Henry Fillipe Desker (1826–1898) and I. R. Belilios (1846–1910), started cattle trading in British Malaya in the 1840s.[33] Belilios came from Calcutta to Singapore during the 1860s and founded Belilios & Co. for importing horses, cattle and feedstuff. As mentioned in Chapter 4, he employed mostly Bengali staff for his company. He owned some sheep pens and cattle sheds and was a pioneer in developing the area around Belilios Road in the 1890s.[34] After the death of I. R. Belilios in 1910, Mrs Belilios looked after the business but could not compete with other cattle-trading companies.

By the late nineteenth century, the cattle trade was primarily dominated by Indian ethnic groups, in particular, the Bengalis and the Tamils.[35] One Tamil Muslim, Moona Kader Sultan (1863–1937), came to Singapore in the 1870s and established the Singapore Cattle Trading Company in 1898.[36] After the death of Belilios, Kader Sultan expanded his company and dominated the cattle trade throughout the Malay Peninsula. In 1914, two companies, Belilios & Co. and Straits Cattle Trading Co., jointly named Belilios, Kader Sultan & Co. and started cattle business in co-partnership in the Straits Settlements.[37]

One Bengali cattle trader, Annukul Chander Chander (commonly known as A. C. Chander), was very influential and prominent among South Asian communities in Singapore.[38] Chander was a partner of the Belilios, Kader Sultan & Co.[39] Their company imported and retailed sheep and goats. They supplied meat throughout the Straits Settlements, particularly in Singapore and the Federated Malay States. They had wholesale and retail shops and daily advertised the price of meat in the newspapers. The retail shops were located on Rochore Road, Bridge Road and Selegie Road, whereas the wholesale shop was on Queen Street. Their meat business was so brisk that they had to ask customers to make advance orders for fresh meat.[40]

All cattle trading companies, including the Belilios, Kader Sultan & Co., imported cattle from India, Burma, Bengal and Australia to British Malaya. For instance, in 1901, the steamer *Lightning* transported over 1,300 cattle from Calcutta to Singapore.[41] A Bengali deck passenger named Hurrish Banarjee, who came to Singapore in 1901, noted that a considerable number of sheep, goats and cows were brought to Singapore every week.[42] However, during the early 1920s, the price of cattle was high so the joint venture company could not cope with the new price. Therefore, the partnership of Belilios, Kader Sultan & Co. broke apart in January 1923.[43]

Due to a lack of access to data, I cannot provide details about Bengali cattle traders in other parts of the Malay States. However, the equally significant extent of trade in other parts of the Malay Peninsula can be guessed from a grant of twenty acres of land at Petaling Hills by the Government of the Federated Malay States to the Bengali cattle keepers for the erection of sheds and dwelling houses.[44]

Most South Asian cattle traders resided in present-day Serangoon areas in Singapore. These areas were the centre and ideal place for cattle traders because of the abundant water for cattle rearing. Some current street names in this area are reminiscent of the cattle trade of the time, for instance, Kandang Kerbau (buffalo enclosure), Lembu Road (cows/cattle) and Buffalo Road. Desker Road, Belilios Road and Chander Road were named after affluent and leading cattle merchants. As of now, these areas, including Lembu Road, Kerbau and Desker Road, are filled with Bengali restaurants and their other commercial outlets.

The cattle trade was lucrative because traders sold the imported cattle to butchery shops or dealers and retailed meat at their own slaughterhouses— often with large profit margins. Moreover, cattle were used as a means of transportation, such as pulling bullock carts, which were popular in Singapore until the mid-twentieth century. It was a source of fresh milk for which there was a high demand, and a good number of Bengali dairymen met these demands.[45] Rajesh Rai argues that the milkmen (*doodhwallahs*) and washermen (*dhobis*) were mainly 'Hindustani' migrants in Singapore who arrived from present-day Uttar Pradesh and northwestern Bihar.[46] There is, however, much evidence to suggest that the Tamils, Punjabis and Bengalis played an equally significant role in dairy farming and the supply of milk in Singapore.[47] This connects back to the traditional bases of these professions in Bengal itself. Various contemporary observers, including Taylor, Clay, Hunter and Wise, reported that there were a good number of dairy farmers (*gowala*) both in Hindu and Muslim communities in Dacca.[48] Many Chittagonians dealt with milk products and groceries in Burmese towns.[49] As the Bengali milkmen were found frequently in Bengal and Burma during the nineteenth century, it is assumed that either they willingly migrated to the Straits Settlements or the British government brought them to supply milk to colonial staff and soldiers.[50]

The cattle industry declined in the 1930s in Singapore due to several factors. First, the Great Depression of 1929 affected the cattle business. Second, the places of cattle rearing were reduced because the government filled up ponds and cleared swamps for infrastructure developments.[51] Third, a worldwide outbreak of cattle diseases like rinderpest and anthrax affected the animal stock. The cattle disease broke out earlier in Bengal and Assam.[52] More than 18,000 and 1,500 cattle died from rinderpest and anthrax in Bengal in 1934 and 1935, respectively.[53] The colonial government restricted the importation of livestock in Singapore by the Municipal Ordinance of 1936. As per the ordinance, the importation of cattle, goats and sheep was strictly prohibited from southern India, Burma, Bengal, Siam and conditionally from the Dutch East Indies, citing the unhealthy environment of slaughterhouses, cattle sheds and dairies.[54] The government finally banned the keeping of livestock at Kandang Kerbau in 1936.[55] As the cattle industry declined, the cattle traders shifted their business to shophouses or other trades.[56] For example, a Bengali cattle trader, A. C. Chander, went back to Calcutta to develop his new business interests.[57]

Bengali Grocery Shops

As the South Asian communities continued to migrate to Malaya, corresponding demands for goods and services increased. Bengali petty traders set up new shops and started selling daily necessities. In his travel account, Ramnath Biswas wrote about a Bengali grocery shop at Seremban, which many Bengali customers used to visit. Lakshmi Naidu recalled that near the Kaliamman Temple in Singapore, businesses thrived—including a bar, a tailor and a barbershop—where many Bengalis traded all sorts of Bengal foodstuff, including *dal*, flour, ghee, tea, rice and a variety of vegetables.[58] Some of them, like M. A. Kader, a chandler[59] from Sylhet, supplied goods and equipment to ships and engine boats.[60] As per Anwarul Haque's oral testimony, his father, Muniruddin, was an electrician and a supplier of electrical equipment in the Serangoon area. After the Second World War, Muniruddin's family resided in a shophouse on Bras Basah Road that served as both a home and a trading centre.[61]

During the 1930s and 1940s, a few bookshops were owned by the Bengalis. For instance, the father of Noorul Islam started a bookshop named 'Modern Book Store' (Figure 5.1) around 1938, located near Muniruddin's electrical equipment store.

Again, it was a shophouse where his parents and siblings lived upstairs. Islam learnt the book business from his father. There were several competing bookstores on Bras Basah Road, which made it a bookworm's haven.[62] Mushahid Ali recalls that the proprietor of a bookstore named Muslim Khan

Figure 5.1   Modern Book Store, 1939
Source: Noorul Islam.

came from Dacca, while Yusuf Ali, another book trader, migrated from Nankhar in Sylhet.[63]

During the 1990s, the Singapore government demolished and renovated the Bras Basah area. Therefore, Islam's family moved to a flat provided by the Housing and Development Board at Pasir Ris. He transferred the bookshop to the Far East Plaza at Scotts Road and renamed it ANA Book Store after his mother. Islam also told me that many Bengali businesspeople worked in other areas in Singapore during the 1960s.[64]

Bengali Boarding Houses

To meet the demand of seamen and new migrants, different types of businesses emerged around seaport areas, including residential hotels and restaurants. The Bengalis, among others, started to set up *makan* houses (traditional food shops) and boarding houses. Shafiya Khatoon remembers that her father, M. A. Majid, set up a *makan* house in the early 1930s for the convenience of seamen. It was located on the seafront of Collyer Quay (presently Marina Bay Sands in Singapore). His adopted son, Akbar Ali, and his Malay friends ran the shop.[65]

A good number of boarding houses were operated by the Bengalis, particularly in Singapore and Malaya. Many newcomers from Bengal were referred to a specific boarding house located at 91 Birch Road, Seremban, which was owned by a Bengali, Priya Lal Dutt. Later on, Dinesh Chandra Chowdhury took charge of the boarding house.[66] The seamen from Bengal stayed at different residential hotels in the Serangoon areas. Khatoon and Mushahid Ali mentioned three individuals, Mozammel, Majid and Mukhles Khan, who managed a few boarding houses. Boarding houses run or owned by the Bengalis were dotted around Singapore in the 1950s but concentrated at Serangoon Road, Rangoon Road, Norris Road, Lembu Road and Cuff Road. Most of these were owned by migrants from Chittagong, Naokhali and Sylhet.[67]

Dhobis *and* Feriwalahs

As noted earlier, Rajesh Rai argued that the 'Hindustani' migrants were responsible for developing Singapore's *dhobi* or laundry industry. The term 'Hindustani' is ambiguous because the geographical area of Hindustan is debatable. *Dhobi* or *dhoba* denotes a skilled washerman, an established professional class in Bengal. For example, Dacca washermen were famous for their skill and dedication. Sometimes, young *dhobi*s from other distant places were sent to Dacca to learn the skill.[68] The *dhobi*s were a thriving class in Bengal; the number of *dhobi*s was 210,763 and 232,407 in Bengal and Orissa in 1872 and 1881, respectively.[69] The British army and administrative and medical staff required the service of *dhobi*s. During the Second World War, the Commanding Loyal Regiment of Singapore sent an urgent telegram to Calcutta to send *dhobi*s to Singapore. In response to the telegram, the protector of emigrants of Calcutta immediately dispatched some *dhobi*s with reasonable remuneration and a repatriation guarantee to Singapore in 1940.[70] It seems to be expected that the 'Hindustani' *dhobi*s included those from Bengal.

Bengali *feriwalah*s (hawkers or mobile vendors) were familiar in the streets across Malaya. A number of Bengali hawkers sold *sarabat* (ginger juice) outside of the St Joseph's Institution compound.[71] Some Bengali vendors or breadmen sold bread in the morning and evening around River Valley Road, Fort Canning Hill and Pearl's Hill in Singapore (Figures A.5 and A.6).[72]

Conclusion

This chapter has explored the symbiotic relationship between transregional trading connectivity and Bengali mobility in Malaya. The EIC merchants reshaped economic corridors, dominated maritime trade across the Bay of Bengal and integrated markets between South and Southeast Asia and beyond. During the second industrialisation in Britain, more inter-regional migration and mobility of British capital took place worldwide. In Southeast Asia, British capital was invested in rail, telegraph, navigation, oil and plantation industries. Chinese and Tamil labourers migrated and worked in the tin and plantation industry in the Malay Peninsula. As the British established a direct commercial and administrative connection between Bengal and the Malay world, new horizons opened up for Bengali migration.[73] Initially, members of Bengali diasporas started small-scale businesses. Later, they were involved in different enterprises, including the cattle trade, grocery shops, bookshops and boarding houses, and created business marketplaces or commercial spaces. Such marketplaces still survive in Singapore and Malaysia, some known as 'Bangla Town' or 'Bangla Bazaar'. This business community promoted Bangla culture and brought over a new generation of Bengali migrants to assist their businesses. They created social and cultural convergences between Bengal and Malaya during the time and space under consideration. As the Bengali diaspora settled and became involved in formal and non-formal professions, their lives were entangled with the flow of social life around their homes and workplaces—a topic that will be covered in the next chapter.

Notes

1. 'Micro' denotes the trading links within the Malay Archipelago seaports, 'meso' refers to the trading ports between the Malay seaports and its adjacent areas and 'macro' indicates the trading connections between the Malay Peninsula and other parts of the world.

2. Mann, *South Asia's Modern History*, 216–217.

3. Atsushi Kobayashi, 'The Role of Singapore in the Growth of Intra-Southeast Asian Trade, c. 1820s–1852', *Southeast Asian Studies* 2, no. 3 (2013): 443.

4. John Phipps, *A Practical Treatise on the China and Eastern Trade: Comprising the Commerce of Great Britain and India, Particularly Bengal and Singapore, with China and the Eastern Islands* (London: W. H. Allen, 1836), 296, 266.

5. Dwarkanath Tagore founded the Bengal Coal Company in the 1840s, and Bengal's coal was exported to Singapore through different ships, including *Labuan* and *Mascotte*. See Dietmar Rothermund, *An Economic History of India: From Pre-colonial Times to 1991* (New Delhi: Routledge, 1993), 24, 59; Dutt, *Economic History of India*, vol. 1, 286–287; SFPMA (Weekly), 19 September 1901, 7; SFPMA (Weekly), 15 May 1902, 296.

6. *Appendix to the Report on the Affairs of the East India Company, Volume III, External and Internal Commerce of Bengal, Madras, and Bombay* (London: The House of Commons, 1831), 5.

7. Phipps, *A Practical Treatise on the China and Eastern Trade*, 294.

8. During the mid-twentieth century, Chittagong port was considered the second largest port in Bengal. *Singapore Free Press* (hereinafter *SFP*), 3 September 1948, 3.

9. Phipps, *A Practical Treatise on the China and Eastern Trade*, 268, 274.

10. *SFPMA*, 24 October 1844, 6.

11. Phipps, *A Practical Treatise on the China and Eastern Trade*, 266.

12. Sarah Deming, 'The Economic Importance of Indian Opium and Trade with China on Britain's Economy 1843–1890', Economics Working Papers no. 25, Whiteman College, Spring 2011, Washington, USA.

13. Samuel Warren, *The Opium Question* (London: James Ridgway, Piccadilly, 1840), 51; Phipps, *A Practical Treatise on the China and Eastern Trade*, 208.

14. *SCCR*, 17 January 1828, 1.

15. *SCCR*, 1 March 1827, 2.

16. Phipps, *A Practical Treatise on the China and Eastern Trade*, 238, 296; C. P. Holloway, *Tabular Statements on the Commerce of Singapore, During the Years 1823–24 to 1839–40 Inclusive. Shewing the Nature and Extent of the Trade, Carried on with Each Country and State. Compiled from Official Documents* (Singapore: Singapore Free Press, 1842), 2.

17. *SCCR*, 6 February 1834, 4; *SCCR*, 15 May 1834, 4.

18. Holloway, *Tabular Statements on the Commerce of Singapore*, 4.

19. *SCCR*, 1 March 1827, 1.

20. Judith M. Brown, *Global South Asians: Introducing the Modern Diaspora* (Cambridge: Cambridge University Press, 2006), 36.

21. *SFPMA*, 4 September 1840, 2.

22. B. C. Allen, *Eastern Bengal District Gazetteers: Dacca* (Allahabad: The Pioneer Press, 1912), 108; James Taylor, *A Sketch of the Topography and Statistics of Dacca* (Calcutta: Military Orphan Press, 1840), 180–184, 311.

23. *ST*, 19 October 1883, 28.

24. *SFP*, 6 May 1960, 10.

25. For details on the trade of the European merchants of Bengal jute and its products across the world, see Tara Sethia, 'The Rise of the Jute Manufacturing Industry in Colonial India: A Global Perspective', *Journal of World History* 7, no. 1 (1996): 71–99; Tariq Omar Ali, *A Local History of Global Capital: Jute and Peasant Life in the Bengal Delta* (New Jersey: Princeton University Press, 2018).

26. *SFPMA*, 25 August 1842, 1; *SFPMA*, 15 October 1853, 5.

27. In 1856, Borneo Company Limited was founded in East Malaysia (Sarawak and Sabah). The company invested in different industries, including jute, sugar and tea, in Bengal. Its directors consisted, among others, of Raja James Brooke from Sarawak and two partners from Singapore; thus, they made international mercantile networks. See Howard Cox and Stuart Metcalfe, 'The Borneo Company Limited: The Origins of a Nineteenth Century Networked Multinational', *Asia Pacific Business Review* 4, no. 4 (1998): 53, 60–65.

28. Tirthankar Roy, *The Economy of South Asia: From 1950 to the Present* (London: Palgrave Macmillan, 2017), 245; Geoffrey Jones, *Merchants to Multinationals: British Trading Companies in the Nineteenth and Twentieth Centuries* (Oxford: Oxford University Press, 2000), 290.

29. In 1907, the total area under jute cultivation was 3,859,500 acres in East Bengal, whereas only 932,500 acres were in West Bengal. See *Eastern Daily Mail and Straits Morning Advertiser* (hereinafter, *EDMSMA*), 29 July 1907, 3.

30. Turnbull, *A Short History of Malaysia, Singapore and Brunei*, 104–105; Liu, *Singapore: A Pictorial History*, 82. The Bengali traders were also seen active in Java. For details, see J. S. Furnivall, *Netherlands India: A Study of Plural Economy* (New York: Cambridge University Press, 1944), 141–142.

31. *The Daily Mail* (1903–1926), 18 April 1925, 7.

32. Koh et al., *Singapore*, 60.

33. *Little India: Historic District*, 17.

34. Siddique and Puru Shotam, *Singapore's Little India*, 40–45; 'The Cattle Trade and Related Cottage Industries', in *Little India Heritage Trail* (Singapore: National Heritage Board, Ministry of Culture, Community and Youth, 2018), 7.

35. Sharon Siddique and Nirmala Shotam-Gore, *Serangoon Road: A Pictorial History* (Singapore: Educational Publications Bureau, 1983), 74.

36. In 1902, Moona Kader Sultan founded another trading company, Straits Merchants Cattle Co. He was known as 'Cattle King' in the Serangoon area. In 1912, he merged both companies and renamed them Straits Cattle Trading Co. See Torsten Tschacher, 'The Impact of Being Tamil on Religious Life among Tamil Muslims in Singapore' (PhD dissertation, National University of Singapore, 2006); Siddique and Puru Shotam, *Singapore's Little India*, 58; 'The Cattle Trade and Related Cottage Industries', 8.

37. *ST*, 6 July 1914, 5; *SFPMA*, 7 July 1914, 2; *MaT*, 6 July 1914, 16.

38. The road in front of his house was called Chander Road, named after him. NAS, OHI, Ronendra Karmakar, 10 October 1983, Acc. No. 000343; Koh et al., *Singapore*, 60.

39. *SFPMA* (Weekly), 10 August 1922, 88; *SFPMA*, 7 August 1922, 6.

40. *MaT*, 19 February 1919, 7; *SFPMA*, 25 January 1919, 5.

41. *SFPMA* (Weekly), 19 September 1901, 7. The Powell and Co. auctioned some Bengal cows and calves in Singapore. See also *ST*, 23 November 1906, 8.

42. *ST*, 22 April 1903, 1.

43. *SFPMA*, 30 June 1925, 11; *ST*, 25 June 1925, 14.

44. NAM, PRA, 'Bengali Cattle Keepers in Petaling Hills Land', Selangor, file no. 1957/0101700W, 11 March 1902.

45. Earl, *The Eastern Seas*, 361.

46. Rai, 'Sepoys, Convicts and the "Bazaar" Contingent', 2.

47. Lakshmi Naidu, born and brought up in Singapore in the early twentieth century, recollected that the Bengali milkmen supplied milk in Singapore. See NAS, OHI, Lakshmi Naidu, 27 November 1981, Acc. No. 000110; 'The Cattle Trade and Related Cottage Industries', 9.

48. Taylor, *A Sketch of the Topography and Statistics of Dacca*, 232, 234; James Wise (ed.), *Notes on the Races, Castes and Trades of Eastern Bengal*, with an introduction by Ananda Bhattacharyya (London; New York: Routledge, 2017), 86, 82, 313, 332; Hunter, *Statistical Account of Bengal*, vol. V, 48, 50, the number of 'Goala' on page 48; A. L. Clay, *Principal Heads of the History and Statistic of the Dacca Division* (Calcutta: Calcutta Central Press Company Limited, 1868), 5, 6; H. H. Risley, *The Tribes and Castes of Bengal, Ethnographic Glossary* (Calcutta: P. Mukherjee, 1998), 282–290.

49. Das, *Banger Bahire Bangali*, 471, 476; Iqbal, 'The Space between Nation and Empire', 80.

50. Earl suggested that Bengali dairymen supplied milk to the breakfast table of the Europeans. See Earl, *The Eastern Seas*, 360–362.

51. Khun Eng Kuah, *Social Cultural Engineering and the Singaporean State* (Singapore: Springer Nature Pvt. Ltd, 2018), 133.

52. *ST*, 29 September 1908, 6.

53. *ST*, 30 May 1936, 19.

54. Siddique and Puru Shotam, *Singapore's Little India*, 75–76.

55. 'The Cattle Trade and Related Cottage Industries', 9.

56. Limin Hee, *Constructing Singapore Public Space* (Singapore: Springer Science, 2017), 99; Siddique and Puru Shotam, *Singapore's Little India*, 59.

57. *ST*, 28 August 1936, 12; *SFPMA*, 28 August 1936, 9. A. C. Chander died in Calcutta in 1936.

58. NAS, OHI, Naidu, 27 November 1981, Acc. No. 000110; see also NAS, OHI, Kannusamy s/o Pakirisamy, 17 November 1983, Acc. No. 000081; Koh et al., *Singapore*, 249.

59. A person who supplies or sells equipment for ships and boats.

60. Interview with Mushahid Ali.

61. Interview with Haque.

62. Interview with Islam.

63. Interview with Mushahid Ali.

64. Interview with Islam.

65. Interview with Khatoon.

66. Sengupta, *Malaysia and Bengali Doctors*, 47–48, 195.

67. Nathan, *S. R. Nathan*, 94; Nathan, *An Unexpected Journey*, 183.

68. Risley, *The Tribes and Castes of Bengal*, 232.

69. Risley, *The Tribes and Castes of Bengal*, 232–233.

70. NAB, Proceedings A, Dept.: Revenue, Br.: Emigration (Calcutta: Government of Bengal), December 1940.

71. Sin Ee Goh recalled that he used to drink *sarabat* from Bengali hawkers. He was Chinese and was born in Java in 1906. He migrated from Java to Singapore with his parents and studied at St Joseph's Institution. See NAS, OHI, Sin Ee Goh, 8 December 1982, Acc. No. 000225.

72. Kannusamy remembered that Bengali breadmen were found regularly in Singapore streets. See NAS, OHI, Kannusamy s/o Pakirisamy, 11 October 1983, Acc. No. 000081.

73. The recruitment process and relevant issues of Bangla-speaking employees in the administration and port offices were discussed in Chapter 2.

6

Tales of Tears, Fears and Pleasures

Like the migrants from many other regions of India, Bengalis cherished high hopes of better lives when they left for British Malaya. As seen in the preceding three chapters, a group of migrants improved the conditions of their lives throughout the late nineteenth and twentieth centuries, and some became quite successful in their professions. A majority, however, continued to suffer existential challenges under colonial and postcolonial conditions. From their journey to their settlement, the life and times of Bengali expatriates in the Malay world were full of stories of aspiration and struggle. This chapter captures a glimpse of these stories.

Pre-embarkation Difficulties

The embarkation process for migrant labourers was generally dreadful. Their grievances started at the very beginning of their journey. The Government of Bengal erected many depots and sub-depots to collect potential labourers in rural areas. The labourers were taken to a *musafir khana* (like a modern shelter house) at Calcutta port for overseas embarkation from these depots. One sub-depot at Goalundo[1] (presently Rajbari district in Bangladesh) sent labourers to Calcutta port or the Assam tea gardens. Government medical officers had to prepare annual reports on these depots, which often positively depicted sanitary issues, accommodation and food supplies. However, such positive reports contradict the reality as reflected in other historical sources. For instance, about 615 emigrants were registered in the sub-depots at Garden Reach in Calcutta in May and June of 1918. Although a majority of them were able to reach the Calcutta shelter house, some emigrants were returned on account of their lack of physical fitness, by demand of their relatives, or simply because some of them refused to go any further than the Goalundo depot.[2] Therefore, the pre-embarkation process was anything but easy.

In addition to the contracted or indentured labourers, 'free' migrants also embarked from the Calcutta port and experienced a frustrating process. They left their villages and found their way to the Calcutta port by trains or bullock carts. After that, they boarded a ship for a ten- to fifteen-day voyage to Southeast Asian ports. Thousands of them disembarked at Penang or Port Swettenham. The remaining passengers completed their journey at Singapore port.[3] Asmat Ali and his cousins migrated from Sylhet to Penang port via Calcutta in 1922. They went to Calcutta port by train and stayed at the *musafir khana* for a few days, which was located near the port. They boarded a ship named *SS Sanghola* or *Rajula* for Malaya.[4]

After arriving in British Malaya, some Bengali migrants aspired to settle there. They adjusted to their new workplaces, learnt the Malay language and customs and tried to integrate within mainstream society.[5] This aspiration of integration is still among the postcolonial migrants. A Bangladeshi migrant worker, Md Sharif Uddin,[6] for example, composed poetry reflecting on his engagement with Singapore:

> You are not in the sweat of the workers.
> You are in their hearts, in every moment of life.
> The creator has given to you such a beauty
> That sometimes I feel we are part of the maker.[7]

Across the Bay of Bengal

Earlier maritime voyages across the Bay of Bengal could be frightening and uncomfortable. Those who travelled during the southeast monsoon suffered seasickness and encountered heavy storms in the Indian Ocean. The unpleasant and some enjoyable experiences during the voyages have been depicted in several travel accounts written by Bengali migrants.

Hurrish Chander Banarjee visited Singapore during the early twentieth century. He was a government employee in Bengal but left the job due to the insufficient salary. As per his travel account, published in the *Straits Times* in 1903, he bought a deck ticket and embarked at Calcutta port along with cattle and passengers in the sweltering heat and had a near-death experience by almost drowning before finally arriving in Singapore. The travel account of Banarjee illustrates some irregularities involving the 'wharf business' at the Singapore harbour. When the ship was anchored to the pier, he was struck by a moving iron bar and suffered injuries. On being asked why the broken wharf remained unrepaired, his rescuer, a Tanjong Pagar Dock Co. staff member, replied, '[W]e are waiting for an accident'. He went on: if a ship break the harbour, the ship would be charged 30,000 for repairing the broken pier and 250 dollars per day for a temporary harbour. They will build a new pier for 20,000 dollars; the net profit will be 10,000 dollars. If the ship were damaged, it would be brought to his company's dockyard to repair it. This entire process was called 'wharf business'. Banarjee's story reflects the corruption and irregularity of the port authorities as well as the vulnerable position of many unknown migrants.[8]

Hena Sinha's travel account reflects the relatively better experiences of middle- or upper-middle-class migrants. After marriage, Hena Sinha and A. C. Sinha left Rangoon port for Singapore by a cargo ship on 25 November 1937. She remembered that the ship belonged to the British Indian Steam Navigation Company, and it was a relatively small ship of about 8,000 tonnages, which usually plied between Calcutta and Singapore. Hena Sinha and her family were in a cabin in the second class, where about half a dozen passengers were lodged. The cabin comprised two beds, a separate bathroom and enough space to move around the cabin. For the cabin passengers, shipping companies supplied three meals daily and sometimes provided extra snacks and tea in the evening. After morning tea, cabin crews served a variety of food for breakfast, including fruit juice, egg, sausages, bacon, cereal, butter and bread, or sometimes fried or baked fish with butter. In addition, there were options to have English or Indian dishes during lunch and dinner. For the Indian dishes, they served a cup of soup, then rice, fish or chicken curry, meat, dessert, and coffee or tea. Unfortunately, the ship had no provision for amusements, so they mostly played cards.

At Penang port, the ships used to take a few hours to discharge goods and passengers. Those moving on to Singapore could take the opportunity to meet and greet near and dear ones there. Like other passengers, during his travel in 1937, A. C. Sinha met a Bengali friend and lunched with his family. Hena Sinha and her husband were newly married, so their relatives and friends received them with garlands. It was Hena Sinha's first visit to Singapore, and she enjoyed the entire journey compared to other accounts. She recalled that Singapore city resembled Rangoon. A. C. Sinha's house was a double-storeyed building with a little compound on Rangoon Road, which his father had bought. Coincidentally, Hena Sinha had left the Rangoon City of Burma for Singapore and resided on Rangoon Road in Singapore.[9]

Indeed, the voyage of the earlier migrants or travellers in the Bay of Bengal was frightening and unpleasant, but sometimes it was enjoyable. Most travellers used steamboats, which were considerably more pleasant than sailing vessels before the 1870s. It needs to be clarified when Bengalis first used the aircraft for travelling to Malaysia and Singapore. The remembrance of Dolly Sinha Davenport helps to determine the approximate period of using the aircraft by the Bengalis. Davenport came to Singapore by plane in 1966 when the airport was at Paya Lebar. Therefore, it is well assumed that the Bengalis used the aircraft from the 1960s, though it did not become a means of mass transport from Bengal to Malaya. However, this technological advancement made human mobility more effortless and more convenient.

Health and Diseases

Indentured labourers mostly worked on plantations and in mining areas. As a result, they consumed unhygienic food and suffered from severe health hazards, as reflected in their mortality rate (Table 6.1).

Many fatal diseases—including malaria, tuberculosis, dysentery, pneumonia, beriberi and cholera—were prevalent across British Malaya, and these diseases caused the death of thousands of estate labourers every year.[10] The cholera epidemic, which is believed to have started in Bengal in the early

Table 6.1 Mortality of adult indentured labourers in Province Wellesley

Years	Death per 1,000 per year
1871–1880	57.3
1881–1890	39.7
1891–1900	49.6
1901–1910	56.9

Source: David Northrup, *Indentured Labor in the Age of Imperialism 1834–1922*, Studies in Comparative World History (Cambridge: Cambridge University Press, 1995), 122.

nineteenth century, began to spread through British troops to Malaya, China and Japan, as well as to the Persian Gulf and East Africa.[11] The Governor of Singapore in the 1860s was justifiably anxious; there were no laws to prevent the spread of diseases and protect its inhabitants from fatal epidemics like cholera.[12]

Beriberi was one of the most severe infections that could have been contracted in the early twentieth century. People suffered from this disease due to a lack of vitamins B1 and B2, and it spread among the consumers of polished rice, primarily Chinese labourers. However, it was absent among Europeans and Tamils who ate 'Bengali rice', also known as unpolished and parboiled rice. Malays also did not suffer from beriberi because they consumed home-milled rice.[13]

The Bengalis, among other diasporic communities, suffered greatly from cholera. Reports showed that some 210 Bengalis died within three years (1880–1883) in the Malay Peninsula.[14] The Federated Malay States started to take preventive measures and gave more attention to the Health Branch, which was established in 1911, primarily in response to the high mortality among Indian labourers.[15] However, cholera continued to cause a high rate of death until the 1920s.

Malaria was another fatal disease. More South Asian labourers died of malaria in Malaya, Mauritius and Assam than in any other British colonies.[16] It happened due to the prevalence of virulent species of malaria and ignorance about the necessity for sanitary water supplies.[17] In the 1890s, a Chinese traveller reported that about 75 per cent of labourers died from malaria in an estate at Broga in Selangor.[18] L. H. Clayton, Superintendent of Immigrants of the Straits Settlements and the Federated Malay States, reported that the health condition of indentured labourers was at its worst in 1908. The employment rate dropped in four estates, and the situation was critical in three estates in Perak. The percentage of mortality rates was 17.64, 18.4 and 11.62 in Changkat Salak (presently, Kuala Kangsar District), Chenderiang (presently, Batang Padang District) and Pondon Tanjong (presently, Pondok Tanjung, Perak). All job contracts were terminated in Changkat Salak and Pondon Tanjong. For a few months, the mortality rates were excessive in those estates: 23.74 per cent in Changkat Salak, 66.66 in Chenderiang and 21.43 in Pondon Tanjong. The record of Bukit Asahan Estate reflected almost the same percentage, estimated at 29.95 per cent.[19]

In 1911, the Singapore government took some initiatives to prevent malaria-related death because such disease killed about 3,000 people yearly.[20] Besides, the Government of the Federated Malay States secured medical facilities for labourers by providing compulsory specialised treatment and care. The owners of estates bore the expense of the labourers' treatment. The government directed reserving at least four beds in estate hospitals for every 100 labourers, hiring qualified dressers and stocking sufficient drugs. The estate hospitals were run under the supervision of government medical officers.[21] The situation improved gradually in the 1930s, as the planters provided some basic facilities, such as sanitation and a better water supply.[22]

Wages and Accommodation

The indentured labourers came to Malaya on the credit ticket system[23] but were unaware of the loopholes in the contract. They received low wages, poor housing and were subject to severe regimentation.[24] In 1909, the superintendent of emigration of Calcutta reported in a letter that the Governor of Bengal fixed the wage of 7 annas for adult male and 5 annas for female indentured labourers per day (where 1 rupee = 16 annas). This meant that male labourers earned around 13 rupees per month, which was insufficient. Even the wage of day labourers of Dacca city was comparatively better than the indentured labourers of British Malaya in 1905. For example, labourers were paid around 10–12 rupees per month in Dacca.[25] However, indentured labourers used to earn lesser wages than non-indentured labourers in British Malaya.[26] The Governor deliberately fixed the minimum wage and served the interests of planters and capitalists, foreclosing the possibility of bargaining in favour of the workers. Even when the plantation industry boomed, the labourers suffered from starvation.[27] Sometimes, workers were kept unpaid for a certain period. These sufferings, including the non-payment of wages, led to mental depression for many labourers. In 1908, one Bengali worker in Singapore attempted to hang himself because his wage of 120 dollars remained unpaid.[28]

Most of the migrants in Singapore lived like missionary families with small salaries. One of Banarjee's friends resided in a messy house on Queen Street, an undeveloped part of the town inhabited mainly by clerks and low-paid workers. House rent increased from 7 to 14 dollars in 1903.[29] As the number of new immigrants increased in Singapore, house rents and the price of daily necessities rose accordingly. Followed by the introduction of new rules and regulations in the 1910s and 1920s, planters slowly began to provide better wages and accommodation to the labourers.[30] Housing was generally livable;

however, in some cases, it was overcrowded in the plantation estates. The heat of the place was oppressive. The drainage system was not sufficient, leading to an unhealthy environment. There was no privacy, and the workers' dormitory was the scene of frequent disputes and quarrels.[31]

The Singapore Employment Act, 1968, which provided basic terms and conditions for the labourers' well-being, was modified frequently. However, throughout the colonial and early postcolonial periods, labourers were exploited. *Stranger to Myself* by Md Sharif Uddin is the narrative of the quotidian life of migrant labourers in Southeast Asia, particularly in Singapore, from the 1990s.[32] The narrative reflects the experiences of all migrant workers. Agents and employers were responsible for the workers' betterment and inhuman treatment. For example, Sharif Uddin's recruiters did not even offer him food on his first night in Singapore.[33] His experiences in postcolonial Singapore are the continuation of the experiences of migrant labourers in colonial times.

Some of Sharif Uddin's poetry and prose reflect the life of indentured and *kangany* labourers. His literary works narrated that cruel and unsympathetic employers forced workers to meet production targets. Employers deducted money from the labourers' monthly salaries if they could not meet prospective targets. These target-oriented working conditions came at the cost of physical and social well-being. Employers often stopped workers from celebrating their social or religious events unless their work was completed. Sometimes, they had to work while sick as employers were inflexible regarding labourers' illnesses. One postcolonial example from Sharif Uddin relays how he was forced to work with a fever of 103°F.[34] Gwee Li Sui wrote in his foreword to Sharif Uddin's book:

> While the city prospers under the government's plans, millions of workers have made it dynamic and enriched it economically. The sacrifices of migrant workers are written in every inch of Singapore—in the bricks of buildings, ship irons, under the floor of houses.[35]

In the capitalist economic system, most low-paid workers cannot meet their aspirations despite working hard. Sharif Uddin worked for about six years for twelve hours a day, starting at seven in the morning, but he could hardly change anything in this life. He assisted in constructing a crowd of mansions but could not make a cottage for himself. Therefore, his economic and social conditions remained the same.[36] In his words:

We toil as labourers for years for a little money. Does anyone know how many of us are really happy? How many are stable economically? Over the past six years, I have never heard anyone take a sigh of pleasure. Only wailing sounds can be heard.[37]

On another note, he says:

Of course, now I do not have the same expectations as before. I have understood that the life working abroad stretches out to punish the greed in me. I am not greedy or dreamy as before. Now I am roaming just to find the lost confidence. I no longer want to hear the list of what I do not have and the list of what I demand. I am too tired of that. What I want is love, a little magic touch. I want my child to come running towards me and give me a tight hug.[38]

The Life of Bengali Seamen

Bengali *lascar*s worked in merchant or military ships and travelled across the world. They were seen frequently in British colonial harbours, particularly Southeast Asian ports. Sometimes, their life and health were at risk as they worked in a challenging and unhygienic environment.[39] A New Zealander wrote about the Malays in every cot, Bengali *lascar*s in shoals and the unpleasant smell everywhere in Singapore harbour.[40] By the early twentieth century, the number of Bengali *lascar*s had decreased in Singapore, as WWI affected maritime transportation as well as causing unemployment and irregularities in the Master Attendants' Office. This trend continued throughout the late colonial period. In 1938, a Bengali named Mirza Abdul Majid (1906–1973), commonly known as M. A. Majid (Figure 6.1),[41] came forward to secure the interest of the working classes, including the Bengalis.[42] He noted the grievance, injustices and unemployment of the Bengali seamen in Malaya. He asked foreign shipowners to improve the working conditions of Asian seamen.[43] In the 1930s, more than 60 per cent of Bengali *lascar*s remained unemployed for an indefinite period in Singapore, and the Master Attendants' Office was indifferent to their grievances. Majid appealed to the officials of the Board of Trade for their patronage, kindness and justice towards Bengali and Malay seamen.[44]

Figure 6.1   M. A. Majid (1906–1973)
Source: Fazlur Rahman, grandson of Majid.

The poor Bengali seamen needed food, shelter and sometimes legal assistance. Majid provided such assistance and relentlessly petitioned the government on their behalf. Majid and his union also worked towards securing the interests of seamen, including calling for a fourteen-day strike to demand an increase in the seamen's salary by 70 per cent in 1954. Organised by the Indo-Malay-Pakistani Seamen Union, between 200 and 460 seamen of the Straits Steamship Company demonstrated, but the company refused to negotiate. Therefore, the strike was extended to 112 days.

Meanwhile, the colonial government appointed T. A. White to the Master Attendant's Office to build a healthy trade union in Singapore. He was an officer of the National Union of Seamen in Britain. After three consecutive meetings between Majid and White, the company raised wages by about 20 per cent, following which Majid ended the long strike.[45] Furthermore, Majid disputed the new working agreement of the Singapore Maritime Employers' Federation, the Malaya Seamen's Union and the Singapore Chinese Seafarers' Federation, labelling the process of seamen recruitment as unsatisfactory and discriminatory. His union considered calling a strike ballot against the agreement.[46] Majid even recommended that the government amend the outmoded shipping laws in Malaya.

Encountering Wild Animals and Planters

As mentioned earlier, plantation labourers worked in forest areas, which could be dangerous and frightening. Tiger attacks were common in the Malay Peninsula during the early colonial period. Colonel Butterworth, the Governor of the Straits Settlements (1843–1855), reported that tigers killed about 200 people annually in the 1850s, and they threatened the plantation worker's life in the following decades.[47] However, many incidents of tiger attacks were not disclosed; planters even prevented officials from investigating because they feared the lousy reputation of their estates would discourage coolies from working there. A Chinese traveller recollected a giant rubber estate in Selangor where about 15,000 labourers were working in 1891. He remembered that many labourers of earlier workforces were either killed by tigers or died from malaria.[48]

The colonial government took a few initiatives to reduce the number of fatalities from tiger attacks. For instance, they granted financial rewards for tiger killing, constructed pits for catching tigers and involved Bengali convicts as hunters.[49] Even the Governor of Singapore requested the Bengal government send half a dozen *shikaris* (hunters). The governor employed convicts to beat in the jungle once a month with *tom-tom*s (native drums) to frighten and drive away the tigers. McNair made three parties with some South Asian convicts, and each party consisted of three transportees. The first party was sent to the Bukit Timah or Central district, another to the Serangoon and Changi or Eastern district and the remaining group was sent to the Choo Choo Kang or Western district.[50] A Bengali killed a tiger at Chasseriau Estate in Singapore and received an award of 50 dollars.[51] The menace of tiger attacks continued in Singapore into the early twentieth century.[52] Although the killing of tigers is judged environmentally sensitive today, in those days, they posed an immediate and direct threat to poor and vulnerable workers. However, a far graver threat came from other human beings.

Most planters practised corporal punishment, forcing and whipping labourers to work. Two English planters were imprisoned for flogging two labourers to death, but the Governor of the Straits Settlements, Andrew Clarke (c. 1873–1875), showed them leniency. Sometimes, exemption from legal punishment made English planters more free-handed in dealing with the workers. The *Indian Daily News* rebuked the Straits governor for acquitting the English planters and advised people to stop patronising them.[53] The workers, on their part, often reacted with violence. Sometimes, the demonstrations of the Tamil and Bengali labourers on rubber plantations in Malaya were unmanageable.[54]

Racism

British officials lived in specific areas that were well planned and more urbanised compared to those inhabited by Asian communities. Colonial racial segregation was maintained through social distance and the possession of spacious housing and numerous servants.[55] European communities created a wide range of recreational associations, including clubhouses for soccer, cricket and billiards, which further excluded the local population.[56] Such policies were often reflected in many corners of public life, ranging from public offices to sporting clubs as well as everyday lives.[57] In one example, the Secretary of the Singapore Sporting Club suggested making a railing around the racecourse to keep off the 'native' people. No wonder Ramnath Biswas was refused passage onboard a boat with three white officers of a rubber plantation when he was crossing the Muar river.[58]

In the medical profession, South Asian doctors, mainly from Bengal and Madras, were treated as 'second class' doctors by the Europeans.[59] They were not given incentives or proper professional training. P. R. Sengupta remembered that the Bengali doctors were given a shorter period of training than their European counterparts so that they would serve as assistants. Even a few Bengali doctors who had completed full medical courses in Europe and passed the relevant examinations were not given equal opportunities vis-à-vis their European counterparts.[60] Asian doctors were not promoted to high ranks in the department because it might have a professional risk for the European medical practitioners to be subordinated by the Asians.[61]

In the Immigration Department, racial discrimination affected Bengalis' careers; Salil Kumar Chakravarti recollected the racial discrimination in his working life that led him to quit his job early.[62] During the Great Depression in the 1930s, unemployed white people received extra government support. In contrast, locals did not.[63] Racial slurs did not always come from the Europeans, but on some occasions, from local people. Sometimes, the Bengali migrants were teased with 'Mang Gha Lee' as a corrupted version of 'Bengali'.[64]

The idea of Bengali racial inferiority was unavoidable in the Malay world. For example, when Biswas cycled across British Malaya, Majid gave him some dollars and said that the Sylheti people would be proud of him if his travels were successful. Majid further remarked that 'the White [Europeans], Chinese, and Malay would know that we [the Bengalis] are *Manus* [human beings] too'.[65] Majid was suggesting that the Bengalis possessed admirable skills and qualities, revealing that it was often assumed that they did not.

A Bengali Globetrotter in British Malaya

Biswas first aspired to be a global traveller while working at the Singapore harbour. He spoke many languages—including Bangla, English, Malay and Hindi—and from 1931 to 1940, Biswas travelled on a bicycle in most parts of Asia, Europe, Africa and America (Map 6.1). He was the first Bengali globetrotter in British Malaya and was known as 'bhoo-paryatak [globe traveller] Ramnath'. Biswas kept notes of his experiences; based on them, he wrote about thirty books. Some of these are significant in the context of this chapter as they are a remarkable reflection of Bengali mobility and socio-economic conditions in Malaya and Singapore.[66]

Biswas received support in many forms, including food, shelter and donations, from Bengalis and other communities, including Chinese, Malay, Tamil, Punjabi and Japanese. Within the Bengali diaspora, Majid, a well-known personality in Singapore's public life with good connections to colonial administrators, helped Biswas in every stage of preparation for his trips, including raising funds and securing visas for different countries.

Following all necessary arrangements, Biswas' departure date was set for 7 July 1931. The news was published in three newspapers: the *Straits Times*, *Malay Tribune* and *Morning Post*. Upon his departure, Bengali migrants of different socio-economic backgrounds arranged a public gathering. Biswas' farewell procession was participated by both Bengali Hindus and Muslims, reflecting communal harmony among South Asian diasporic communities. The crowd included *sareng* and *sukani* (*lascars*) from Sylhet and Bengalis from other places. After socialising with his South Asian, Chinese and European acquaintances, Biswas began his journey from the Bengali Mosque[67] at Queen Street in Singapore. Several thousands of South Asian expatriates[68] gathered to wish him success in front of the mosque. When they saw Biswas on the bicycle, they expressed excitement with terms like 'Allah-hu-Akbar' or 'Vande Mataram'. The mosque's imam offered a special *dowa* (prayer) for Biswas. Some literate *lascars* spoke at the meeting.[69] The Government of Singapore provided him with identification cards in different languages (mainly English,

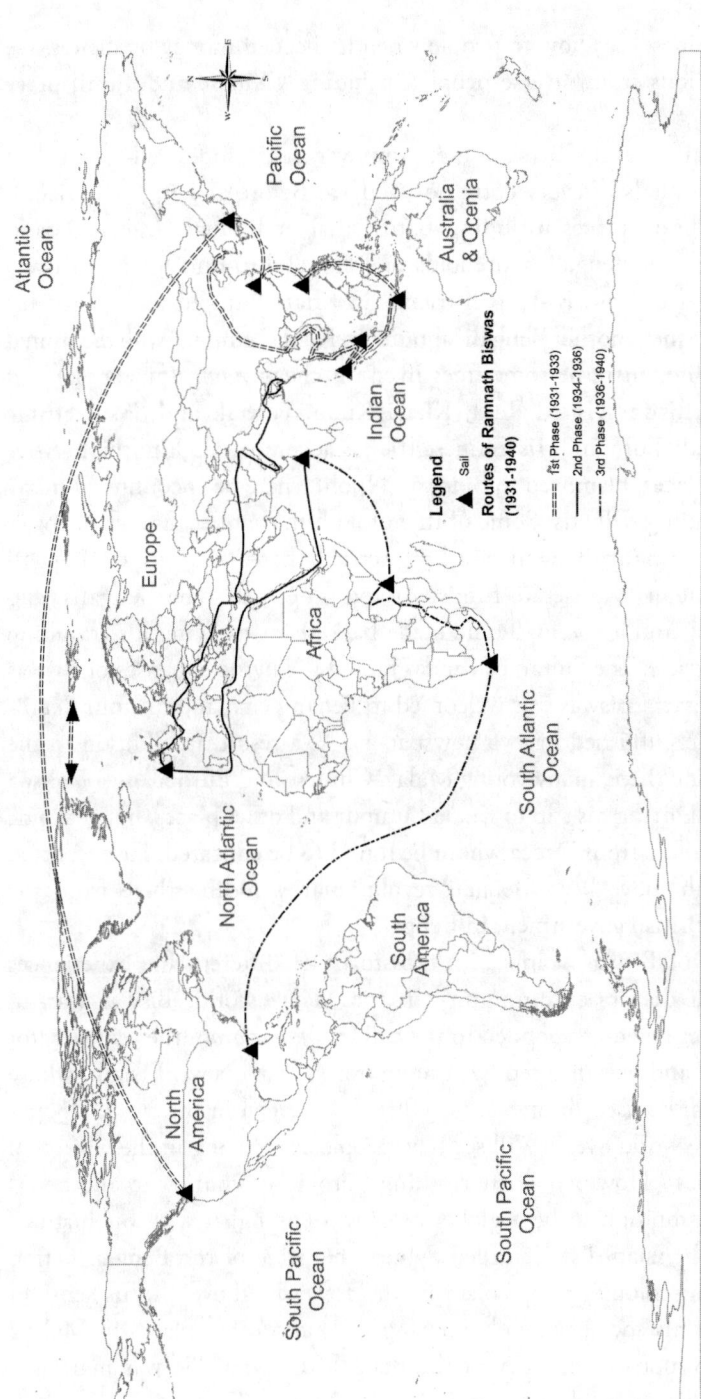

Map 6.1 Projected map of Ramnath Biswas's biking routes

Source: Adapted by Gazi Mizanur Rahman from Google Maps.

Note: Map not to scale and does not represent authentic international boundaries.

Malay and Chinese) to show to people when he needed money or shelter. He received donations from diverse people, including Chinese and Tamil petty shopkeepers.[70]

During his travel, Biswas met impoverished and well-established Bengali professionals in every corner of Malaya. Before arriving at Malacca, he met Bengalis in places including Batu Pahat and Muar (Map 6.2) and stayed overnight in Bengali households in Johor Bahru and Skudai. Biswas incidentally met one of his Bengali friends in Kuala Lumpur and visited his house. Later, he met another Bengali labourer in Kuala Lumpur, who recounted his miserable life where he sometimes lived on cheap *nanas* (pineapple) and durian fruits. Biswas visited Rasa, Kuala Kubu, Peretak and Sakai ethnic areas from Kuala Lumpur. His Chinese friends accompanied him there. After visiting these places, he moved to Bidor and Ipoh, where he encountered many Bengalis, including Sylhetis. Some of them told him that because of the lower living expenses, many Bengali Muslims settled there.[71] He visited Bengali clubs in Seremban to generate funds. At Ipoh, he met some Bengalis who donated money and a *khalur* (home-made basket) for carrying his travelling stuff on the bicycle. The Sultan of Perak granted the living expenses of Biswas in Kuala Kangsar.[72] Biswas was welcomed to Penang city, and his tour details in Penang were published in two newspapers. As a result, in addition to the Bengalis residing there, many young Malay, Chinese and Europeans socialised with Biswas.[73] During his trip to Kuala Lumpur and other places, he met some hawkers and tailors from Dacca whom he found to be educated. He suspected that they might have been Bengali revolutionaries hiding there from the torture of the British government in Bengal.

The story of Biswas points to a crossroads of different life experiences of the Bengali diasporic community in the Malay world. Biswas was an ambitious traveller who responded to the call for *ojanar aroti* (the yearning for the unknown) and was inspired by, among others, Kazi Nazrul Islam, whose following poem he used to invoke: 'I refuse to be caged in the closed doors / I will travel the world over / Will see how people are moving in the whirlpool of turning times / How people are running / From one country to another!'[74] However, his ambition to be a globetrotter was entangled with his birth in a remote South Asian district called Sylhet, the pride of the Bengali nation and India's anti-colonial nationalism itself. However, above all, his sense of adventure and his social networks in Singapore and other places in Malaya reflect the enormous complexity of the Bengali diaspora. He was making a place both for himself and his community.

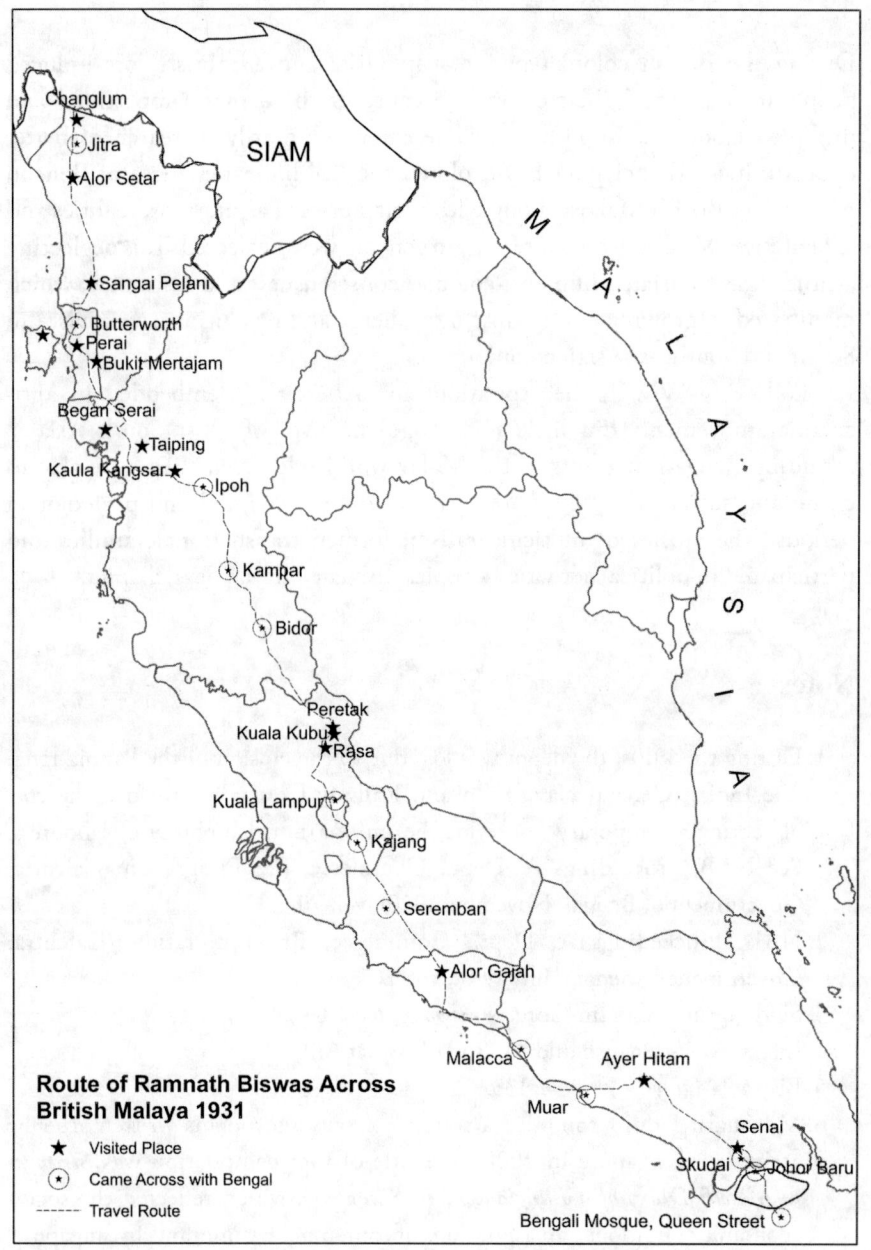

Map 6.2   Estimated bike routes in Malaya

Source: Adapted by Gazi Mizanur Rahman from Google Maps.

Conclusion

During the British colonial period, capitalists and administrators induced people to migrate to their colonies because of the demand for skilled and unskilled labourers. In addition, some came voluntarily in search of better opportunities. This chapter has explored the real-life experiences of Bengali migrants in British Malaya, along with their stories of aspirations, realities and exploitation. Working-class interests, in general, were neglected. This neglecting attitude was translated into anti-colonial consciousness and resistance, which manifested in growing communist movements and revolutionary activism in South and Southeast Asian colonies.

Following WWII, the aspirations for a better life embedded in anti-colonial movements did little to change the lives of most South Asians, including Bengali migrants in the Malay world. However, they were able to create and sustain their diasporic space across the colonial and postcolonial periods. They fostered multiculturalism, formed transnational families and participated in political activities—topics discussed in the next chapter.

Notes

1. During the 1910s, the depot was lost due to the erosion of the Padma river. The Indian General Navigation and Railway Company provided the cost of renting a temporary house for the uninterrupted mobility of labourers. See NAB, Proceedings A, Dept.: Commerce, Br.: Emigration (Calcutta: Government of Bengal, November 1920), vol. 70.
2. NAB, Proceedings A, Dept.: Commerce, Br.: Emigration (Calcutta: Government of Bengal, July 1918), vol. 20.
3. Siddique and Shotam-Gore, *Serangoon Road*, 6.
4. Interview with Mushahid Ali (son of Asmat Ali).
5. Biswas, *Malaysia Vromon*, 133.
6. Md Sharif Uddin compiled a series of essays and poems written after he arrived in Singapore in 2008. The title of that compilation was *Stranger to Myself: Diary of a Bangladeshi in Singapore*, which reflected the socio-economic conditions and aspirations of contemporary migrants in Singapore. The book won the Singapore Book Awards in the non-fiction category. See also *Nikkei Asian Review*, 27 February 2019.

7. Md Sharif Uddin, *Stranger to Myself: Diary of a Bangladeshi in Singapore*, ed. Theophilus Kwek (Singapore: Landmark Books, 2017), 71.

8. *ST*, 22 April 1903, 1.

9. NAS, OHI, Hena Sinha, October–November of 1983, Acc. No. 000354.

10. J. Norman Parmer, 'Health and Health Services in British Malaya in the 1920s', *Modern Asian Studies* 23, no. 1 (1989): 49.

11. Gwyn Campbell, 'Introduction: Abolition and Its Aftermath in the Indian Ocean World', in *Abolition and Its Aftermath in Indian Ocean Africa and Asia*, ed. Gwyn Campbell (London; New York: Routledge, 2005), 4; Ghee, *The History of Medicine*, 31; Nasution, *Chulia in Penang*, 62.

12. *STOJ*, 12 April 1870, 3.

13. Lenore Manderson, *Sickness and the State: Health and Illness in Colonial Malaya, 1870–1940* (Cambridge: Cambridge University Press, 1996), 90.

14. *STOJ*, 8 May 1880, 3; *STOJ*, 14 February 1881; *STWI*, 2 April 1883, 7.

15. Parmer, 'Health and Health Services in British Malaya in the 1920s', 66.

16. Ralph Shlomowitz and Lance Brennan, 'Epidemiology and Indian Labor Migration at Home and Abroad', *Journal of World History* 5, no. 1 (1994): 58–64, quoted in Northrup, *Indentured Labor*, 121.

17. Manderson, *Sickness and the State*, 85–89.

18. *SFPMA*, 8 June 1939, 4.

19. *ST*, 6 April 1912, 9.

20. Ghee, *The History of Medicine*, 52.

21. Wright, *Twentieth Century Impressions of British Malaya*, 249.

22. Aiyar, *Indian Problems in Malaya*, 58.

23. *Kanganies* or any other forms of intermediaries paid the cost of the passage in advance to workers and retained control over their services until they repaid their debt in full.

24. Rajeswary Ampalavanar, *The Indian Minority and Political Change in Malaya 1945–1957* (Kuala Lumpur: Oxford University Press, 1981), 23; Hefner, Introduction, 30.

25. Allen, *Dacca*, 85.

26. From the Protector of Emigrants and Superintendent of Emigration of Calcutta to the Secretary to the Government of Bengal. NAB, Proceedings A, Dept.: General, Br.: Emigration (Calcutta: Government of Bengal), January 1912, vol. 13.

27. Biswas, *Malaysia Vromon*, 135.

28. *SFPMA*, 3 November 1908, 4.

29. *ST*, 22 April 1903, 1.

30. Aiyar, *Indian Problems in Malaya*, 58.

31. Aiyar, *Indian Problems in Malaya*, 61.

32. Uddin, *Stranger to Myself*.

33. Uddin, *Stranger to Myself*, 19.

34. Angus Whitehead, 'Review of *Stranger to Myself: Diary of a Bangladeshi in Singapore*, by Md Sharif Uddin', *Asiatic* 12, no. 1 (2018): 220.

35. Gwee Li Sui, foreword to *Stranger to Myself: Diary of a Bangladeshi in Singapore*, by Md Sharif Uddin, ed. Theophilus Kwek (Singapore: Landmark Books, 2017), 13.

36. Uddin, *Stranger to Myself*, 124.

37. Uddin, *Stranger to Myself*, 113.

38. Uddin, *Stranger to Myself*, 124.

39. *SFPMA*, 20 July 1896, 2.

40. *SFPMA*, 16 November 1891, 3.

41. Majid has already been mentioned in Chapter 2 of this book. Born in Sylhet, he was a unionist, benevolent politician and pious Muslim. He received primary and secondary education in Sylhet, and his uncle sent him to London to study Law. However, he discontinued his study and left for Tokyo, where he spent one year before coming to Singapore in 1925 and spending the rest of his life there. More discussions of Majid's involvement in public spaces can be found in Chapters 7 and 8.

42. NAS, SSOC, 273/639/1-14 (CO). M. A. Majid to J. Foley, the Under-Secretary to Board of Trade, Mercantile Marine, 2 September 1938.

43. *ST*, 20 October 1953, 4.

44. NAS, SSOC, 273/639/1-14 (CO).

45. *SFP*, 12 July 1954, 1; *ST*, 13 July 1954, 7.

46. *ST*, 31 October 1955, 4.

47. Peter Boomgaard, *Frontiers of Fear: Tigers and People in the Malay World, 1600–1950* (New Haven; London: Yale University Press, 2001), 103.

48. *SFPMA*, 8 June 1939, 4; *ST*, 14 June 1939, 12.

49. McNair and Bayliss, *Prisoners Their Own Warders*, 50.

50. McNair and Bayliss, *Prisoners Their Own Warders*, 51–52.

51. *STWI*, 7 May 1884, 2.

52. Orfeur Cavenagh, *Report on the Progress of the Straits Settlement, from 1859–60 to 1866–67* (Singapore: Straits Government Press, 1867), 16; Boomgaard, *Frontiers of Fear*, 103; Wright, *Twentieth Century Impressions of British Malaya*, 930.

53. *Straits Observer* (Singapore), 21 March 1876, 3.

54. Nawab Syed Mahomed, President of the Indian National Congress, noted in a meeting in Karachi that he had seen the painful experiences of the plantation labourers and their resistance. See *The Advertiser* (Adelaide, SA: 1889–1931), 29 December 1913, 9.

55. John G. Butcher, *The British in Malaya 1880–1941: The Social History of a European Community in Colonial Southeast Asia* (Kuala Lumpur: Oxford University Press, 1979), 77; Kenneth Ballhatchet, *Race Sex and Class under the Raj: Imperial Attitudes and Policies and Their Critics, 1793–1905* (New Delhi: Vikas Publishing House Pvt. Ltd 1979), 2–3.

56. Harper, 'Globalism and the Pursuit of Authenticity', 272.

57. *STWI*, 30 August 1883, 2.

58. Biswas, *Malaysia Vromon*, 95.

59. Lee, 'The Founding of the Medical School in Singapore in 1905', 5. Doctors were categorised under two heads—Europeans and Asians—in British Malaya. The Asian doctors were mainly trained in South Asian medical colleges.

60. Sengupta, *Malaysia and Bengali Doctors*, 37.

61. Parmer, 'Health and Health Services in British Malaya in the 1920s', 71.

62. NAS, OHI, Chakravarti, 3 August 2007, Acc. No. 003209.

63. *ST*, 28 August 1932, 9.

64. NAS, OHI, Nora Anny Samosir, 13 May 2010, Acc. No. 001811.

65. Biswas, *Malaysia Vromon*, 65–66.

66. Biswas, *Malaysia Vromon*, 28; Muntasir Mamun and Ujjal Ashrafuzzaman, 'Legend of the East: Ramnath Biswas Who Wheeled before WWII', *Trino (Adventure Quarterly)* 3, no. 1 (January–March 2012): 49, 52, 53; Mousumi Biswa Das Gupta, 'Ramnath er Bishho Vormon' [World Travel of Ramnath], *Banik Barta*, 6 October 2017, https://www.revolvy.com/page/Ramnath-Biswas, accessed 13 June 2018.

67. This mosque was a popular place for Bengali Muslims, many of whom lived around the Queen Street area. A Bengali migrant, Moulvi M. Idris Gowhary, was the imam of the Queen Street Mosque and a licentiate in Muslim Law in Arabic. He was also the Secretary of the Bengal Muslim Association. See *Morning Tribune* (hereinafter *MoT*), 28 April 1938, 7.

68. Majid estimated that at least 5,000 expatriates would attend the mass gathering. See Biswas, *Malaysia Vromon*, 64.

69. Biswas, *Malaysia Vromon*, 66.

70. Biswas, *Malaysia Vromon*, 133.

71. Biswas, *Malaysia Vromon*, 155, 168.
72. Biswas, *Malaysia Vromon*, 171.
73. Biswas, *Malaysia Vromon*, 189–190.
74. Quoted in Iftekhar Iqbal, 'The Bengali Muslim: Language and Space-Making at the Ocean's Margins', in *Oceanic Islam: Muslim Universalism and European Imperialism*, ed. Sugata Bose and Ayesha Jalal (New Delhi: Bloomsbury Publishing, 2020), 197–198.

7

The Making of a Diasporic Space

Social and Political Dimensions

Bengali migrants became distinctly visible in the Malay public space in the late nineteenth century. Their professional world has been discussed in Chapters 4 and 5, showing that they gradually created a diasporic space with other migrant communities, such as the Chinese and Tamils. When it comes to social spaces, the Bengalis carved them out in several ways: by maintaining intergenerational communication, fostering multiculturalism, continuing interaction with other diasporic communities and forming transnational families in Malaya. These multidimensional aspects of space-making made the Bengali diaspora an integral part of the Malay cosmopolitan world, a role only enhanced by the contributions to Malaya's decolonisation process after WWII. This chapter explores how the Bengalis carved out a place for themselves through interactions with other communities, political practices and involvement in making institutions of social and political importance.

Intergenerational communication

When Ramnath Biswas was travelling in Malacca, an elderly 'Sundarban Bengkalis' invited him to have dinner with his family. The Sundarban Bengkalis served eastern Bengal food and spoke in an unusual accent, prompting Biswas to learn more about the so-called Sundarban Bengkalis.[1] He later had another opportunity to learn about them from a Bengali named Deepak, who spoke in the Barisal dialect and lived in a Portuguese *mahalla* (a residential area or unit).[2] According to Deepak, when Buddhism declined in Bengal, many Bengali Buddhists from the Sundarbans migrated to Pulau Bengkalis.[3] This dispersion continued during the Portuguese and Maghs plunder at the Bay of Bengal and Sundarban areas.[4] This diffuse community was mostly composed of fishermen in Bengal. They upheld the same profession at Pulau Bengkalis. After fishing in the Straits, they brought the fish to sell in the Malacca market. Later, some settled in Malacca and converted to Christianity.[5] Deepak said that the Bengalis who migrated from Pulau Bengkalis to Malacca were known as Sundarban Bengkalis. A few primary and secondary sources corroborate Deepak's narrative. For instance, Lloyd and Moore suggested that the Indians settled in the tiny fishing village and married local girls before the Muslim arrival. The *Suma Oriental* and the Report of Balthasar Bort, Dutch–Malacca Governor (1665–1677), both explain that the Bengali fishermen settled and engaged in the fishing profession in Malacca.[6]

Shafiya Khatoon remembers that when her father, M. A. Majid, came to Singapore in the early 1920s, he was sheltered by Osman Ali, a Bengali migrant who had already settled there. Majid married the widow after Osman Ali's death and affectionately raised Osman Ali's two young kids. Majid had no children with the widow, and one of his foster sons, Akbar Ali, helped him run a hotel at Collyer Quey. Ali married a girl from a wealthy family in Singapore, and Ali's daughter, Dr Balkis, presently also lives in Singapore.[7]

Majid himself sheltered many Bengali immigrants in Singapore. Khatoon recalls how her father had a rented shophouse with two units. The Bengali seamen needed to be accommodated during the repairing or refuelling of vessels. The ground floor was used as a lodging house for them, and her father provided food for the unemployed seamen. Sometimes, the tenants cooked their own food and only paid rent for accommodation, which Majid took according to the financial capacity of the guests.[8]

Intergenerational connections among the Bengalis sustained an increasingly visible social network that promoted further diasporic settlement. Many returned to Bengal to marry a Bengali bride or bridegroom. Others sent remittances to their relatives, and some regularly visited their ancestral homes to foster the connections between Bengal and Malaya. For example, K. C. Sinha migrated from Calcutta to Singapore around 1900 and went back home to marry a Bengali girl. His eldest son, A. C. Sinha (married in 1937), and grandson, Ranjit Sinha (married in 1966), went back to Bengal to marry Bengali brides. Hena Sinha, the wife of A. C. Sinha, maintained relationships with relatives in Burma and Bengal. The descendants of four generations of the Sinha family still live in Singapore, and sometimes, they visit their relatives in Kolkata and Dhaka.

Mushahid Ali remembers his connection to his ancestral homeland in Bangladesh. His father, Asmat Ali, went back to Taltala in Sylhet and married

Sairabanu in 1923. Mushahid Ali and his siblings were born and brought up in Kota Tinggi, Johor. However, his father returned to Bengal permanently in 1959. Mushahid Ali used to send remittances, and most of the Bengalis in Singapore did so during that time, as he remembers. When he was a Singaporean diplomat (1970–1974) in Kuala Lumpur, he met Sheikh Mujibur Rahman (the first president of Bangladesh) and Abdus Samad Azad (the first foreign minister of Bangladesh) in 1972. Azad was from Sylhet; therefore, he spoke with Mushahid Ali in the Sylheti dialect, reflecting on their emotional bond with their ancestral homeland. In 1992, he went to Bangladesh to meet his sisters and their offspring. His nephews and grand-nephews are still living in Sylhet, and his siblings occasionally visit relatives there.[9]

Anwarul Haque recalls that his father, Muniruddin, went back to Bengal in the 1930s to marry a Bengali woman at Fenchuganj in Sylhet and returned to Singapore. Haque was born in Singapore and visited his ancestral homeland in Sylhet in 1949 for the first time. Out of his eight siblings, six are living in Singapore. He is the eldest, and the youngest one is Hamidul Haque (b. 1963), a lawyer. His eldest sister, Zarina, has a strong bond with the homeland and visits Bangladesh quite often.[10]

Transnational Families and Interracial Marriage

Human mobility and territorialism are opposed to one another. Territorial authorities such as the nation state control people on the move, and mobilities beyond national spaces face challenges constantly in different ways.[11] Miscegenation is the one way that facilitates mobility beyond nation states' territory.[12] Miscegenation in the Malay cosmopolitan world fosters de-territorialisation, transnational family and multiculturalism and began in Malaya well before the colonial period.[13] During the colonial period, however, Muslim marriage rules played a significant role in assimilating Indian Muslims into Malay society. Indian Muslims could easily make a marital relationship with Malay Muslim women, whereas non-Muslims needed to convert to Islam. There were few hurdles for Bengali Muslims who wished to marry local Malay Muslim women.[14] The EIC brought 'Free Bengalis' from Bengkulu to Penang in 1824, who were already a mixed community because they had married Sumatran women and created transnational families.[15]

The children of Malay mothers and Indian fathers, mainly Tamil and Bengali, were known as *jawi pekan* or *jawi peranakan*. These multiracial families created cultural potpourri in Malaya. For instance, J. D. Vaughan[16] noted that the offspring of mixed parentage adopted a portion of the costume worn by their Indian father and classified it as Malay. However, their dress more accurately could be described as Kling and Bengali.[17] The Jawi Pekan adopted the cultural characteristics of both ethnic groups[18] and developed a cultural synthesis.

It was mentioned earlier that some Bengali Muslims intermarried with partners from other Muslim ethnic groups, including Malay, Sumatran and Chinese communities. In her oral testimony, Khatoon recalls how Majid and his Chinese wife became a key example of a transnational and multiracial family in the Malay Peninsula. Majid first married a Bengali widow (Akbar Ali's mother), but that marriage was short-lived. After that, a Malay woman, the wife of a Bengali migrant, helped Majid marry for the second time. Majid and the Chinese girl whom he married, renamed Hamidah Binte Abdullah Sani, had ten offspring.

In 1965, the eldest daughter of Majid, Khatoon, married Kamsani Hasan, a mixed Malay. His father was an Indonesian Malay, and his mother was a Bruneian who had a connection with the Brunei royal family by marriage. Hasan's maternal aunt, Mrs Kadayang Amas Ampuan Salleh (commonly known in the family as Maskatun), was the first wife of Sultan Ahmad Tajuddin (the twenty-seventh sultan of Brunei Darussalam).[19] Khatoon visited her husband's relatives in Brunei on several occasions since 1969. The first time, she travelled by ship and, coincidentally, celebrated her son's (Fazlur Rahman) first birthday in Brunei.

Hasan had a close connection with his three maternal cousins, namely Y. A. M. Pengiran Anak Datin Seri Setia Hjh Siti Saerah Al Mahrum Sultan Ahmad Tajuddin (Belabab Basar, 1928–2013), Y. A. M. Pg Anak Siti Zubaidah Al Mahrum Sultan Ahmad Tajuddin (Belabab Tangah, c. 1932–1986) and Y. A. M. Pengiran Anak Datin Seri Setia Hajah Siti Halimah ibni Al-Marhum Sultan Ahmad Tajuddin (Belabab Damit, 1935–2009). Khatoon attended the wedding of Saerah, daughter of Sultan Ahmad Tajuddin, at Darul Hana (Old Royal Palace) and her funeral. The twenty-ninth sultan of Brunei Darussalam also attended the *janazah* (funeral) prayer for Saerah.

One of Khatoon's sisters married a Bengali bridegroom in London, whereas other siblings married people of different ethnic groups, including those of Chinese and Malay backgrounds. Their offspring are now identified as Chinese or Malay. Her second sister, Sharifa Majid, married a Singaporean Malay named Sidek bin Saniff. He was a popular and respected teacher of the Malay language.[20] After M. A. Majid's death, Sidek bin Saniff was invited by Prime Minister Lee Kuan Yew (r. 1959–1990) to join the People's Action Party (PAP), and he stood in the general election in 1976. He was elected a parliament member and served the city-state for twenty-five years, including in the capacity of Senior Minister of State for Education until 2001.[21] Fazlur Rahman, a grandson of Majid, is now working at Doha Bank in Singapore. He married the daughter of mixed-racial parentage. On a lighter note, Rahman claims to be 25 per cent Bengali, as his maternal grandfather and grandmother were Bengali and Chinese, while his paternal grandmother and grandfather were Bruneian and Indonesian, respectively!

To add to the list of Bengali transnational families, Mushahid Ali married a Malay girl when working as a diplomat in Malaysia in 1974. His brother Mashhur Ali (b. 1943) married the daughter of a mixed-race family; her father was a Bengali, and her mother was a Tamil. Most of Mushahid Ali's offspring, nieces and nephews married people of different ethnicities, and they live across the world, particularly in Bangladesh, England, Canada and the USA. Three of Mashhur Ali's children had spouses of Malay and Indian origin.[22] Muniruddin's (1903–1980) younger brother, Kamruddin, married a Malay woman named Saleha binte Yusoff.

V. Kanda Pillay was a renowned Tamil medical practitioner whose brother married a Bengal woman. However, his mother was not happy about it.[23] Urmila Nandi, a Bengali daughter of an inter-ethnic parentage, drew the attention of S. R. Nathan, the sixth president of Singapore, and they were married after an affair, although initially, Nandi's family had not welcomed this relationship. Nathan wrote:

> Umi's [Nathan called her by this name] parents would not have seen me as a suitable match. My family origins are Tamil. They were Bengali, and they would no doubt have preferred a Bengali suitor, ideally a nice lawyer or doctor. Nevertheless, I started to leave her notes. She would leave her reply, and I would sneak by and collect it.[24]

More recently, marriage between the Bengalis and other ethnic or religious communities is more frequent, forging more transnational, multiracial and inter-religious connections in Malaya.[25] The offspring of Muniruddin and Kamruddin have married different nationals, including Malay, Pakistani and Dutch. Haque is the eldest son of Muniruddin—he married a Eurasian woman in 1973. One of his three sons has married a Bengali Hindu girl.[26] Dolly Sinha

Davenport recollected her married life and described her transnational family in the following words:

> I have three offspring. Ranjit was the father of two kids. One kid is with Davenport [after the death of Ranjit, Mrs Sinha married Brand Davenport]. My eldest daughter is settled in the USA. She got married to an American who had two sons. My son, Robin Sinha, is a doctor, settled in Singapore, and married a Chinese girl. The youngest daughter, Roya, is settled in Singapore.... She got married to a boy who is mixed race, mother Chinese and father Irish. Brand [her second husband] was an Anglo-Indian. His father was pure English, and his mother was mixed-race.[27]

The ratio of inter-ethnic marriage has been increasing gradually in the Malay Peninsula, particularly in Singapore and Malaysia. For example, 22.1 per cent of total marriages in Singapore were inter-ethnic in 2017, a remarkable increase from 16.4 per cent in 2007 and 7.6 per cent in 1990.[28] In this context, the Singapore government introduced a 'double-barrelled' policy in 2010 to decide the children's identity in an inter-ethnic family.[29] This new policy is flexible. Children can choose their father's and mother's ethnic identity— for instance, Indian-Chinese, Malay-Indian, Chinese-Malay or Eurasian-Chinese. However, South Asian ethnic groups' offspring are categorised using the umbrella term 'Indian'. This leaves room for much ambiguity as each 'Indian' may have a distinct cultural identity.

M. A. Majid: A Bengali's Quest for Resistance and Political Space

During the early twentieth century, diverse South Asian migrants formed the 'Indian Association', and its numbers rose gradually across British Malaya.[30] Initially, such associations served as a platform for South Asian communities, bringing them under one umbrella and protecting and promoting their rights. Later, some leaders of these associations were involved in politics. For instance, Dwijendra Majumdar, a Bengali doctor, was involved in social work and became the Negeri Sembilan Indian Association President for three successive years during 1937–1939.[31] He continued his political struggle until his death.

S. C. Goho was politically active from the 1930s and worked for the Indian labourers' interest in Singapore. In 1939, the Johor Indian Labourers Association was formed thanks to his generous efforts. He helped to mediate between the striking Indian labourers in Singapore and the Federated Malay States between 1938 and 1941, demanding better wages and an improved working environment for Indian labourers.[32] He was elected Vice-president and President of the Central Indian Association of Malaya (CIAM) in 1939 and 1940. Later, he became the President of the Singapore Indian Association in 1940. He formed the Indian Youth League (IYL) in 1938, and its membership rapidly increased to 2,000 at the outbreak of WWII. It later merged with the Indian Independence League (IIL).[33]

On the eve of WWII, Goho was an influential leader in the Indian independence movement and took the initiative to achieve the well-being of the Indian community in the Straits Settlements.[34] His popularity among the Indian community was a threat to the British, and his worsening relationship with the colonial authority led to his arrest immediately before WWII.[35] After the war, the Malayan Security Service (MSS) secretly reported on A. N. Mithra[36] and Goho, noting that they were capable leaders who might return to politics in the future.[37] The prediction proved correct. Goho contested in the first general election of 1948 under the Singapore Legislative Council Election Ordinance 1947.[38] As an independent candidate, Goho became one of the first elected legislative councillors from the Rural West constituency. Three candidates stood for the constituency, and Goho received 981 votes, which was 50 per cent of the total turnout. The following issues were in his electoral manifesto: 'no' to sectarianism, communalism and provincialism; the abolition of racism; equal treatment to all under British rule; the protection of minorities; the betterment of working-class conditions; reconsideration of the back pay question; more seats for the people in the Legislative Council and democratic government; better housing; and the improvement of rural areas.[39] Unfortunately, after the election, he became seriously ill and left Singapore for Calcutta, where he died in July 1948.

Of all the Bengali politicians with a diasporic background, Majid has touched the most political spheres with his significant influence. He has already been referred to in this book, and in what follows, we will focus on his political career. He symbolises the Bengalis' struggle for political space as a mostly peripheral diasporic people in the messy world of colonial and early postcolonial Malaya. Following the Great Depression of 1929, which foregrounded a time of unrest in British colonies across the globe, he was

involved in trade unionism and labour politics.[40] In Singapore, workers
in rubber plantations and tin mines, municipal council coolies, bus and
construction labourers, pineapple cutters and harbour labourers called
strikes.[41] The Government of the Straits Settlements was aware of the Chinese
communist activities in Malaya. Communist leaders could easily influence
low-wage earners or suppressed people. Therefore, the government allowed
trade unionism by introducing a Trade Union Bill in 1940 to contain the
spread of communism among the working class.[42] In this context, the leaders
of port labourers formed different seamen unions. Majid formed the Indo-
Malay Seamen Union in the early 1940s, including members from India
and Malaya. Later on, he became the President of the Indo-Malay-Pakistani
Seamen's Union.

After WWII, Majid transitioned into national politics and stood in
municipal commissioner and legislative councillor elections. In 1948, two
candidates from the Progressive Party and Majid, an independent candidate,
competed for the Municipal South-West constituency (Map 7.1) in the first
Legislative Council election. Though Majid was defeated in the election,
his electoral manifesto was as follows:[43] the removal of illiteracy from the
colony; free compulsory vernacular education up to primary and secondary
grades; the improvement of medical and health services; cheaper transport;

Map 7.1   Area of constituencies during the Legislative Council election, 1948
Source: *ST*, 20 March 1948, 8.

full encouragement for trade unionism; a comprehensive programme of social welfare and achievement of self-government; supporting income tax; suspension of immigration into the colony; and priority of local people for recruitment to top positions of government services.[44] He promised that he would remove all forms of injustice to the workers.[45]

Majid endeavoured to achieve a self-government system in Singapore. He showed his dissatisfaction with other political leaders, who were not sincere in obtaining self-government, and called them 'political opportunists'.[46] Singapore was one of the advanced British colonies; therefore, he urged the people to elect 'representatives and achieve self-democratic rule.[47] After the Legislative Council election of 1948, Majid contested for the City constituency in the 1951 Legislative Council election and the Cairnhill by-election of 1957. Along with standing in the elections, Majid was vocal against malpractices. Of the eight candidates, Lee Kuan Yew and Majid were particularly concerned about electoral malpractices in different forms as they obstructed constitutional development. Lee Kuan and Majid alleged that a few electoral candidates entertained potential voters and used 'women of doubtful virtue' to tempt the voters during the by-election of 1957. They offered to provide evidence of these malpractices.[48] The Singapore Governor, Sir Robert Black, appointed a commission consisting of three members, headed by S. H. D. Elias, to enquire about the allegations of malpractice during the election and prevent future corruption.[49]

Majid promoted a democratic culture and ethical values in politics. He invited opponents and other contestants to join his meetings during the election campaign.[50] He appealed to the people to be 'more conscious about civic responsibility' and register as voters. His democratic practices were reflected in an open letter, wherein he asked a legislative councillor about his liability and reminded him of his election pledges to the people of Farrer Park in Singapore.[51] Majid had good connections with some prominent contemporary politicians, including David Marshall,[52] Tengku Abdur Rahman and Lim Yew Hock. They used to visit Majid's house and discuss contemporary political issues in British Malaya.[53] The leading political parties, namely the Malayan Democratic Union, the Singapore Progress Party and the United Malays National Organisation (UMNO), were not concerned about labourers' welfare. After the Legislative Council election of 1948, Majid initiated the formation of a new political party, the Singapore Labour Party (SLP), to protect labourers' interests. He was the 'principal organiser' of the party and had the following aims and objectives:

1. Majid attempted to break the dominance of the Malayan Communist Party in the labour movement.[54] He declared that his political party's membership would be open to all British and non-British, men and women wage-earners aged above eighteen years, except communists.

2. His party aimed to achieve self-government rule in Singapore by 1954; therefore, he and his party would participate in municipal commissioner and Legislative Council elections. It further aimed to acquire independence through the merger with the Federation of Malaya and form a 'socialist society in Malaya' through constitutional means.

3. The party projected compulsory national service after attaining full responsible self-government.

4. The party would promote the rights and better living conditions of workers.

5. It vowed to fight for a minimum-wage policy and employment insurance for workers.

6. It demanded a more equitable distribution of wealth.

7. The party would advocate for the state ownership of the tin and rubber industries.

8. It supported the formation of a Fraternity and Welfare Committee.

9. It favoured granting subsidies for fishing and agricultural industries.

10. The party aimed to revise the Trade Union Ordinance and allow trade unions to participate in politics.

11. It demanded increasing income tax and imposing an inheritance tax.

12. It suggested the elimination of illiteracy through implementing free and compulsory vernacular education in primary and secondary grades.

13. The party advocated for adult literacy.[55]

Majid was inspired by the success of the 'welfare state' in the United Kingdom. Therefore, he suggested that the party constitution would be like the British Labour Party.[56] He called a meeting to adopt the party constitution, where about 200 guests were invited from various trade unions, associations and individuals interested in the labour movement.[57]

On 1 September 1948, the new political party was inaugurated officially through a public meeting chaired by Majid, held at Clifford Café on Prince Street. An ad hoc committee was formed consisting of seven members; Majid and S. S. Manyam (President of the Army Civil Service Union) were elected as president and vice-president, respectively.[58] Francis Thomas attended the meeting and was elected a member of the SLP.[59] The SLP was rocked by internal conflicts and became defunct by 1959, and when the new Societies Ordinance was passed on 16 May 1960, the party did not re-register and ceased to function.

The SLP collapsed despite Majid's better leadership. There are a few factors behind the collapse that require exploration. In diasporic spaces, supporters of political leaders often come from their own diasporic community. This practice played a significant role in the early stages of the legislative assembly and city council elections in Singapore. Majid was born in Bengal and lived in Singapore for about twenty-three years, lending him a significant support base. Majid spoke against corruption in the legislative council election and endeavoured to establish social welfare programmes and a self-government system in Singapore. Even the Singapore government adopted policies based on some aspects of his election manifestos and the objectives of his political party. For example, in 1948, Majid proposed compulsory National Service after attaining full responsible self-government in Singapore; however, British authorities introduced National Service in 1954 at the height of the Malayan Emergency (1948–1960). National Service is still being practised in Singapore. Moreover, the Singapore government prioritised eradicating illiteracy from the colony and improved medical and health services, which were significant election agendas in Majid's campaign.

Things, however, soon changed. A significant ethnically defined pool of voters began to be dominant in the Singapore election process. In the late 1940s, Chinese political leaders could easily influence the Chinese people, which formed nearly 80 per cent of the total population in Singapore.[60] Table 7.1 shows the racial composition and birthplace of three early political parties' leaders. It further illustrates that the SLP had a multiracial composition. However, most leaders were South Asians born in British India. For example, in the General Council of the SLP, members constituted seventeen Indians, one Pakistani and three Chinese in 1950.[61]

Majid had a good relationship with the British administration until 1950 as he did not criticise government employees; instead, he supported the government's containment policy for the communists. However, this relationship started deteriorating when he took a stance against the discrimination and corruption of the Master Attendants' Office and Bureau Office. His criticism of a colonial institution irritated the authorities. While

Table 7.1 Diversity in the leadership of early political parties, Singapore, 1945–1955

Name of Political Parties	Races and No. of Leaders	Birthplaces and No. of Leaders	Languages and No. of Leaders
Singapore Progressive Party (1945–1955)	Chinese: 9	Singapore: 9	English: 18
	Indians: 5	Federation of Malaya: 4	Bilingual: 2
	Malays: 1	Abroad: 7	
	Others: 5		
Total	**20**	**20**	**20**
Malayan Democratic Union (1945–1948)	Chinese: 8	Singapore: 8	English: 10
	Indians: 1	Federation of Malaya: 5	Bilingual: 5
	Malays: 2	Abroad: 2	
	Others: 4		
Total	**15**	**15**	**15**
Singapore Labour Party (1948–1953)	Chinese: 4	Singapore: 5	English: 15
	Indians: 10	Federation of Malaya: 2	Bilingual: 3
	Malays: 0	Abroad: 11	
	Others: 4		
Total	**18**	**18**	**18**

Source: Excerpt from Yeo Kim Wah, 'A Study of Three Early Political Parties in Singapore, 1945–1955', *Journal of Southeast Asian History, Singapore Commemorative Issue 1819–1969* 10, no. 1 (March 1969): 124, 129, 134, 135.

facing the government's ire, his political rivals criticised him. Moreover, his political activities focused mainly on the labourer's interests, so he failed to attract the support of other professionals in elections. After being defeated in several elections, he lost interest in politics. When his rival groups sued him in the mid-1960s, he gradually withdrew himself from social and political activities. In short, Majid played a vital role in constitutional politics in Singapore and prevented communist penetration into labour politics. However, his centre-left, life-long commitment to working-class people often caused him to clash with mainstream politics and bureaucratic corruption. He would be remembered as a significant political figure in the history of modern Singapore.

Participation in Anti-British Activities during the Pacific War

In 1905, the anti-British movement and revolutionary activities started in the context of the partition of Bengal during Lord Curzon's tenure and soon spread throughout the Indian subcontinent and beyond. Some Bengali revolutionaries migrated to Malaya, creating fertile ground for the anti-British movement there.[62] WWII brought a colossal opportunity for opposition groups to organise movements against British colonialism in Southeast Asia. When Japan formally joined the war on 7 December 1941 and rapidly took control over the British colonies in Southeast Asia, a new strategic possibility opened up for a Bengali revolutionary, Netaji Subhas Chandra Bose (1897–1945) and his supporters.[63]

Rash Behari Bose (1886–1945)[64] had already formed the IIL in Thailand to organise Indians who were living outside India. In February 1942, he led the formation of the Indian National Army (INA).[65] He held a conference in Tokyo, where many Bengali leaders from various parts of Southeast Asia attended.[66] During the Bangkok Conference of 1942, R. B. Bose was elected as the President of INA. Soon afterwards, at the invitation of INA, S. C. Bose arrived from Germany in Singapore by submarine. A rapturous reception was given to him on 2 July 1943.[67] On 4 July 1943, the IIL leaders and INA senior officers assembled at the Cathay Cinema, where R. B. Bose handed over the supreme control of both wings to S. C. Bose.[68] Many Bengalis in Malaya answered Bose's clarion call to join the INA or the Azad Hind Fauj. The INA, consisting of 40,000 personnel who were mainly Punjabis, Bengalis and Tamils, together with the Japanese units, were led against British India in 1943.[69] Sengupta noted that at least one member of every Bengali diasporic family volunteered to serve at the frontier of Burma and donated generously in cash, kind or both.[70] Though it is difficult to provide an exact figure for Bengali troops and civilians, it can be safely inferred that it was significant.

First, the British Indian Army consisted of the Malays, the Madrasis and the Bengalis during WWII, and they were deployed in the Straits Settlements and Hong Kong. Some Bengali combatants were often handy with bombs and good at sabotage.[71] Second, they were captured as prisoners of war (POWs) during WWII in Malaya and consequently joined the INA.[72] Third, many of the organisers and leaders of the INA in Kuala Lumpur were Bengali. Tarrith Babu, another Bengali revolutionary, planted the thought of nationalism among the young Bengali migrants. Even a Bengali named Surat Ali led a Chinese communist revolutionary group.[73] All these activities helped to create an anti-British sentiment in Malaya. As a result, Subhas Chandra Bose was able to recruit many Bengalis from Kuala Lumpur.[74] Fourth, radio was a major means for forming public opinion in favour of the movement, and radio programmes were aired every day for 230 minutes in English and seven South Asian languages, including Bangla.[75] The INA and the Japanese Army disseminated propaganda posters in different languages, including Bangla.[76] Therefore, it seems that a significant number of Bengalis joined the INA and Indian Independence League (IIL).

A few Bengali doctors voluntarily joined the INA and were sent to the Burmese front. Khitish Chandra Roy was deployed in the medical wing of the INA camp in Rasah, Seremban. He was transferred to Burma with the rank of captain. He returned by the end of the war and witnessed some Bengali casualties in Burma.[77] Dinesh Chandra Chowdhury (1899–1971) worked at the Jeram Padang Estate Hospital in Bahau district until WWII. A section of his hospital was used to train Bengali youths.[78] Major General A. C. Chatterji was a medical practitioner in the Indian Medical Service; when the British surrendered, he joined the INA. He efficiently organised the Independence League and helped collect and manage funds. He was appointed minister for finance to the Azad Hind Provisional Government.[79]

Both the INA and IIL ran 'spy schools' and training camps in Malaya and Burma. Some Bengali migrants were involved as trainees, trainers and administrators in those institutions. For example, Sudhinanda Roy administered a Bengali Spy School, which was founded in May 1943 at Port Dickson[80]; N. K. Banerjee was the Director of Penang Free School, which was used as a training camp[81]; and B. N. Sengupta's nephew was an officer at an Azad Hind Fauj training camp. This camp recruited many youths from Singapore and Johor, mainly Tamils, Sikhs, Punjabis and Bengalis.[82] Such institutions and their personnel played a significant role during the Pacific War against the British Raj.

The British forces were aware of training camps and spy schools and were keen to identify the trainees who fought against them. The British government secretly prepared a report about the Swaraj Training Institute in Penang, where some Bengali trainees attended the first long course.[83] This provided a fragmentary physical description of the trainees, their origins and place of work in Malaya. Moreover, the Commander-in-chief (C&C) in India made a list of agents or spies and sent them secretly to the War Office in 1944. This document described different ways to identify the agents, including names, origins, physical features, training places and professions. As per the commander's secret notes, the Bengali spies were educated, mainly originated in eastern Bengal, and were below thirty years old.[84] C. D. Bhattacharya was a spy who worked in the intelligence department of the INA. He received training at the Penang Hill camp and was sent to Burma.[85] Ronendra Karmakar's father also left his job, joined the INA and was assigned to the Burmese front.[86]

When D. K. Majumder was the President of the IIL, Balak and Balika Sena, the youth sections of INA, were formed for recruiting and training boys and girls who were below eighteen years old in Malaya.[87] Initially, Kishore Battachary enlisted in the Tokyo Cadets and then the Balak Sena. Finally, he joined the regular INA force. He received two weeks of training with the Tokyo Cadets at Gilstead Road. Colonel Loganathan sent him to Seletar Camp to attend the Nihon class, where he learnt Japanese and trained for the police force. He was not yet fifteen years old when he began training. Therefore, he was recruited for the second batch of the Balak Sena, where he met other young Bengalis. They learnt drilling and propaganda skills at the Hindi School in Penang under the Japanese Liaison Office.[88]

The Rani Jhansi Regiment was the INA's female wing and consisted mainly of rubber plantation workers in Malaya. Still, a few members came from educated and privileged families.[89] Before joining the Women's Regiment, young girls joined the Balika Sena Camp located at Waterloo Street in Singapore. Those training included some Bengalis. One Bengali woman in the Rani Jhansi Regiment tried to play up her 'commonality' with S. C. Bose by speaking to him in Bangla.[90] The majority of the trainers were Bengalis and Tamils.[91] Some Bengali Balak Sena and Balika Sena members became doctors in later life, namely Prabir Sengupta, Madhuri Majumder and Anjali Sengupta.[92]

The INA had nine units, and its headquarters was located in Singapore. Hena Sinha voluntarily served as head of the social welfare department of the INA.[93] In her oral testimony, she remembered a series of meetings with S. C. Bose regarding her INA involvement, job responsibilities and experiences. When S. C. Bose came to Singapore, he invited a few Indian women, including Hena Sinha, for a tea party at Chancery Lane and asked her to take charge of the social welfare department. Though S. C. Bose offered her a full-time job, she accepted it as a part-time and honorary position. He appreciated Hena Sinha's attempts to balance public commitment and family responsibility, which required her to care for her children and her blind father-in-law. She carried out the job until the end of the war.[94]

Following the Pacific War and anti-British resistance, the crucial question was how INA soldiers and collaborators would be treated in British Malaya. The Governors' Conference in Singapore recommended that the Indian civilians who were 'collaborators' and 'traitors' and had committed atrocities would be prosecuted. The Headquarters of the Supreme Allied Commander South East Asia (SACSEA) made a list of seven Bengali collaborators on 22 February 1946. The Singapore government aimed to deport some collaborators for security and humanitarian grounds. The Government of India made assurances that the people against whom there were no allegations of collaboration were free to return to India.[95]

While INA personnel were hailed as heroes in India, the situation was quite the opposite in the Indian diaspora in Malaya. They were stigmatised as 'fascists and collaborators with [the] Japanese'.[96] After the Japanese Occupation (1942–1945), some Bengali INA members were either removed from their employment or imprisoned. Karmakar's father was among those who lost their jobs.[97] C. D. Bhattacharya returned to Penang and opened a shop importing rice from Thailand following the end of the conflict. However, the British government discovered his identity and put him in Pudu's jail. After six months inside, he was freed and found work as a surveyor in Singapore's City Council.[98] Kishore Battachary also returned to Penang after working with the INA and hid in a rubber estate, which was twenty miles off Seremban. Later, he joined the police department, guarded Prime Minister Lee Kuan Yew's house and met him personally.[99]

Though nationalist consciousness among Indians in Southeast Asia was primarily focused on their home country, they significantly contributed to the shaping of Malay nationalism.[100] In 1931, the Bengali globetrotter Ramnath Biswas suggested that the Indians should strive to be 'pure' Malay, not expatriates; they should work along with the Chinese and Malay to strengthen Malay nationalism.[101] Such activities made it possible for Subhas Chandra Bose and Rash Behari Bose to recruit a significant number of members for the INA and the IIL from among the Bengalis. Rajeswary Ampalavanar suggests that Subhas Chandra Bose's arrival in Singapore in 1943 stimulated the Indian community and the Malay and Chinese nationalists.[102] He further indicated that the legacy of the IIL was a solid commitment to continue the independence struggle for India and Malaya. Some INA members, including S. Ganapathy and P. Veerasenan, led the Malayan Communist Party (MCP). Even the Malayan Indian Congress (MIC, formed in 1946) was heavily influenced by the anti-colonial ideology inherited from the IIL.[103] Thus, the activities of the

INA and the IIL, which were supported by diverse South Asian diasporas and significantly the Bengalis, geared up Malay nationalism throughout the Pacific War and boosted decolonisation in Southeast Asia within a decade after the Second World War. People of South Asian origin were gradually marginalised in politics as Malay nationalism became firmly established, and the politics of trade unionism—the cornerstone of South Asian diasporic politics—became weak. Moreover, most political leaders of South Asian descent split along communal lines under the headers of the MIC and the Penang Indian Muslim League (established in 1941). Consequently, Hindus and Muslims began to organise separately.[104]

Living under Japanese Occupation (1942–1945)

Singapore experienced the impacts of two world wars under British rule. The Bengali diaspora, like all residents, faced a terrifying situation when the Japanese Army dropped bombs for the first time in Singapore.[105] During the Japanese invasion, people of many ethnic backgrounds left Singapore for the countryside for safety until mid-February 1942. Anwarul Haque recalls that his family left Singapore for his uncle's house in Johor during the war and returned when the Japanese Army surrendered to the British force in 1945. Some Bengali refugees took shelter temporarily at a rubber estate in Port Dickson (presently at Esso Refinery), which belonged to a Bengali doctor, Paresh Nath Sen.[106]

Many suffered and lost their lives during the Japanese invasion, including Bengali migrants. Hena Sinha's brother-in-law, Bimol Sinha, and Victor Norris were killed, and K. C. Sinha lost his eyes.[107] The Japanese authorities did not pay salaries for a few months at the beginning of their occupation. Hena Sinha's husband did not get salaries for three months. Even when he started receiving monthly wages in yen, his salary decreased because the newly introduced currency carried less fiscal value and was not widely used. In addition, the dollar became unacceptable, and the price of commodities soared towards the end of the occupation due to high inflation rates. The occupying government rationed different items, like rice and bread, but these were of inferior quality. To make up for the financial hardship, Hena Sinha grew vegetables in her front yard with a Chinese *amah* (domestic assistance).[108]

Some Bengali professionals continued their respective jobs under the Japanese administration. Most European doctors in Malaya were either evacuated or interned by the Japanese Army, making the public health sector understaffed.[109] Asian doctors, mostly Bengalis, stepped in to manage hospitals throughout the occupation in British Malaya.[110] The working atmosphere was one of fear; the Japanese authorities were poised to arrest and behead those suspected of being anti-Japanese. Japanese officials also dominated and disrupted people's lives. For example, a Japanese officer intended to take the quarter where A. C. Sinha and his family lived. A. C. Sinha was afraid to refuse and replied, 'Okay, you want to stay, you can stay, but I have a blind father and a mother, and a wife with an infant. Where am I to go and live? You give us a place to stay, I will go'. The Japanese officer took the house, and the Sinha family moved elsewhere and stayed there throughout the Japanese Occupation.[111] Others did not escape so lightly. Nripendra Kumar Sen[112] was interned for an unknown reason and released by the end of the Japanese Occupation from the Changi prison in poor health. During his captivity, the Japanese Army forced him to issue a few prisoners' death certificates, citing false reasons such as dysentery rather than torture, which was against his conscience.[113] Ronendra Karmakar worked in the City Council. He remembered that the Japanese were cruel and most police were corrupt officers. However, their attitudes became more favourable or merciful towards the end of the occupation.[114]

The Japanese Army committed war crimes, including forced prostitution, kidnapping and rape.[115] Four hundred Chinese women were abducted in Singapore in 1943.[116] Mushahid Ali's family was worried about his younger sister, who was then ten years old. To avoid being taken away by the Japanese military, she was married off to a Bengali working in Singapore as an electrician.[117] Hena Sinha also had similar concerns; her family worried about her sister-in-law, who was sent to Calcutta for safety.

During the Japanese invasion, the British administration was in disarray, and many diasporic community members volunteered to alleviate the dire situation. Goho (1891–1948), a Bengali, came to the forefront and played a pivotal role in evacuating both Indians and non-Indians from 1941 to 1942.[118] He formed a group of volunteers named the 'Indian Passive Defence Force' to protect Bengalis and other Indians.[119] Under the Passive Defence Force, 800 volunteers worked at sixteen relief depots and a first-aid hospital, providing treatment to more than 10,000 casualties regardless of race. Goho set up two camps where 25,000 Indian refugees were fed and took shelter.[120] Two Indians lent Goho 50,000 dollars to help evacuate Indian refugees. When the British regained administrative power from the Japanese government, the Governor of Singapore, Shenton Thomas, praised Goho in a note sent to the Government of India for his valuable service 'in the evacuation of women and children, and the fine example of courage and determination which he has set to his countrymen, and indeed to us all'.[121] One of Goho's most treasured possessions was a letter he received after the liberation from Lt Col Chudhuri OBE, former commanding officer of the Nee Soon POW Camp. Mr Chudhuri remarked: 'You were the first Indian in Singapore who came forward to help us at the risk of your life. You saved many lives, and for this our gratitude can never be wanting.'[122]

The Bengalis: A Major Component of Malay Cosmopolitan Society

The port cities of the Malay Peninsula were meeting points for people from all over maritime Asia and beyond to start from a 'neutral ground', and by the late nineteenth century, a cosmopolitan space began to be clearly visible.[123] Arnold Wright describes it as a 'kaleidoscopic' society.[124] Its multicultural background fostered a cosmopolitan and pluralistic society that generated cultural fusions. In the 1940s, J. S. Furnivall coined the term 'pluralistic society' when describing the Southeast Asian port cities. By using this term, he referred to the medley of people, such as European, Chinese, Indian and Malay, who coexisted under a single political regime while upholding their distinct religions, cultures, languages, ideas and customs.[125] The Bengali diaspora was an integral component of the pluralistic society in Malaya. Sociocultural events sometimes displayed the cultural cross-section of Malaya. For example, in 1917, the Straits Chinese British Association (SCBA) staged a multi-ethnic display representing the fact that the infantry for the Second Troop Singapore Boy Scouts was recruited from different ethnicities and cultures, including those of Tamil, Bengali, Chinese, Malay and Jewish backgrounds.[126] The traits of a multicultural society were aptly reflected in the following comment from Lee Kuan Yew: 'We start now in Singapore. Whether you are a Tamil, Punjabi, Bengali; whether you are a Malay, Cantonese, Hokkien, we together constitute the people of Singapore.'[127] In another speech, he suggested, 'We no longer live together in groups of Cantonese, Hokkien, Teochew, Hainanese, Malay, Bugis, Arab, Tamil, Punjabi, Bengali or Ceylonese. We have neighbours of all dialects and races in the same block in the new towns.'[128]

The Bengalis interacted in various capacities with other diasporic communities. A. C. Sinha had many friends of different religious, ethnic and professional backgrounds. During the Japanese Occupation, Sinha helped a Chinese rickshaw puller by providing medicine and money, even during his marriage and the pregnancy of the rickshaw puller's wife. Every Chinese New Year, the rickshaw puller and his family used to visit Sinha's house.[129] During the Pacific War, Goho rescued many Chinese residents, including his impoverished clerk, the father of Danny Chue.[130] Chue remembered that Goho provided shelter and food and also sent her aunt to Calcutta, saving her from forced prostitution by the Japanese Army. After the war, Goho adopted Chue's aunt as a daughter. In the 1960s, Chue's father visited the aunt at Goho's residence in Calcutta. She also used to come and see her family in Singapore in the 1980s after settling down in Calcutta with relatives of Mrs Goho. Communication between the two families continued through letters, greeting cards and phone calls.[131]

Mushahid Ali remembers having many childhood friends, mainly Chinese, Indian and Eurasian. They visited each other's houses during cultural and religious festivals, such as Chinese New Year and Eid-ul-Fitr. Shafiya Khatoon remembers that her father (M. A. Majid) helped people irrespective of race and religion. He adopted a Chinese girl, gave shelter to a Bengali Hindu engineer and assisted a Malay woman, Che Aminah,[132] in 1950. As her father was a politician and social worker, he attended many diverse social events, including Chinese and Christian funerals. Despite not being a professional lawyer, he was knowledgeable enough to advise those in need. He helped an Angullia family regain property lost due to a colonial government decree. Like Majid, his descendants still practice interracial, religious, social and multicultural bonding with other migrating communities.

Conclusion

The Bengalis migrated to the Malay world either under duress or voluntarily, but once they arrived, they cautiously sought to create and nurture a relationship with their host society. Part of this relationship was formed by engaging with the nuances of their professional and political world. The Bengali diasporic community contributed to the Malay pluralistic society through biracial marriage and daily interactions with other communities, which fostered multiculturalism and multi-ethnic entanglement. A few Bengali migrants who permanently made their home in Malaya participated in political activities to help create a more democratic country and a better quality of life. However, their political activities sought to enlarge the number of voters, primarily among maritime workers. This endeavour failed to develop a broad-based support group, unlike the movements of the Chinese or Tamils. Yet, even if met with mixed success at a mainstream political level, these political activities were part of a far broader social and civic life—a topic that will be explored in greater detail in the following chapter.

Notes

1. Biswas, *Malaysia Vromon*, 110, 111.
2. Biswas, *Malaysia Vromon*, 109.
3. It is an island in the Strait of Malacca under the Riau province of Indonesia.
4. J. J. A. Campos, *History of the Portuguese in Bengal with Maps and Illustrations* (Calcutta; London; Sydney: Butterworth & Co., 1919), 158–159, 163–164.
5. Biswas, *Malaysia Vromon*, 105.
6. For details, see Lloyd and Moore, *Malacca*, 60; Cortesao, *The Suma Oriental of the Tome Pires*, vol. 1, 93; Bort, *Report of Governor Balthasar Bort on Malacca 1678*, 9.
7. Interview with Khatoon.
8. Interview with Khatoon.
9. Interview with Mushahid Ali.
10. Interview with Haque.
11. David Ludden, 'Presidential Address: Maps in the Mind and the Mobility of Asia', *Journal of Asian Studies* 62, no. 4 (2003): 1062.
12. The miscegenation process created transnational families through interracial marriage across the world. See Elise Lemire, *'Miscegenation': Making Race in America* (Philadelphia: University of Pennsylvania Press, 2002); Dan Rodríguez García, 'Mixed Marriages and Transnational Families in the Intercultural Context: A Case Study of African/Spanish Couples in Catalonia', *Journal of Ethnic and Migration Studies* 32, no. 3 (April 2006): 403–433.
13. For a brief history of interracial marriage among different ethnic groups, including Malay, Hindus, Chinese, Bengali, Siamese and Arabs in the Malay Peninsula during the pre-colonial and colonial periods, see Sandhu, 'Indian Settlements in Melaka', 179; Winstedt, *Malaya and Its History*, 16; Lloyd and Moore, *Malacca*, 29; Timothy P. Daniels, *Building Cultural Nationalism in Malaysia: Identity, Representation, and Citizenship* (New York; London: Routledge, 2005), 20, 38–39, 52; Hoyt, *Old Malacca*, 59.

14. Khondker, 'Bengali-speaking Families in Singapore', 184–185.

15. Amrith, *Crossing the Bay*, 76; Winstedt, *Malaya and Its History*, 16.

16. J. D. Vaughan (1825–1891) was a sailor of the EIC's naval ship. He was an active soldier of the British force during the campaign against Brunei. He was appointed superintendent of police in Penang in the early 1850s and served as assistant resident councillor of Singapore in 1861. He eventually became a prominent lawyer.

17. Nasution, *Chulia in Penang*, 121.

18. Paul Kratoska and Ben Batson, 'Nationalism and Modernist Reform', in *The Cambridge History of Southeast Asia, Vol. 2, The Nineteenth and Twentieth centuries*, ed. Nicholas Tarling (Cambridge: Cambridge University Press, 1992), 314.

19. Interview with Khatoon.

20. Interview with Khatoon.

21. *ST,* 11 July 2018; *AsiaOne,* 29 March 2015; *ST,* 29 March 2015. Sidek Saniff was a critic of the education policy of Lee Kuan Yew's government; therefore, his decision to accept Lee's offer to contest as a PAP candidate in the general election created quite a stir in the Malay community.

22. Interview with Mushahid Ali.

23. NAS, OHI, Dr V. Kanda Pillay, 8 December 2006, Acc. No. 003106. Dr Pillay was born in 1929 in Malaysia. He worked there until 1956; later, he joined Singapore General Hospital in 1957.

24. Nathan, *S. R. Nathan: 50 Stories from My Life*, 81.

25. See NAS, OHI, Karmakar, 18 October 1983, Acc. No. 000343; NAS, OHI, Kannusamy s/o Pakirisamy, 17 November 1983, Acc. No. 000081. Kannusamy was born in 1914 in Singapore. His father and mother were also born in Singapore in 1855 and 1892.

26. Interview with Haque.

27. Interview with Davenport.

28. *Statistics on Marriages and Divorces, 2017* (Singapore: Department of Statistics, Ministry of Trade and Industry, 2017), 8; *ST,* 10 July 2018.

29. *ST,* 13 January 2010.

30. They formed about twenty-one new Indian Associations between 1939 and 1941. Joyce Lebra, *The Indian National Army and Japan* (Singapore: ISEAS, 2008), 39; M. Stenson, *Class, Race, and Colonialism in West Malaysia* (Vancouver: University of British Columbia Press, 2011), 58–59.

31. Ho, *Doctors Extraordinaire*, 79. Another example of the Bengali involvement in organising Indian Associations was that the Indian Association of Kuching

was formed in 1931 mainly through two well-known Bengali, namely Krisna and R. K. Bhattacharyya. D. S. Ranjit Singh, 'Indians in East Malaysia', in *Indian Communities in Southeast Asia*, ed. K. S. Sandhu and A. Mani (Singapore: Times Academic Press and ISEAS, 1993), 579, 584.

32. Indian labourers called a strike at the Singapore Traction Company in 1938. Two years later, another strike was called by 20,000 Indian labourers due to the British repression in the Federated Malay States (FMS) in 1941. Rai, *Indians in Singapore*, 185–186; Stenson, *Class, Race, and Colonialism*, 93.

33. Nilanjana Sengupta, *Singapore My Country: Biography of M. Bala Subramanion* (Singapore: World Scientific Publishing Co., Pvt. Ltd), 2016, 60–61.

34. Stenson, *Class, Race, and Colonialism*, 73.

35. K. K. Ghosh, *The Indian National Army: Second Front of the Indian Independence Movement* (Meerut: Meenakshi Prakashan, 1969), 43.

36. A Bengali living in Malaya during the Japanese Occupation, A. N. Mithra, was elected the President of the New Democratic League of Indians. He did not participate in the INA, but he was closely connected with Goho and assisted in releasing political prisoners.

37. NAS, 'Activities of the Indian National Army (INA) and the Indian Independence League (IIL)', Secret-Migrated Archives, FCO 141/14392, D2014040111; 1 January 1945–31 December 1946.

38. Singapore became a Crown Colony in 1946 and was administered separately from Malaya. Revised Singapore's constitution allowed the local people to participate in the colonial government, which led to obtaining Singapore's self-government. *ST*, 20 March 1948, 1; Kim Wah Yeo, *Political Development in Singapore, 1945–55* (Singapore: Singapore University Press, 1973), 252.

39. *ST*, 20 March 1948, 8.

40. L. J. Louis, 'Recovery from the Depression and the Seamen's Strike 1935–6', *Labour History* 41 (November 1981): 74–86.

41. Yeo Kim Wah, 'The Communist Challenge in the Malayan Labour Scene, September 1936–March 1937', *Journal of the Malaysian Branch of the Royal Asiatic Society* 49, no. 2 (230) (1976): 45.

42. Loh Oun Hean, *Industrial Relations in Singapore: Practice and Perspective* (Singapore: World Scientific Publishing Co. Pte Ltd, 2018), 13; Tan Pheng Theng, 'A Conspectus of the Labour Laws of Singapore', *Malaya Law Review* 10, no. 2 (1968): 220.

43. *ST*, 17 February 1948, 1.

44. *ST*, 20 March 1948, 8.

45. *SFPMA*, 9 March 1948, 5.

46. *ST*, 27 May 1957, 7.

47. *ST*, 7 July 1950, 6.

48. *ST*, 18 September 1957, 5; *ST*, 13 September 1957, 4; *ST*, 24 September 1957, 4.

49. *ST*, 4 September 1957, 9.

50. Majid invited other contestants, including S. C. Goho, to join his election meetings. *MoT*, 13 March 1948, 15; *ST*, 31 March 1951, 4.

51. *ST*, 13 November 1956, 9.

52. David Saul Marshal D. K. J. P. (1908–1995) was the first chief minister in Singapore from 1955 to 1956. After his resignation, the Governor appointed Lim Yew Hock to form the next government in Singapore. He was also the Minister for Labour and Welfare and Francis Thomas for Communications and Works.

53. Interview with Khatoon.

54. Koh et al., *Singapore*, 319; *ST*, 2 September 1948, 4; *SFPMA*, 2 September 1948, 8.

55. *SFPMA*, 1 July 1948, 5; *ST*, 2 September 1948, 4; *MaT*, 24 March 1948, 3; *SFPMA*, 1 July 1948, 5; Sharon Teng, 'Singapore Labour Party', SingaporeInfopedia, National Library Board, Singapore, https://eresources. nlb.gov.sg/infopedia/articles/SIP_2018-01-26_111726.html, accessed 7 July 2019; Yeo Kim Wah, 'A Study of Three Early Political Parties in Singapore, 1945–1955', *Journal of Southeast Asian History, Singapore Commemorative Issue 1819–1969* 10, no. 1 (March 1969): 134.

56. *MaT*, 8 June 1948, 2.

57. *ST*, 28 November 1948, 7.

58. The remaining interim committee members were G. Saragapany (the editors of the *Indian Daily Mail* and the *Tamil Murasu*), Francis Thomas (teacher of St Andrew's School), Eric J. Woodford, A. Mohd Kamal and A. Latif. About 100 prospective members of the new party and a few observers, including Silcock of Raffles College, and A. Simpson, assistant trade union adviser to Singapore, M. P. D. Nair, an Indian who was a founding member of the Army Civil Service Union (ACSU), and Peter Williams, a Ceylon-born Tamil, a leader of the ACSU, attended the meeting.

59. *ST*, 31 August 1948, 7; *ST*, 2 September 1948, 4.

60. Wah, 'A Study of Three Early Political Parties in Singapore, 1945–1955', 116.

61. Wah, 'A Study of Three Early Political Parties in Singapore, 1945–1955', 135.

62. Ramnath Biswas met some Bengali revolutionaries in Malaya. See Biswas, *Malaysia Vromon*, 126, 129, 130–131, 133–134.

63. S. C. Bose was a left-leaning leader of the Indian National Congress, but he resigned from Congress and founded the Forward Bloc Party in 1939. Deshabandhu Chittaranjan Das and Aurobindo, leaders of Anushilan Samity and Jugantar, two major radical organisations in Bengal, inspired S. C. Bose in revolutionary activities. For more about S. C. Bose's feelings towards Bengal, the Bangla language and revolutionary activities, see Sugata Bose, *His Majesty's Opponents: Subhas Chandra Bose and India's Struggle against Empire* (Massachusetts; London: Harvard University Press, 2011), 20, 23, 63, 166, 231, 182, 265–266; Joyce Lebra, *Women against the Raj: The Rani of Jhansi Regiment* (Singapore: ISEAS, 2008), 17; Jensrani Thangavel, 'The Indian National Army and the Singapore-Malayan Indians (1942–1945)' (BA dissertation, Nanyang Technological University, 1979).

64. Born in West Bengal and secretly involved in Jugantar, a revolutionary group led by Jatin Mukherjee (popularly known as Bagha Jatin in Bengal), Rash Behari Bose fled to Japan after attempting to assassinate Lord Hardinge of Penshurst, Viceroy of India, in Delhi in 1912. Rai, *Indians in Singapore*, 213; Ghosh, *Indian National Army*, 44.

65. The Indian National Army (INA) or the Azad Hind Fauj is known as the Fifth Column. As an active member of the IIL in Thailand, Pritam Singh accompanied the Japanese forces and organised the Fifth Column. See Lebra, *The Indian National Army and Japan*, 40.

66. A few names are Rash Bihari Bose, B. D. Gupta, Dwijendra Majumdar, S. C. Goho and Swami Satyananda Puri. See Ghosh, *Indian National Army*, 45, 47; Lebra, *Indian National Army*, 41–43; Bose, *His Majesty's Opponents*, 239.

67. E. Bruce Reynolds, 'The Indian Community and the Indian Independence Movement in Thailand during World War II', in *Southeast Asian Minorities in the Wartime Japanese Empire*, ed. Paul H. Kratoska (Oxon: Routledge, 2002), 170; Bose, *His Majesty's Opponents*, 194. There is a debate on the place of embarkation of S. C. Bose. He arrived in Singapore, either from Tokyo or Berlin. The debate was described in Bose, *His Majesty's Opponents*, 244.

68. Lebra, *Women against the Raj*, 71.

69. Mann, *South Asia's Modern History*, 76.

70. Sengupta, *Malaysia and Bengali Doctors*, 25–26.

71. *WN* (Sydney), 6 August 1938, 4.

72. *The Daily Telegraph* (Sydney), 16 January 1943, 6. The INA consisted of different races, including Bengali and Sikh. See NAS, OHI, Damodaran s/o K. Kesavan, 9 November 1981, Acc. No. 000127; NAS, OHI, Girishchandra

Kothair, 14 October 2013, Acc. No. 003824. Damodaran, born in Madras in 1918, came to Singapore in 1939. Later, he joined the INA and left Singapore for Burma. The British caught him as a POW. Kothair was born in Gujarat and came to Ipoh in 1941. He joined the INA and trained at INA's Officer Training School.

73. Biswas, *Malaysia Vromon*, 203–204.

74. Biswas wrote about a Bengali revolutionary leader, Tarrith Babu, who migrated from Sylhet. He could speak fluently in Tamil. Though he was a medical practitioner in Seremban, he frequently visited labourer slums in Kuala Lumpur to raise awareness about anti-colonialism or nationalism among the working class. Kuala Lumpur was a secure and fertile place for the revolutionaries. Therefore, the British encountered massive resistance in Kuala Lumpur until 1948; and they marked it as a home of 'dacoits' or 'terrorists'. Biswas, *Malaysia Vromon*, 129, 134–135.

75. Bose, *His Majesty's Opponents*, 225.

76. *Toodyay Herald*, 23 April 1943, 3.

77. Sengupta, *Malaysia and Bengali Doctors*, 39, 55.

78. Sengupta, *Malaysia and Bengali Doctors*, 47–48.

79. Zahida Ahsanuddin, *India's Freedom Struggle and the Great INA: Memoirs of Maj. Gen Mohammad Zaman Kiani* (New Delhi: Reliance Publishing House, 1994), 220.

80. Tapan Chattopadhyay, *The INA's Secret Service in Southeast Asia: Its Background, Infrastructure, Resources and Activities during World War II* (Kolkata: Readers Service, 2011), 110.

81. NAS, OHI, Bhattachary, 8 March 2010, Acc. No. 003490.

82. NAS, 'Malaya: Disposal, Status and Brief History of the INA', Microfilm-NAB 2147; file number: WO 203/2298, 1 August 1945–31 August 1945.

83. The training schools taught a range of subjects, including spreading anti-British propaganda, using weapons, drilling, physical training, Indian history, Congress nationalist movement, first aid, preparation of sketches and maps, and behaviour under interrogation.

84. NAS, 'Indian Traitors and Fifth Columnists Trained by the Japanese: Formation of Indian Independent League and Indian National Army', Image: NAB 2575, file number-W 208/803, 1942–1945.

85. NAS, OHI, Bhattachary, 8 March 2010, Acc. No. 003490.

86. NAS, OHI, Karmakar, 18 October 1983, Acc. No. 000343.

87. Sengupta, *Malaysia and Bengali Doctors*, 55.

88. NAS, OHI, Bhattachary, 8 March 2010, Acc. No. 003490.

89. Notably, Gauri Bhattacharya, Neau Roy, Kalpana Dutt, Aruna Chatterji and Lobanya Chatterji. Bose, *His Majesty's Opponents*, 247; Lebra, *Women against the Raj*, 82, 104–105; Meira Chand, 'Warrior Women: The Rani of Jhansi Regiment', *biblioasia*, National Library Board, Singapore, https://www.meirachand.com/wp-content/uploads/2019/10/Jhansi-Regiment.pdf, accessed 21 March 2018.

90. Arunima Datta, 'Social Memory and Indian Women from Malaya and Singapore in the Rani of Jhansi Regiment', *Journal of the Malaysian Branch of the Royal Asiatic Society* 88, no. 2 (309) (2015): 98.

91. Sengupta, *Singapore My Country*, 74; see also NAS, OHI, Bhattachary, 10 March 2010, Acc. No. 003490.

92. Sengupta, *Malaysia and Bengali Doctors*, 25–26.

93. NAS, 'Indian Traitors and Fifth Columnists Trained by the Japanese', file number-W 208/803; Image no.- NAB 2575, 1942–1945.

94. NAS, OHI, Hena Sinha, 21 October 1983, Acc. No. 000354.

95. For details of the INA members and their trial after the war, see NAS, 'Activities of the Indian National Army (INA) and the Indian Independence League (IIL)', Secret-Migrated Archives, FCO 141/14392, D2014040111, 1 January 1945–31 December 1946.

96. Rai, *Indians in Singapore*, 268.

97. NAS, OHI, Karmakar, 18 October 1983, Acc. No. 000343.

98. NAS, OHI, Bhattachary, 8 March 2010, Acc. No. 003490.

99. NAS, OHI, Bhattachary, 8 March 2010, Acc. No. 003490.

100. Kratoska and Batson, 'Nationalism and Modernist Reform', 314–315.

101. Biswas, *Malaysia Vromon*, 131.

102. Ampalavanar, *The Indian Minority and Political Change*, 8.

103. Ampalavanar, *The Indian Minority and Political Change*, 9.

104. Brown, *Global South Asians*, 124.

105. Hena Sinha's family lived on the top floor of the Kandang Kerbau Hospital quarter. When the Japanese Army dropped bombs in the early morning of 8 December 1941, and the British blew an air-raid siren pointing to the hospital, the cacophony of fighter aircraft and sirens made the environment frightening. Her husband, A. C. Sinha, went downstairs immediately and told Mrs Sinha, 'Switch off all the lights; the Japanese are bombing.' See NAS, OHI, Hena Sinha, 21 October 1983, Acc. No. 000354.

106. Sengupta, *Malaysia and Bengali Doctors*, 40, 52.

107. NAS, OHI, Hena Sinha, 21 October 1983, Acc. No. 000354.

108. NAS, OHI, Hena Sinha, 21 October 1983, Acc. No. 000354.

109. Abdul Majid Ismail, 'The History of Early Medical and Health Services in Malaysia', *Malaysian Historical Society* (December 1974), 11.

110. A. N. Ray, S. K. Mitra and A. Ganguli continued to work at the Johor Bahru General Hospital during the Japanese Occupation. Capt. Dutta and K. C. Sengupta continued their service in the oil palm estate near Labis, Johor, while B. C. Majumder remained in the Health Department, Seremban. D. K. Majumder continued his private practice in Seremban. K. N. Ghosh had just commenced his private practice in Kuala Lumpur before WWII and continued throughout the occupation. Sengupta, *Malaysia and Bengali Doctors*, 45–46, 55; see also Ho, *Doctors Extraordinaire*, 78–79.

111. NAS, OHI, Hena Sinha, 21 October 1983, Acc. No. 000354.

112. Dr Nripendra Kumar Sen graduated from Calcutta Medical College. He was brought to Singapore in 1929 and posted to the Department of Bacteriology as chief assistant to Dr W. A. Young at the King Edward VII College of Medicine. Dr Sen stayed back in Singapore and continued the job under the Japanese government. See Sengupta, *Malaysia and Bengali Doctors*, 45–46.

113. Sengupta, *Malaysia and Bengali Doctors*, 46.

114. NAS, OHI, Karmakar, 18 October 1983, Acc. No. 000343.

115. For detailed activities of the Japanese soldiers and authorities in Malaya during the occupation (1942–1945), see Lee Geok Boi, *The Syonan Years: Singapore under Japanese Rule 1942–1945* (Singapore: National Archives of Singapore and Epigram, 2005).

116. Edward Drea, Greg Bradsher, Robert Hanyok, James Lide, Michael Petersen and Daqing Yang, *Researching Japanese War Crimes Records: Introductory Essays* (Washington, DC: Nazi War Crimes and Japanese Imperial Government Records Interagency Working Group, 2006), 69.

117. Interview with Mushahid Ali.

118. R. Jumabhoy, *Multiracial Singapore* (Singapore: Tak Seng Press, Pte Ltd, 1970), 98–99; Rai, *Indians in Singapore*, 206–207; Sengupta, *Singapore My Country*, 60–61.

119. Ghosh, *Indian National Army*, 44; Koh et al., *Singapore*, 60.

120. *ST*, 26 July 1948, 5; Solomon, *A Subaltern History of the Indian Diaspora*, 167; 'S. C. Goho and Wartime Singapore', Memory of Danny Chue, Singapore Memory Project, 2015.

121. *ST*, 26 July 1948, 5.

122. *ST*, 26 July 1948, 5.

123. Anthony Reid, ed., *Southeast Asia in the Early Modern Era: Trade, Power and Belief* (Ithaca; London: Cornell University Press, 1993), 77; *SFPMA*, 25 June

1857, 3; W. G. Shellabear (trans.), *The Autobiography of Munshi Abdullah Abdul Kadir (1796–1854)* (Singapore: Methodist Publishing House, 1918), 141.

124. Wright, *Twentieth Century Impressions of British Malaya*, 603.

125. J. S. Furnivall, *Colonial Policy and Practice: A Comparative Study of Burma and Netherlands India* (Cambridge: Cambridge University Press, 1948), 304; see also Hefner, Introduction, 4, 13; Reid, *Southeast Asia in the Age of Commerce*, 66.

126. *MaT*, 23 October 1917, 6.

127. NAS, Speeches and Press Releases (hereinafter SPR), address by Prime Minister Lee Kuan Yew, 19 February 1966.

128. NAS, SPR, address by Lee Kuan Yew, 14 April 1978.

129. NAS, OHI, Hena Sinha, 21 October 1983, Acc. No. 000354.

130. Rai, *Indians in Singapore*, 211–212; Ghosh, *Indian National Army*, 44.

131. 'S. C. Goho and Wartime Singapore', Memory of Danny Chue, Singapore Memory Project, 2015.

132. Che Aminah was a language teacher who translated manuscripts from Japanese to Malay at Bandung's Japanese Military base. She adopted Maria Hertogh (1937–2009) in 1942. This story is discussed at length in Chapter 8.

8

The Making of a Diasporic Space

Civil Society

International migrants in Malaya frequently engaged in social and associational activities, often leading to the growth of what may be termed a diasporic civil society. Civil society organisations created a public space in urban areas to secure their interests and represent themselves through various activities, including social services, acts of community solidarity, policy advocacy and cultural activities. Each generation of migrants made its imprint by creating new organisations or promoting existing ones.[1] The Bangla-speaking diaspora shared a similar historical process for space-making in Malaysia and Singapore. The previous chapter focused on Bengali place-making from the lens of political organisations and activism. This chapter explores further Bengali contributions to place-making from the vantage point of civil society, including associational and other activities. The binary processes of globalisation, that is, 'globalization of the local' and 'localization of the global', could help to articulate the role and engagement of Bengali migrants in the local and international sphere, especially since the end of WWI.[2]

Bengali Civic Spaces within the South Asian Diaspora

During the early twentieth century, South Asian transnational communities formed different organisations under the umbrella term 'Indian' mainly for three reasons. First, despite different ethnic backgrounds, the Indian diasporic communities were open to forging cooperation. The Bengalis, among other diverse South Asian migrants, played a vital role in forming organisations and associations of a social and religious nature. For example, Hindu migrants disseminated the idea of reforming Hinduism in Malaya. S. N. Bardhan, a Bengali, was a founding member of the Arya Samaj Sangam, established in

1910. Later, he served as its president from 1911 to 1919.[3] Adi Dravida Sangam, another Hindu reformist organisation, was founded in the 1920s in Singapore. S. C. Goho frequently arranged dialogues there on the Hindu religion.[4] Apart from the religious debates, members of Hindu religious associations occasionally placed their demands before the government. For instance, delegates from the Arya Samaj, Dravida Sangam and Vivekananda Sanmarga Sangam appealed to Singapore's government to introduce an ordinance for the registration of Hindu marriage in the Straits Settlements.[5]

In 1914, the Hindu Association was founded. It had social and religious functions and organised spiritual debates. In 1946, when the Singapore authority decided to move the Hindu burial ground to the state-owned Choa Chu Kang Cemetery, which was opened in 1947, the Hindu Association brought the issue to the authorities.[6] The new cemetery was located far from the Hindu concentrated area, causing inconvenience to the Hindu community in Singapore. To maintain internal cohesion and friendly relations among its members, the association had a soccer team and arranged football tournaments.[7] Members also showed their broader societal solidarity by offering special prayers at Hindu temples to end WWI and the King George VI's victory.[8] Bengali Hindus, including A. C. Chander, were in leading positions in the association. He was elected president of the association and a vice-chairman of the Hindu Advisory Board for Penang and was a member of the Hindu Advisory Board for Singapore.[9] Later, the association celebrated the silver jubilee of King George V on his fiftieth birthday; they congratulated him and sent a telegram through the local authority.

The visits of Bengali intellectuals to Southeast Asia contributed to disseminating ideas and news about political and social activities from Bengal among the South Asian community. On his way to the USA to attend the Parliament of Religions, Swami Vivekananda, a Hindu religious reformer, visited Singapore on 12 June 1893. After that, priests of the Ramakrishna Order[10] from Calcutta occasionally visited Singapore to draw people's attention to the mission's activities. Finally, Swami Adyananda was sent to Singapore in 1928 to open a mission branch. From then, Bengali priests were sent regularly from Calcutta to operate the branch.[11] The bond between Bengali Hindu devotees and the Ramakrishna Mission was deep from its inception. In 1928, seven members were on the executive committee of the Mission, including Chander, K. C. Ghosh and M. N. Das.[12] The visit of Rabindranath Tagore twice in the 1920s energised the Bengali civic space in Malaya. During his second visit in 1927, the Bengali diasporic community formed a reception committee with other South Asians. The Singapore Indian Association published a flyer in Bangla and Tamil and organised a mass gathering to ensure a warm reception for the poet.[13]

The Bengalis took up remarkable leadership of several 'Indian' committees and associations. In 1916, an Indian multi-ethnic committee was formed at 1 Jalan Besar in Singapore to support the wounded of the British Army during World War I. Muslim and Hindu committee members were migrants from Bengal, Punjab and the United Provinces. The committee's president, vice president, secretary and treasurer were Bengali. The committee organised a mass gathering at the racecourse to generate a fund for the British Army. In his address there, K. C. Sinha expressed that it was an excellent opportunity to show 'undying loyalty and devotion to the British Raj'. F. Seton James, colonial secretary to the Straits Settlements, attended as the chief guest, and the meeting instantly raised 3,000 dollars for the Red Cross Fund.[14]

Another example of Bengali leadership involved the Singapore Indian Association (SIA), which was established in 1923.[15] Chander, the justice of peace,[16] emphasised the necessity of such an association[17] and became its founding chair. It organised social, religious and political programmes and even had different sports teams with seasonal leagues for football, cricket and hockey.[18] The association also provided financial assistance to distressed people. For instance, it remitted a sum of 1,500 rupees to British India for the Quetta (now in Pakistan) earthquake relief fund.[19] Indian national days and the birth or death anniversaries of prominent Indian personalities were also marked by the SIA.[20] When Indian representatives visited Singapore, it arranged reception or farewell programmes.[21] During these events, association leaders spoke in different languages, including Bangla, Hindi and Tamil, but English was a common medium of communication.[22] Chander was elected the Vice-president of the SIA in 1923 and the President in 1925.[23]

The 1920s saw diverse South Asian migrants forming associations based on racial and geographical identities. While this highlighted specific cultural and economic features of smaller diasporic communities, some diasporic leaders felt the need for a broader 'Indian' platform. A. K. Surattee, President of the SIA, appealed for the unity of Indians during the thirteenth annual general meeting in 1936. He urged all Indian ethnicities in Malaya to unify under a parent body, such as the Central Indian Association of Malaya (CIAM).[24]

CIAM, established in 1936, was more politically inclined than other civil society organisations. It aimed to use this political clout for the immediate betterment of the Indian diasporic community in Malaya. The leaders of CIAM promoted Indian nationalism and the activities of the Indian National Congress and sponsored visits from Indian nationalists, including Pandit Jawaharlal Nehru (1937), Pandit Hridoy Nath Kunzru (1938) and A. K. Gopalan (1939).[25] At the same time, the CIAM donated money for social welfare, collected funds and presented an ambulance to the China Relief Committee.[26] The council of the CIAM also opened a high school in Malaya for the Indian multi-ethnic offspring.[27] Those at the head of the CIAM were English-educated and sensitive to ethnic and religious diversity. One of their priorities was migrants' social and economic well-being in Malaya[28]; they advocated fair wages for labourers and supported better educational facilities for their children.[29] Out of about 800,000 diverse South Asian migrants, nearly 90 per cent were labourers. Therefore, their well-being was a vital issue for associations, as Goho maintained.[30] Goho was President and Vice-president of the CIAM in 1939 and 1940, respectively. During his tenure, he helped to form the Indian Association in Johor.[31]

These discussions reflect the remarkable development and impact of civil society associations and their activities within the Indian multi-ethnic diaspora. The Bengalis were a significant part of this diasporic community and played an important leadership role. The following section will discuss the exclusively Bengali associations and their activities.

Bengali Associations and Their Religious and Cultural Activities

The Bengalis, both Hindu and Muslim communities, formed several associations and initiated many social, religious and cultural activities during the interwar period in British Malaya. The Malayan Bengalee Association (MBA), one of the earliest Bengali associations, started functioning in Malaya in the 1920s. Its members came from the same ethnic group and language. Fresh Bengali migrants and the descendants of those who had arrived from mainly Calcutta, Dacca, Chittagong and Midnapore were also members of the MBA. The association's pioneering members were P. N. Sen, A. B. Paul and B. C. Majumdar. In 1952, the MBA was formally registered, and H. K. Choudhury was its first elected President (1951–1956). After the formation of Malaysia in 1963, the MBA renamed itself the 'Malaysian Bengalee Association'. K. K. Mandal, A. M. Tarafder and J. B. Ray served as presidents of the Malaysian Bengali Association in the 1970s.[32]

South Asian multi-ethnic Hindus started celebrating their religious festivals publicly in British Malaya in the early nineteenth century.[33] The Bengali Hindus began to celebrate religious festivals separately in the 1920s. Under the auspices of the MBA, they celebrated Durga Pooja and Kali Pooja (Deepavali) in Seremban in 1928 with a significant amount of funds provided by Dr Paresh Nath Sen.[34] In the 1930s, the Bengali community built a 'Kali Temple' at Rasah in Seremban. During the same period, they purchased land in Seremban to open a hostel for Bengali students. The hostel never aterialized, but the land was used to celebrate *pooja* festivities from the 1950s. Still, the MBA celebrates many religious occasions, including Laxmi Pooja, Saraswati Pooja and Dol/Holi.

As mentioned earlier, the SIA encountered internal chaos during the early 1930s as some members became increasingly sensitive to racial, linguistic and territorial identity.[35] Bengali Muslim migrants and their descendants founded the Bangiya Moslem Sammilani (the Bengal Muslim Association) in Singapore in the 1920s. The Sammilani arranged different social and religious events and programmes. In 1935, they celebrated the silver jubilee of George V (1865–1936) at Rangoon Road in Singapore with a three-day-long programme. Most of the participants were Bengali *lascars*, merchants and seamen. *Doa selamat* (prayers) was offered for the king and his empire at the Queen Street Mosque on the first day. A Bangla music concert was arranged on the second day, and on the last day, a special dinner was served at M. A. Majid's house as the secretary of the Sammilani.[36] More than 150 guests attended the dinner. At this event, Majid wrote a congratulatory message to the Viceroy of India.[37]

In 1938, a new Management Committee was appointed for the Sammilani. A Bengali descendant, S. I. M. Ibrahim, became the President of the Sammilani.[38] They interacted with other diasporic communities and forged strong ties with them, as illustrated by the appointment of H. S. Moonshi, a renowned Tamil Muslim doctor and justice of peace, as a patron of the Sammilani. Many guests from other diasporic communities were present at the reception for Moonshi's acceptance.[39] He was the vice-chairman and joint secretary of the Mohammedan Advisory Board and was involved in the Muslim community's well-being in Singapore.[40]

In 1938, on the birthday of the Prophet Muhammad (peace be upon him), Ibrahim invited people for a *meelad shareef* (celebration of the birth anniversary of Prophet Muhammad) and arranged a religious talk given by Hafiz Fazlur Rahman Ansari, editor of the *Genuine Islam*, at Angullia Mosque in Singapore.[41] Munshi Muhammed Ally conducted the programme. Imam

Moulana Idris Gowhary of the Queen Street Mosque recited the *meelad*. After the religious function, the Sammilani served a public feast, where more than 1,000 guests from different diasporic communities were present.[42]

In 1939, during a preliminary meeting at the G. H. Café, the Sammilani generated a fund of 2,000 dollars for establishing a rest house for Muslim travellers in Singapore.[43] Concurrently, World War II broke out, and the activities relating to the rest house were stalled. However, after WWII, Majid founded the Social Service Club for Indian Muslims at Collyer Quay Road in 1947. The club confined its activities to social services among Muslims. It aimed to finance the needy, including widows and orphans, and donate money to establish schools and scholarships to spread education among Muslim students. Membership was open to Indian Muslim residents in Singapore and the Malay states. The club was renamed the Indian Muslim Welfare Association, and Majid became its President.[44] However, both the Sammilani and the Indian Muslim Welfare Association failed to register under the Society Ordinance, which disqualified them from functioning in the early 1950s.

The Bengali Muslim diaspora created social spaces in other port cities in Southeast Asia, particularly in Rangoon. Didarul Alam of Chittagong came to Rangoon in the 1920s and became the editor of two Bengali periodicals, namely *Juger Alo* (Light of the Era), a monthly magazine, and the weekly *Sammilani* (Rendezvous). The Bengali Hindu and Muslim diaspora formed different civic associations in Rangoon, such as the Bengal Mohamedan Association (club and library), Khadim ul Islam (caretakers of Islam) and the Chittagong Moslem Society. Forty Hindu and Muslim literary activists founded the Bangla Sahitya Sammilon (Bengali Literature Rendezvous), which launched a literary journal named *Sammilon* at a later date, and Moulvi Muhammad Abdul Monem became its editor.[45]

For Bengali Hindus, Ronendra Karmakar and his father, along with a few notable persons, founded the Bengali Association Singapore (BAS) in 1947.[46] However, association members were inactive for a few years before A. C. Sinha registered it with the Registry of Societies in 1956 and was elected its first president. Members of the association were primarily second- or third-generation Bengalis whose forebears had migrated from undivided Bengal.[47] Though Bengali Hindus used to celebrate Durga Pooja in-house in Singapore, from the 1950s, it began to be celebrated publicly on a large scale.[48] The BAS played a significant role in organising this and other religious festivals, such as Laxmi Pooja, Saraswati Pooja and Dol.[49] About 23,000 people, regardless of race and religion, used to join the Durga Pooja in Singapore in the early twentieth century.[50]

Before the independence of Bangladesh, the BAS was the sole registered association of the Bangla-speaking community in Singapore. During the early 1970s, some Bengalis of eastern Bengal met informally and arranged social functions through the Bangladesh High Commission. Meanwhile, a new wave of Bangladeshi migrants started arriving in Singapore. In 1977, a Bangladeshi businessman, M. Kader, sought to establish a new organisation for Bangladeshi migrants. However, the Registry of Societies rejected his request, citing that there was already an organisation for the Bengalis. Later, under M. A. Aziz's leadership, a group of Bangladeshi professionals, mainly academics,[51] successfully set up the Singapore Bangladesh Society (SBS).

Founding SBS members were of diverse professional backgrounds and permanent residents who had migrated to Singapore from the 1970s onwards. Aziz was the first President and held the post from 1981–1985.[52] Bengali descendants whose parents had migrated in the early colonial period were not involved in the SBS. The society continues to organise various activities to promote mutual understanding and friendship between the people of Singapore and Bangladesh. Its members embrace both Bangladeshi and Singaporean cultures and traditions. It arranges social, cultural and recreational activities—including celebrating the national days of Bangladesh and Singapore—and maintains brotherhood and cordial relations with all communities in the country. Among its other activities are blood drives and *iftar* (the breaking of fasting) parties. Some temporary Bangladeshi migrants attend these events regularly and enjoy them alongside the Bangladeshi resident community. For both groups, these events create a feeling of a home away from home.[53]

The SBS has assisted many Bangladeshi itinerant workers experiencing difficulties in Singapore. For instance, it provided some fifty Bangladeshi migrant labourers with food and shelter for seven days in the Jurong Mosque after a labour recruiting agent cheated them. After that, the society arranged a free passage home with Biman Bangladesh Airlines.[54] Two Bangladeshi workers came to Singapore after being defrauded in Brunei; they were hospitalised and received support from the SBS to return home.[55] In another example of personal support for the Bangla-speaking diaspora, Dolly Sinha continues to grant a discount for students from Bangla schools during the Tagore Society programme.[56]

In general, most Bengali Muslims were members of the SBS, whereas Bengali Hindus joined the BAS. Members of these two Bangla-speaking communities continue to perform parallel activities with minimal social interaction. This interaction, such as it is, could be best described as 'constructive disengagement', a mutual and respectful distancing from each other. The idea of 'civil indifference' helps us understand this social relationship.[57]

Though the Bengalis from West Bengal of India and Bangladesh share common cultures, including language and food habits, they were split into two communities in Malaysia and Singapore in the late 1970s. The primary reason for this division was the independence of Bangladesh, which separated the Bangla-speaking community along national lines. However, other historical aspects should be considered. During the late colonial and postcolonial periods in South Asia, politics took a communal turn among the Bengali Hindu and Muslim communities. The first Partition of Bengal in 1905 seeded separatism along communal lines among educated Muslims and Hindus. Though it was annulled in 1911, what both communities experienced during the anti-partition movement in Bengal tied Bengali ethnic identity to religious affiliation, which rippled and impacted the Bengali diasporic community in Malaya after the Partition of 1905. The communal division was apparent in forming civil society organisations in British Malaya in the 1920s; for example, the Malayan Bengalee Association was formed predominantly by Hindu religious-based migrants, whereas the Bangiya Moslem Sammilani was the association of the Muslim community.

The communal-based networks of Bengali migrants also appeared after the 1947 Partition. The failure of Chitta Ranjan Das's Bengal Pact (1923) and the United Independent Bengal Movement (1946), initiated by Huseyn Shaheed Suhrawardy, led to the partition of Bengal in 1947. Consequently, during the second partition of Bengal, many Bengali Hindus and Muslims were displaced forcibly from East Bengal to West Bengal and vice versa.[58] These partitions based on communal lines affected Bangla-speaking expatriates in the Malay Peninsula. Some Bengali Hindus who had migrated from Eastern Bengal to Malaya before the partition of 1947, their descendants in East Bengal, opted to leave for Calcutta after the partition. For instance, Sarojininath Bardhan (1874–1927) and Bhupendra Chandra Majumder (1890–1983) migrated from Eastern Bengal to Malaya before the Bengal divide of 1947. Still, after the partition of 1947, their descendants in Malaya continued a kinship with the Calcutta-based relatives. Most South Asian political leaders were split along communal lines under the banners of the Malayan Indian Congress and the Penang Indian Muslim League. Consequently, Hindus and Muslims began to organise separately in post-1947 British Malaya. For example, the BAS celebrated only Hindu religious and Bangla cultural functions, though a significant portion of Bengali migrants in Singapore were Muslim.[59]

In more recent times, relations among the Bangladeshi diasporic community have often been influenced by national politics within Bangladesh. For example, during the election of the Management Committee of the Bangla Language School in 1992, two Bangladeshi lecturers at the National University of Singapore contested for the post of the president. They tried to draw their compatriots' attention by using both 'communal' and 'liberal' sentiments.[60] Referring to a school textbook that contained an Indian flag, one candidate criticised the other for his silence about the matter and argued that Bangla schools' textbooks should be kept away from national identity. This faction raised why the recommended textbooks had been selected from Calcutta-based Hindu writers, whereas most students were from Bangladesh. They wanted a proportionate representation of textbooks and authors from both West Bengal and Bangladesh. However, the other faction argued that the school aimed to teach the Bangla language and equitable representation was unnecessary. It appears that the specific dividing line between the two competing blocks was drawn by a subtle sense of communalism and liberalism.[61]

Since the early twentieth century in the Malay Peninsula, some Bengali migrants have been known to perform music at home, particularly in Singapore. K. C. Sinha's family was culturally minded. Occasionally, they arranged a Bangla music night where they sang and played many musical instruments, including the guitar, organ, violin and piano.[62] Bengali leaders of Indian associations sometimes patronised Bangla music by organising cultural functions, and following the visit of Rabindranath Tagore and the establishment of the Ramakrishna Mission, they started to perform Bangla music publicly. A non-Bengali recalled listening to *Rabindra sangeet* or Tagore songs at the Ramakrishna Mission on Rangoon Road. Though he did not understand the music, he was fascinated by the tune. After that, he read every English translation of Tagore's work.[63] The Bengalis from different organisations arranged open concerts. For instance, Majid organised a Bangla music concert at Rangoon Road to celebrate the silver jubilee of George V. After forming the MBA, the BAS and the SBS in Malaya and Singapore, the Bengali diaspora regularly organised musical events and competitions. An interviewee recalled seeing a Bengali female singer competing with Tamil and Punjabi contestants in a classical music programme. The Bengali competitor returned to Bengal and never came back to Singapore.[64] By the 1930s, the

Bangla cultural space was remarkably shaped, and their cultures became well-known to other communities.

As with their celebration of Bangla music, the Bangla-speaking community celebrated some common traditional events, such as Bengali New Year (Pahela Baishakh/Bangla Nabobarsho), from their early days in Malaya. Later, they came to celebrate the anniversary of Rabindranath Tagore and Kazi Nazrul Islam (Rabindra–Nazrul Jayanty). In 1961, during the Tagore centenary, the BAS screened a documentary on Tagore's life and works and the theatrical performance of his short story 'Kabuliwala'.[65] It also celebrated Tagore's 150th birth anniversary with various shows.[66]

Apart from observing common Bangla traditions and culture, the SBS organises diverse activities such as magic shows, indoor and outdoor games, and cooking and decoupage classes.[67] As part of the Singapore Heritage Week 1987, the SBS staged its annual cultural event at the Public Utilities Board auditorium on 4 July 1987, featuring *Nakshi Kathar Math* (The Field of the Embroidered Quilt), among other regular performances. Other artistic efforts took the form of *Sapurey nreetha* (Snake Charmer Dance), a snake dance based on a folk tale; *Mayur nreetha* (Peacock Dance), a pure dance portraying the antics of a peacock; and *Monipuri nreetha* (Manipuri Dance), a modified version of the Manipuri dance.[68] Performing Bangla folk culture in a distant place reflects the deep bond between the diasporic community and their original land and contributes towards creating a multicultural space.

By the mid-twentieth century in Singapore, Bangla movies were being screened publicly. Satyajit Ray's *Apur Sangsar* (The Household of Apu) was shown on 28 February 1962.[69] The Singapore Broadcasting Corporation introduced Channel 12 in 1983, transmitting different programmes in foreign languages and aired the movie *Mahanagar* (The City) on 25 April 1987. The movie was directed by Satyajit Ray and won an award at the Berlin Film Festival in 1964.[70] Moreover, Bangla theatrical dramas were staged publicly in Singapore, for instance, *Aparajito* (Undefeated), *Darpan* (The Mirror) and *Kanchenjunga*.[71] Such stage performances reflect a Bengali cultural space that had matured even prior to the arrival of the new wave of itinerant labourers from the 1980s, alluding to a settled diaspora. Members and patrons of Bengali associations sponsored cultural and film exhibitions to support government initiatives toward developing cultural consciousness and multiculturalism.[72] For example, in 1979, the BAS collaborated with the Singapore Cultural Foundation to organise concerts and dance shows.

The nature and features of these associations' activities seem to have shifted over time. Dolly Sinha has compared the past and present activities of the BAS. She remembers that the BAS organised music and dance at the school's hall or clubhouses in the 1950s; its members organised and performed without the assistance of modern technological equipment. However, nowadays, the association relies on digital equipment and event management companies. It frequently arranges programmes and hires artists from Dhaka and Kolkata, further blurring the boundaries between home and away. People now prefer comedy shows rather than classical music, films and art exhibitions shown during the early days. These days, members of the international diaspora from across the world increasingly attend these events.[73]

Language plays a significant role in transmitting culture from generation to generation. Some Bengali migrants, whose parents migrated to British Malaya many years ago and formed transnational families, have lost language, culture, and *Bangalitto* (Bengaliness) in modern times. The families of Ismail Ballah and Majid have testified to being disconnected from Bengali cultural practices. Many multilingual Bengalis began to stop speaking Bangla with their children in the twentieth century, leading Bengali migrants to worry in the late 1940s about the next generations losing touch with Bangla. Therefore, they organised Bangla language classes for their children.[74] This attempt continued for a short period. Still, after some time, Lee Kuan Yew realised the significance of children's mother tongues in promoting bilingualism. In 1977, he eloquently noted:

> When a Singaporean child goes to school, he is exposed to bilingualism.... At home, he speaks Hokkien, Hainanese, Teochew, Hakka, Cantonese, or Hindi, or Bengali. He goes to school and is immediately confounded by a barrage of two verbal artillery systems. He is subjected to two percussion bangs. Into one ear, he gets English, into the other Mandarin.[75]

Lee suggested that Singaporean children had to be bilingual. English was compulsory, but a second language was incorporated into the school curriculum. Students could take their mother tongue or other languages, including Mandarin, Tamil, Bangla and Punjabi, as their second language. Subsequently, Bangla was given importance as a second language in the South Asian languages group, and it was accommodated in the Board of Teaching and Testing South Asian Languages under the Singapore Education Ministry in 1990.[76] Therefore, Bengali students were able to acquire Bangla linguistic skills through pedagogy. Although mainstream schools did not teach second languages, Bengali students could take Bangla at pre-university ordinary and advanced levels. This initiative of the Singapore government opened up new avenues for cultural development for the Bengali diasporic community.

More recently, members of Bengali civil society associations realised the need to open Bangla language schools or centres to educate their children. With the Singapore government's approval, the SBS and Bangladeshi professionals established two Bangla language learning centres in Singapore, namely the Bangla Language and Literary Society (BLLS) and the Bangladesh Language and Cultural Foundation (BLCF), in 1994 and 2000, respectively. The number of students increased steadily, and presently, two more branches of these centres have been opened, and the Singapore government has provided a grant of 54,000 dollars to each centre. The government has allocated public schools for conducting classes every weekend.[77] Rumu Paul remarks that it is such a relief that his daughter can read Bangla novels now.[78] The schools meet every Saturday for three and a half hours, with teachers from both Bangladesh and West Bengal.[79] Currently, there are approximately 4,000 to 5,000 children enrolled in Bangla language courses in these institutions.[80] The majority of the students are the offspring of the Bengali community, which originated from Bangladesh.

Locating Bengalis in Charities, Philanthropies and Sports

It is important to note that Bengali societal engagement was not limited to their own communal and ethnic organisations. Some notable Bengalis extended their public involvement through organisations sponsored by other ethnic and international groups, including the Malay, Tamil, Chinese and Europeans. Here is an outline of such engagements.

Professionals and Their Associations: The Case of Dr Madhuri Majumder

The active life of Madhuri Majumder is particularly remarkable and representative of the way Bengali women engaged with public space in the messy world of ethnic and communal entanglements. Majumder was born in Seremban after her father, D. K. Majumder, arrived in Malaya from East Bengal as a medical officer in 1930. After completing her graduation in

Malaya, Hong Kong and Calcutta, Majumder began her career as a house officer at Melaka General Hospital in 1961.[81] In 1982, she became the first woman president of a branch (Perak) of the Malaysian Medical Association (MMA). During her tenure, she was active in community health services and the development of medical education. She organised different seminars and symposiums associated with the Perak Medical Practitioners' Society and the Ipoh chapter of the College of General Practitioners.[82] When she was the President of the Perak Society for Promotion of Mental Health (PSPMH) in 1986, she rehabilitated developmentally delayed children with various occupational activities, including singing, dancing, orchid farming and ceramic and art projects. Sometimes, she welcomed them at her house and workstations for training and nursing.[83] Her endeavours mainly involved rehabilitating intellectually disabled people to prepare them for mainstream society. She served the PSPMH for 27 years.

Majumder was a founding member of the College of Physicians, Surgeons and General Practitioners. She held top positions in different professional organisations, including the Dermatological Society of Malaysia, the Singapore Dermatological Society and the Malaysian Society of Parasitology. Apart from engaging in professional associations, she was a member of the Equestrian Club, Vice-president of the Ipoh Society of Prevention of Cruelty to Animals and a founding member of the Ipoh Fine Arts Society.[84] Moreover, she was a philanthropist. She began the 'Majumder Scholarship Fund' to assist needy students. Six students from two schools in Perak—S. M. K. Sri Putera Sungai Pari and S. M. K. Buntong—were the first beneficiaries of her endowments. During the International Women's Day celebration in 2012, she was bestowed with the Women of True Beauty Award (Anugerah Wanita Mutiara). Majumder achieved exclusive titles and trophies for service to community health. She is popularly known as the 'Mother Teresa of Ipoh'.[85]

Bengali Athletes and Their Involvement in Sporting Associations

Some Bengali descendants contributed to Malaya's sporting world as sports organisers and players in international and regional tournaments. Ibrahim became an ardent golfer and a member of the Singapore Island and Country Club. He was the Royal Island Cup Champion and won the Meyer Cup in 1932, 1938 and 1939.[86] Benoy Kumar Sen was also a well-known golfer. He represented Singapore in golf in the Putra and Nomura Cup competitions in 1969 and 1979, respectively. J. K. Mitra started his athletic career in 1949 while studying Senior Cambridge at Raffles Institute. He was pitted against a strong competitor named Chan Onn Leng from the Anglo-Chinese School, but Mitra won most of the matches.[87] Later, he became a pilot for the Auxiliary Air Force of Singapore, whereas Leng became a doctor in Malaysia.[88]

Anwarul Haque started playing in the Singapore national team with the 1956 Melbourne hockey squad. He was one of the best hockey goalkeepers in Singapore from the 1950s to 1971. In 1962, Haque participated in the fourth Asian Games in Jakarta. When Singapore merged with Malaysia in 1963, he played for the Malaysian national team. During the 1964 Summer Olympics in Tokyo, the Malaysian national team comprised twenty-two players, of whom four were from Singapore, Haque being one of them. He participated in the sixth Asian Games in Bangkok in 1970 and the sixth Southeast Asian Peninsular Games (SEAP) in 1971, when Singapore clinched a silver medal. He served the Singapore national hockey team while working for the Judicial Department. He was selected as the sportsman of the year in Singapore to recognise his performance in the 1970 Asian Games. He was nominated for the Asian all-star hockey XI, comprised of the best hockey players from Asian countries, including India, Pakistan and Hong Kong. Haque was involved in many sports clubs and associations. He was the Chairman of the Singapore Hockey Association (1986–1992) and the Singapore Cricket Club (2002–2007), the oldest sports club in Singapore, founded in 1852. He was the Deputy President of the club for five years and finally became its president. The Singapore Hockey Association and the Singapore Women's Hockey Association merged in 1992 to form the Singapore Hockey Federation, and Haque became the Chairperson of the Appeals Board of the federation.[89]

Voluntary or Charitable Activities: The Case of the Sinha Family

During the decolonisation process, the Malayan economy was quite unstable. In particular, Singapore could not bring all its citizens under social safety nets. Some Bengalis and philanthropists from other communities came forward to support society through voluntary charitable works. They aided different associations by working to support aged people, family planning and patients with cognitive issues. Two Sinha family members, Hena Sinha and Dolly Sinha (a daughter-in-law of A. C. Sinha), made remarkable contributions.

Hena Sinha, a homemaker and the wife of A. C. Sinha, volunteered for the Family Planning Clinic and Family Planning Association. He was the President of the Inner Wheel Club, affiliated with the Rotary Club. Soon after

WWII, Hena Sinha became interested in voluntary work after many children had become orphans during the war and Japanese occupation. She noticed that many low-income families could not feed and educate their children and was moved to form a volunteer group with the assistance of her friends, requesting the Methodist Church at Kampong Kapor to allow them to use its open space and benches. After that, they started to teach and feed the orphans every morning. They did not have enough funding initially, but a few generous volunteers later joined them and worked to improve the conditions of the underprivileged through different initiatives, including family planning. Hena Sinha left for England in 1949 to accompany her husband, A. C. Sinha, who was awarded the Queen Scholarship to pursue higher medical studies. However, both returned to Singapore in 1951 and continued their social services.[90]

A group of people, including T. P. F. McNeice, Mary Tan and H. B. Amstutz, started a family planning clinic in Singapore. They formed the Family Planning Association (FPA), and McNeice became the President of the association. Upon her return, A. C. Sinha became Vice-president of the FPA, and Hena Sinha resumed her voluntary work with the clinic at Kandang Kerbau Hospital. Her responsibilities included storing and distributing family planning materials and medicines and recording each patient's case. The FPA opened new clinics throughout Singapore, and its officers advised parents not to have many children, providing birth protection components to back up this advice.[91] Its efforts played a significant role in reducing the birth rate and promoting infant and maternal health awareness.

Hena Sinha became Vice-chairman and then Vhairman of the FPA (1962–1965). She also was a member of the International Planned Parenthood Federation's (IPPF) governing body, which was formed in the early 1950s. The IPPF was associated with family planning, and its movement was worldwide. Hena Sinha was involved in running the IPPF from 1962 to 1965. In addition, she became a member of the Young Women's Christian Association's (YWCA) Executive Committee. She organised many social activities, including helping disabled and older men, women and children. She worked there as a policymaker for two years. She continued to work for society and marginalised communities until her last days, only slowed down by the emotional shock of the death of her husband, A. C. Sinha and elder son, Ranjit Sinha, in quick succession.[92]

Dolly Sinha Devanport, a legal practitioner and wife of Ranjit Sinha, was similarly intrepid in her work and was involved in charity associations from the 1970s onwards. She joined hands with Shakuntala Bhatia to establish the Asian Women's Welfare Association (AWWA), a charitable organisation, in 1970. They founded the Ang Mo Kio Community Home in Singapore in 1976, a voluntary service for older men and women without kin or means of livelihood. It still exists today and is known as the Senior Community Home. Dolly Sinha was asked to generate funds for its upkeep and arranged many charity exhibitions, workshops and a carnival to raise funds. For instance, she organised a premiere for the 'Dance of the Orient' at the National Theatre with the assistance of the AWWA and the BAS.[93] Moreover, she and her volunteer group displayed floral designs on different themes that were available for purchase alongside other handicrafts.[94] Dolly Sinha was the President of the AWWA in 1978 but lost touch with it when the Singapore government took charge of the association.[95]

Apart from the AWWA, Dolly Sinha was engaged in fundraising for the Spastic Children's Association and the Saint Andrew's Community Hospital to purchase necessary materials, including bed sheets, bed covers and pillows. She was also attached to creating a fund for the Home Nursing Foundation. People from different ethnicities, including Malays, Bengalis, Chinese and Eurasians, donated money. The Singapore government awarded her twice in recognition of her charity work and community services.[96]

The Localisation of International Communities and the Internationalisation of Locals

Robertson, a theorist of globalisation, shows how dynamic the process in which a 'local' enters the global arena is and how the 'global' flows into the 'local'.[97] His model of globalisation articulates how the multi-directional flows of commodities and corresponding human mobilities shape spatial histories. In their host countries, Bengali migrants were involved in either the Malayan Bengalee Association or the Bangiya Moslem Sammilani; therefore, their attachment was to their Bengali identity and community. Their involvement in civic associations in distant places helped them become a 'local' away from home. However, when the Bengali migrants or their descendants participated in international associations or spheres, such as the Indo-Malay-Pakistani Seamen Union and the Singapore Asian Seafarers' Federation (SASF), they overcame the territorial boundary of British Malaya. They found themselves in a far larger world of engagement. Another example of international networking is crafting connections with the global Muslim community by Bengali Muslims of Malaya, along with others. For instance, members of the Muslim Merchants Society, including those who were Tamil, Arab, Malay and Bengali, collected a fund for the earthquake victims in Anatolia in December 1940, sent through the British representative in Ankara.[98]

After the revolt of 1857 in British India, some South Asian Muslims dispersed across Cairo, Mecca and Istanbul. They made a Pan-Islamic intellectual network between the British and Ottoman empires.[99] Such networks subsequently facilitated the Pan-Islamic Movement or the Khilafat Movement (1919–1924). When the Khilafat Movement ended, Pan-Islamism was increasingly seen among the Muslim community, who tried to reorganise a global network. A General Pan-Islamic Conference was held in Jerusalem in December 1931, a landmark in transforming Jerusalem into a new centre of the Islamic world.[100] Some South Asian Muslim migrants, including Bengali descendants, were involved in the Pan-Islamic movement in British Malaya. A Bengali descendant, Ibrahim participated in the Islamic Conference in Jerusalem, where he performed the funeral prayer for Muhammad Ali, president of the Khilafat Movement. The conference formed a Young Men's Muslim Association (YMMA) similar to the Young Men's Christian Association (YMCA). After returning from the conference, Ibrahim formed the Young Muslim Physical and Literary Union in Malaya in 1932 and became its President. This organisation provided physical (ju-jitsu) and spiritual training to young Muslims.[101]

As the President of the Indo-Malay-Pakistani Seamen's Union, a multi-ethnic trading organisation, Majid tried to unify Asian seamen. He prioritised the rights of the harbour and maritime workers irrespective of ethnic identity, which put him in contact with some international organisations. In 1948, Majid was selected as a reception committee member during the conference of the International Labour Organisation (ILO) in Singapore.[102] After that, in 1949, he went to Calcutta for two months to organise seamen.[103] Majid drew the attention of the ILO to the problems of Asian seamen. He wrote to the chairman of the maritime wing of the ILO regarding the arbitrary treatment of Asian seamen in Singapore.[104] In 1948, Majid was elected the joint secretary of the SASF and the President of the Maritime Union of Malaya.[105] He was also the Secretary of the Asian Seafarers' Advisory Council and the Asian Maritime Officers' Union in Singapore. He assured the seamen that though the federation was formed in Singapore, it would work for Asian sailors' welfare. Some leaders of the SASF, including Majid, met shipowners to achieve mutual interests of the shipping industry and its labourers in Singapore in 1948.[106]

As the President of the Muslim Welfare Association in Singapore, Majid assisted people regardless of ethnicity and religion. One remarkable example was that he helped Che Aminah binte Mohamed during the arbitration process for custody of Maria Hertogh or Nadra Adabi. Aminah, a Malay woman, adopted a Dutch infant named Maria Hertogh in 1942 when the Japanese Army imprisoned her father in Indonesia. After the capture of the family's sole breadwinner, Maria's mother could not afford the expense of six offspring, so she requested Aminah to adopt Maria. After adoption, Maria was converted to Islam, renamed Nadra and was brought up as a Muslim Kampong girl.[107] When WWII ended, the biological parents filed a case against Aminah to repossess their daughter.[108] The incident then took a dramatic turn. Majid raised funds to help Aminah and hired solicitors in the legal battle in 1950.[109] The global community was drawn to the lawsuit when the erstwhile Dutch government became involved. Even Majid's house became a hub of local and international media. In particular, the public sensation was stirred when Nadra's biological parents and the vice consul general of the Dutch Consulate visited Majid's house.

Quest for Citizenship

The Bengali diaspora's involvement and contributions to Malaysian and Singaporean public space were the primary ground for claiming citizenship and civic rights. At the beginning of British colonial rule, migrating communities hardly enjoyed any civic rights in the Malay world. They were considered 'British Subjects' or 'Imperial Citizens'.[110] In Malaya, citizens' rights became an issue in the 1930s. The quest for citizenship opened Pandora's box as it became a burning issue for the offspring whose parents had migrated and settled in Malaya. The problem was rooted firmly in past migrations and took over twenty years to solve. The Federal Legislative Council made some necessary conditions for acquiring citizenship in the proceedings of 1933. The Federal Legislative Council focused on two requirements for acquiring citizenship: (*a*) imperial naturalisation or by birth citizenship, which means the children born in British Malaya, and (*b*) Imperial birthright citizenship, which means that a person acquires citizenship automatically by law. The children whose parents are British subjects or who acquire any of the requirements mentioned earlier are citizens of the British Empire.[111]

Citizenship rights and the question of nationality remained unclear in the naturalisation approach. Both were discussed elaborately at the Asian Relations Conference.[112] A delegate from Malaya stated that his government would allow citizenship only to those who considered Malaya their homeland and firmly advised Indian and Chinese migrants to make a choice; they would have to choose to be a citizen of Malaya. The delegates of the conference agreed that a person could have only one nationality at any one time, but anyone willing to retain their original nationality should be treated in a 'generous and humane spirit' in the country of their residence.[113]

After WWII, the Colonial Office decided to restructure Malaya's administration by separating Singapore as a Crown Colony and forming the Malayan Union by providing equal rights to all residents regardless of ethnic origin.[114] In 1949, Malcolm John MacDonald (Governor General of Malaya and Commissioner General for Southeast Asia) convened a Communities Liaison Committee with the leaders of different ethnic groups to come to a standard agreement on the question of citizenship.[115] As his attempt was unsuccessful, the Reid Commission was sent to Malaya in 1956, just before its independence, to settle the issue of citizenship, among other issues. The leaders of the United Malays National Organisation (UMNO), the Malaysian Chinese Association and the Malayan Indian Congress agreed on some conditions of *jus soli*, which would be implemented only after independence.[116] Thus, about half a million Chinese and a quarter of a million Indians were granted fundamental civil rights in the 1950s while accepting the Malays' dominance in politics, culture and economic rights.[117] In 1957, the British government transferred the state's power to the Government of the Alliance Party (made of UMNO, the Malayan Chinese Association and the Malayan Indian Congress) after assuring exclusive Malay rights, and citizenship was given to the non-Malays.[118]

As special rights of dominance were given to the Malays, some South Asian migrants, including Pakistanis and Bengalis, opted for the Malay identity. For example, although Majid was Bengali by birth and was 'Indian' on his identity card, he did not want to categorise his offspring as Indian. There was no categorical option or space to write the Bengali ethnic identity in the citizenship application form, so all of his offspring took on a 'Malay' identity because his wife was a Chinese Malay.[119] Most Bengalis obtained citizenship through naturalisation. The former diplomat Mushahid Ali remembers that all his siblings and relatives received citizenship through naturalisation because they were born in Malaya.[120] Dolly Sinha Davenport recalls that she gained Singaporean citizenship in 1966 because she married a Bengali doctor who was a Singaporean citizen.

Conclusion

The South Asians who had migrated to British Malaya in the nineteenth century made their presence felt through involvement in social organisations and civic activities in various capacities, becoming a major part of society by the dawning of WWII. They created civil society associations in line with regional or linguistic priorities during the colonial and postcolonial periods.[121] This chapter has explored the development of Bengali public space in the context of the broader cultural and social milieu in Malaya. It has further shown the patterns of interactions among ethnicities, national identities and pluralistic cultural, social and political practices. These converging of Bengali societal, associational and cultural activities created 'Banglascapes' in Malaysia and Singapore.[122] A wide range of societal entanglements of the Bengali migrants facilitated interactions with mixed racial associations, which allowed them to become a truly trans-local community. Mixing between these civil society organisations and their activities, including those continued in the postcolonial period, led to the formation of what has recently been termed 'cosmopolitan thought zones'.[123] Bengali descendants or the offspring of mixed-racial parents lost connections with their fathers' place of origin. Their cosmopolitan traits, more than the Bangla language and cultures, remain strong among them. Therefore, Bengali ethnic identity is weak among the second, third and fourth generations of Bengali migrants; they could be referred to as having 'less Bengaliness'.[124]

Notes

1. N. Theodore and N. Martin, 'Migrant Civil Society: New Voices in the Struggle Over Community Development', *Journal of Urban Affairs* 29, no. 3 (2007): 269.
2. Roland Robertson, *Globalization: Social Theory and Global* (London: Sage Publications, 1992), 5, 173.

3. S. N. Bardhan was appointed Medical Advisor to the Singapore Family Benefit Society in 1919. Sengupta, *Malaysia and Bengali Doctors*, 111.

4. Solomon, *A Subaltern History of the Indian Diaspora*, 200.

5. *MaT*, 27 March 1933, 7.

6. *ST*, 14 May 1946, 4.

7. *Sunday Tribune* (Singapore), 20 June 1937, 19.

8. *MaT*, 4 June 1915, 8.

9. *ST*, 15 September 1922, 10; *MaT*, 14 September 1922, 6; *SFPMA*, 1 September 1930, 7; *MaT*, 2 February 1931, 2.

10. The Ramakrishna Mission is a Hindu religious organisation that started a spiritual movement worldwide. It originated in Bengal following the teachings of a Bengali saint, Ramakrishna Paramahansa (1836–1886), after his chief disciple, Swami Vivekananda (1863–1902), established the Ramakrishna Mission in Calcutta in 1897.

11. *MaT*, 18 August 1928, 13; Jean-Pierre Mialaret, *Hinduism in Singapore: A Guide to the Hindu Temples of Singapore* (Singapore: D. Moore for Asia Pacific Press, 1969), 65–66; Nor-Afidah Abd Rahman, 'Ramakrishna Mission Singapore', SingaporeInfopedia, National Library Board, Singapore, https://eresources.nlb.gov.sg/infopedia/articles/SIP_410_2005-01-18.html, accessed 28 June 2018.

12. *SFPMA* (Weekly), 23 October 1929, 9.

13. Jyotish Chandra Ghosh, *Bishwa Bhramone Rabindranath* [Rabindranath in World Voyage] (Calcutta: Sri Guru Library, 1942), 113, 171; Das, *Banger Bahire Bangali*, 477–478; Chattopadhyay, 'Jabodeeper Path e', 142–145, 482.

14. *SFPMA*, 16 September 1916. The names of leaders and their origins were discussed in Chapter 2. This committee was responsible for holding one of the first South Asian multi-ethnic public gatherings.

15. From the 1910s onwards, diverse South Asian ethnicities formed Indian associations in different Malay states, including as the Kedah Indian Association and the Perak Indian Association.

16. During the colonial period, a justice of peace (JP) was appointed by the government in Singapore. These individuals were picked from prominent community leaders trusted by the government and helped maintain peace.

17. *ST*, 2 March 1923, 10.

18. *MaT*, 28 December 1934, 20; *ST*, 27 February 1936, 14; *SFPMA*, 28 January 1941, 10; *MaT*, 4 December 1941, 4; *ST*, 16 July 1954, 14; *SFP*, 10 September 1960, 12; *NN*, 29 March 1972, 27.

19. *MaT*, 15 July 1935, 10.

20. *SFP*, 13 August 1948, 5.

21. *SFP*, 6 July 1950, 5.

22. *SFPMA*, 6 October 1941, 6.

23. S. C. Goho became the President of the SIA in 1940. R. K. Bhattacharyya and Dr Krisna founded the Indian Association at Kuching in 1931. See Singh, 'Indians in East Malaysia', 579, 584. The arrival of South Asians in Brunei is traced back to the early twentieth century. The Belait Indian Association and Bandar Sri Begawan Indian Association (BSBIA) were formed in the late 1930s. See A. Mani, 'A Century of Contributions by Indians in Negara Brunei Darussalam', in *Rising India and Indian Communities in East Asia*, ed. K. Kesavapany, A. Mani and P. Ramasamy (Singapore: ISEAS, 2008), 186.

24. *ST*, 28 August 1936, 13.

25. *Morning Tribune* (hereinafter *MoT*), 4 May 1939, 2; *SFPMA*, 2 July 1938, 3.

26. *ST*, 30 October 1937, 16.

27. *MaT*, 13 July 1938, 12.

28. *SFPMA*, 8 October 1941, 8; *MaT*, 9 October 1941, 3; *ST*, 12 December 1940, 10; *MaT*, 27 April 1939, 13; *MaT*, 14 July 1938, 6; *ST*, 11 December 1940, 10.

29. *MaT*, 24 July 1941, 11.

30. *MaT*, 17 July 1941, 3.

31. Sengupta, *Singapore, My Country*, 60–61; Jumabhoy, *Multiracial Singapore*, 55.

32. Sengupta, *Malaysia and Bengali Doctors*, 60, 64. See also the Malaysian Bengalee Association, https://www.mba.org.my/history.php, accessed 20 March 2017.

33. Mialaret, *Hinduism in Singapore*. The author is not focusing on pre-modern Hinduism and the Hindu kingdom in the Malay Peninsula.

34. Sengupta, *Malaysia and Bengali Doctors*, 190, 40.

35. Sengupta, *Singapore: My Country*, 151.

36. *Sunday Tribune (Singapore)*, 5 May 1935, 2. *SFPMA*, 6 May 1935, 3.

37. *ST*, 13 May 1935, 13.

38. *MaT*, 17 March 1938, 18.

39. It was mentioned earlier that Munshi Muhammad Ally was a Bengali and the secretary of an Indian multi-ethnic committee in 1916.

40. *MoT*, 28 April 1938, 7.

41. *MaT*, 1 June 1938, 13.

42. *MaT*, 8 June 1938, 13. Notable guests including Capt. N. M. Hashim, A. M. S. Angullia (JP), Dr H. S. Moonshi (JP), Syed Gulab Shah and Syed Abdullah bin Yahya attended the feast.

43. *SFPMA*, 12 January 1939, 2.

44. *MoT*, 31 July 1947, 3; *ST*, 24 March 1948, 5.

45. Iftekhar Iqbal, 'The Bengali Muslim: Language and Space-Making at the Ocean's Margins', in *Oceanic Islam: Muslim Universalism and European Imperialism*, ed. Sugata Bose and Ayesha Jalal (New Delhi: Bloomsbury Publishing, 2020), 185–186.

46. NAS, OHI, Karmakar, 18 October 1983, Acc. No. 000343.

47. NAS, OHI, Karmakar, 18 October 1983, Acc. No. 000343; see NAS, OHI, Hena Sinha, October–November of 1983, Acc. No. 000354.

48. Gopal, 'A Sea of Change, an Ocean of Memories: Migration and Identity', 254.

49. *ST*, 15 February 1959, 11.

50. *Telegraph* (India), 21 July 2013.

51. A Bangladeshi professor worked at the National University of Singapore.

52. *ST*, 27 March 1983, 17; Habibul Haque Khondker, 'Sociological Reflections on the Diasporic Bangladeshis in Singapore and USA', in *The South Asian Diaspora: Transnational Networks and Changing Identities*, ed. Rajesh Rai and Peter Reeves (London; New York: Routledge, 2009), 129.

53. Rahman, *Bangladeshi Migration to Singapore*, 120.

54. *ST*, 27 March 1983, 17.

55. *ST*, 27 March 1983, 17.

56. Interview with Davenport.

57. Khondker, 'Bengali-speaking Families in Singapore', 184, 185.

58. Brown, *Global South Asians*, 24.

59. Khondker, 'Bengali-speaking Families in Singapore', 184, 185; Dolly Sinha Davenport remembers that the BAS celebrated only *pooja*s and Bangla cultural festivals. She was involved in the association's activities in the late 1960s and was President from 1979 to 1988. Interview with Davenport.

60. The term 'communalism' was introduced by the colonial occupants of British India during the nineteenth century for the use and manipulation of religious or ethnic differences for 'political' ends. Communalism has spread beyond the subcontinent amongst the substantial communities of Indians, Pakistanis and Bangladeshis living abroad. See Bates, 'Introduction', 2.

61. Khondker, 'Bengali-speaking Families in Singapore', 185–187.

62. NAS, OHI, Hena Sinha, October–November of 1983, Acc. No. 000354.

63. NAS, OHI, Chengara Veetil Devan Nair, 9 January 1981, Acc. No. 000049; Chengara Veetil Devan Nair was born in Malacca in 1923 and became the President of Singapore in 1981.

64. NAS, OHI, Mohinder Singh, 24 June 1985, Acc. No. 000546.

65. *SFP*, 1 July 1961, 3.

66. *Telegraph* (India), 21 July 2013.

67. *ST*, 27 March 1983, 17.

68. *ST*, 24 July 1987, 5.

69. *SFP*, 28 February 1962, 3.

70. *Business Times*, 25 April 1987, 10; see also *ST*, 2 November 1986, 1.

71. *ST*, 31 August 1958, 11; *ST*, 22 November 1959, 7; *Business Times*, 20 April 1985, 6.

72. *ST*, 21 April 1980, 6; *ST*, 19 March 1982, 4.

73. Interview with Davenport.

74. NAS, OHI, Hena Sinha, October–November of 1983, Acc. No. 000354.

75. NAS, SPR, Lee Kuan Yew, 23 December 1977; *ST*, 29 December 1977, 14.

76. *At the Crossroads: Report on the Action Committee on Indian Education* (Singapore: Promotion and Sales Center, 1991), 58.

77. Interview with A. K. M. Mohsin.

78. *Telegraph* (India), 21 July 2013.

79. Khondker, 'Sociological Reflections on the Diasporic Bangladeshis in Singapore and USA', 129.

80. Interview with Davenport.

81. Sengupta, *Malaysia and Bengali Doctors*, 46, 137.

82. Ho, *Doctors Extraordinaire*, 77.

83. S. Sundralingam, 'Datuk Dr Madhuri Majumder', *Ipoh Echo (Archives)*, *Ipoh's Community Newspaper, Ipoh Food, Ipoh Media*, 16 March 2013, http://www.ipohecho.com.my/v2/2013/03/16/datuk-dr-madhuri-majumder/, accessed 26 March 2018.

84. *SO*, 26 April 2003; Ho, *Doctors Extraordinaire*, 77.

85. S. H. Ong, 'Majumder Scholarship Fund', *Ipoh Echo (Archives)*, *Ipoh's Community Newspaper, Ipoh Food, Ipoh Media*, 16 March 2013, http://www.ipohecho.com.my/v2/page/58/, accessed 28 June 2018; *SO*, 11 May 2012.

86. Rashid, *Research on the Early Malay Doctors 1900–1957*, 179.

87. NAS, OHI, Pathmanaban Selvadurai, 10 September 2002, Acc. No. 002699.

88. *SFP*, 26 July 1952, 4.

89. Interview with Haque; see also *The New Paper*, 21 July 2004, 49; *ST*, 15 July 2017; Roy Tomizawa, 'From Silver to Gold in Singapore: Tan Howe Liang to Joseph Schooling', *The Olympians*, 5 May 2017.

90. NAS, OHI, Hena Sinha, October–November of 1983, Acc. No. 000354.

91. NAS, OHI, Hena Sinha, October–November of 1983, Acc. No. 000354.

92. NAS, OHI, Hena Sinha, October–November of 1983, Acc. No. 000354.

93. *NN*, 16 November 1972, 2.

94. Dolly Sinha was an expert on flower arrangement. She used to supply floral works to clubhouses or sometimes individual homes or hotels. Her entire profit was deposited into the charity fund. Later, she wrote a book based on her flower arrangement experiences entitled *Between Heaven and Earth: A Singapore Story in Flower* (Singapore: Flame of the Forest Publishing Pte Ltd, 2015).

95. Interview with Davenport.

96. Interview with Davenport.

97. Robertson, *Globalization*.

98. *ST*, 12 February 1940, 11.

99. Seema Alavi, *Muslim Cosmopolitanism in the Age of Empire* (Cambridge, MA: Harvard University Press, 2015); Seema Alavi, 'Little Men between Big Empires: Muslim Cosmopolitanism in the Age of Imperial Expansion', in *Oceanic Islam: Muslim Universalism and European Imperialism*, ed. Sugata Bose and Ayesha Jalal (Delhi: Bloomsbury, 2020), 100–124.

100. Thomas Mayer, 'Egypt and the General Islamic Conference of Jerusalem in 1931', *Middle Eastern Studies* 18, no. 3 (1982): 311; Jacob M. Landau, *Pan-Islam: History and Politics* (London: Routledge, 2015), 225.

101. Rashid, *Biography of the Early Malay Doctors 1900–1957*, 119, 896.

102. *ST*, 30 June 1949, 7.

103. *ST*, 12 August 1949, 5.

104. *ST*, 20 October 1953, 4.

105. Singapore Asian Seafarers' Federation (SASF) was formed to pursue the broader interests of seamen from six unions and was composed of 13,000 members. The six unions included the Maritime Union of Malaya, the Indo-Malay Seamen Union of Malaya (formerly the Indian and Pakistani Seamen's Union of Malaya), the Chinese Seamen's Union, the Foochow Seamen's Union, the National Chinese Seamen's Union and the Singapore Seamen's Union.

106. *ST*, 30 November 1948, 8.

107. Maideen, *Nadra Tragedy*, 20–56, 105; Syed Muhd Khairuddin Aljunied, *Colonialism, Violence and Muslims in Southeast Asia: The Maria Hergogh Controversy and Its Aftermath* (New York: Routledge, 2009), 58; Koh et al., *Singapore*, 319.

108. Maideen, *Nadra Tragedy*, 80.

109. Maideen, *Nadra Tragedy*, 78, 201–202; see also Fatini Yaacob, *Natrah: In the Name of Love*, trans. Maryam Abdullah, Zurhaida Mohd Ismail and Flora

Emilia Abdullah (Kuala Lumpur: Institut Terjemahan Negara Malaysia and Penerbit Universiti Teknologi Malaysia, 2011), 66; Joe Conceicao, *Singapore and The Many-headed Monster: A Look at Racial Riots against a Socio-Historical Background—A New Perspective on the Riots of 1950, 1964 and 1969* (Singapore: Horizon Books, 2007).

110. For instance, the Government of Singapore issued a passport for Ramnath Biswas and introduced him as a British subject.

111. For more discussion about awarding citizenship rights, see Aiyar, *Indian Problems in Malaya*, 88–89, 145–148.

112. On the eve of decolonisation, Asia's potential leaders and representatives met at a conference at Purana Qila (Old Fort) in Delhi from March to April 1947. The conference participants encountered a crucial issue in determining citizenship and nationality rights and constituted a sub-committee to consider 'Racial Problems and Inter-Asian Migration'. The sub-committee sought two potential solutions for the citizenship rights of earlier migrants and their descendants and the control of future migration across Asia.

113. *Asian Relations: Being Report of the Proceedings and Documentation of the First Asian Relations Conference, New Delhi, March–April 1947* (New Delhi: Asian Relations Organization, 1948), 91–99.

114. C. M. Turnbull, 'Melaka under British Colonial Rule', in *Melaka: The Transformation of a Malay Capital c. 1400–1980, Vol. 1*, ed. Kernial Sing Sandhu and Paul Wheatley (Kuala Lumpur: Oxford University Press, 1983), 280–281.

115. C. M. Turnbull, 'Regionalism and Nationalism', in *The Cambridge History of Southeast Asia, Vol. 2, The Nineteenth and Twentieth Centuries*, ed. Nicholas Tarling (Cambridge: Cambridge University Press, 1992), 602.

116. Ampalavanar, *The Indian Minority*, 128; see also Cheah Boon Kheng, *Malaysia: The Making of Nation* (Singapore: Institute of Southeast Asian Studies, 2002).

117. Ampalavanar, *The Indian Minority*, 125; Hefner, Introduction, 29.

118. Yat Ming Loo, *Architecture and Urban Form in Kuala Lumpur: Race and Chinese Spaces in a Postcolonial City* (Surrey; Burlington: Ashgate Publishing Limited, 2013), 27. Knowledge of the Malay language was a requirement for Malay citizenship. Consequently, many language training centres were founded, and it became a lucrative commercial industry because most immigrants, including the Bengalis, rushed to learn the Malay language. Harper, 'Globalism and the Pursuit of Authenticity', 272.

119. Interview with Khatoon.

120. Interview with Mushahid Ali.

121. A recent example of how the Bangladeshi diaspora creates visible public space is forming of the All European Bangladeshi Association (AEBA) across European Union countries. See José Mapril, 'Making a "Bangladeshi Diaspora": Migration, Group Formation and Emplacement between Portugal and Bangladesh', *Migration Letters* 18, no. 1 (2021): 13–24.

122. Andrea Priori and José Mapril, 'Banglascapes in Southern Europe: Im-mobilities, Emplacements, Temporalities', *Migration Letters* 18, no. 1 (2021): 1–11.

123. Sugata Bose and Kris Manjapra (ed.), *Cosmopolitan Thought Zones: South Asia and the Global Circulation of Ideas* (London: Palgrave Macmillan, 2010).

124. There has been a decline in the use of the Bangla language among the descendants of the Bengalis who migrated to Malaysia. These weakening cultural bonds among the Bengali community are being referred to as 'less Bengaliness'.

Epilogue

Henri Lefebvre's ideas concerning the production of space have been the subject of nuanced debates since the 1970s. These debates primarily focused on the relationship between physical space, capitalist flows and conscious human actions. This book has combined Lefebvre's notion of the capitalist production of space with the idea of space produced by transnational mobility. The Bengali diasporas and their transnational community in Singapore, Malaysia and Brunei during the colonial and postcolonial periods form the central theme of this book, which has attempted to demonstrate the temporal and spatial dimensions of Bengali mobility, filling a significant gap in the historical migration literature on Asia.

This book has countered the impression that most South Asians in the Malay world were 'Indians', of whom the Tamils constituted a significant portion. The size of the Bengali community was remarkable. However, they were underestimated because many who settled in Malaysia and Singapore adopted Malay identities, forming a highly conspicuous and essential section of the middle classes. Their established 'networks' may promote present-day migration from Bangladesh, especially to Singapore and Malaysia. All these discussions have been categorised into two broad areas. Chapters 1–3 explored the background and processes of the emergence of the Bengali diasporic community in the Malay world and the masking of their identity within the generic term 'Indian'. The second set of aspects, spanning Chapters 4–8, offers a detailed understanding of facets of Bengali space-making in British Malaya, dealing with the professional world, the domain of petty traders and the spaces of politics and civil society.

Historical migrations of diverse ethnic groups from South Asia, as seen today, were generally described as 'Indian' in the historical literature. In recent years, the dominant 'Pan-Indian identity' has been dissected as heterogeneous, with a focus on ethnic and linguistic aspects.[1] In the context of recent trends in the studies of South Asian migration and diasporic communities within Asia, this book has explored the Bengali transnational community through multiple temporal and spatial contexts. Trans-regional connectivity between the Bay of Bengal and the Malay Sea has a historical pedigree. The British colonial authority introduced rules and regulations to govern the flow of human mobility. One system was developed in response to another in light of new challenges. Some of those rules and regulations still exist—for example, providing travel costs and accommodations to the migrating workers.

The colonial legacy of the Bengali migration is seen in the public space of the postcolonial Malay Peninsula. The colonial government prioritised the Bangla language and Bangla-speaking people in the running of the Government of Straits Settlements, which reflects the fact that the Bengalis constituted a large portion of the population. The Singapore Education Ministry selected Bangla as the second language in the South Asian language group during the postcolonial period. Some streets and places named after Bengali migrants in Malaysia and Singapore are marks of a successful spell of place-making by the Bengalis.

Though the majority of Bangla-speaking migrants are itinerant labourers and temporary workers in present-day Malaysia, Brunei and Singapore, this book has assembled a pool of data to show that over the past two centuries, at least, the Bengalis have established a diasporic community that features conspicuous intergenerational lineages and a long-term relationship with the Malay world with a stake in the political, sociocultural and occupational arenas.

Following their disembarkation in the port cities of the Malay Peninsula, Bengali migrants were involved in the skilled and unskilled professional world. Among other skilled professions, Bengali medical practitioners played a significant role in the history of public health services and the development of medical education in British Malaya. Bengali semi-skilled and unskilled labourers and petty traders created commercial spaces. Sunil Amrith has shown the space-making of Tamils primarily in rubber plantations, whereas Bengali semi-skilled workers were involved in harbour labourer and shop-house business, such as boarding houses, groceries, bookshops, hotels, corner shops and restaurants. In postcolonial times, the professional stakes of Bengali migrants were somewhat reversed. Most Bangla-speaking migrants were manual labourers in Malaysia, Singapore and Brunei, whereas only a small number worked in different skilled professions, such as teachers, engineers and doctors. In 2017, Bangladeshi migrants constituted the third-largest number of foreign workers in Brunei and Malaysia,[2] whereas the second-largest number was in Singapore in 2016, making them a significant part of Singapore's public space today.[3] In more recent times, however, Bangla-speaking migrants and diasporic members have again developed a remarkable presence in the skilled labour sector and the professional and commercial world. A growing group of wealthy Bangladeshis, primarily investors, have opted for the Second Home residency programme in Malaysia, sponsored by the Government of Malaysia. With more than 4,000 opting for this, the Bangladeshis are only the third largest group after Chinese and Japanese residents to avail themselves of this opportunity.[4] In Singapore, with assets worth about 1 billion dollars in 2020, a Bangladeshi-Singaporean businessman is the thirty-seventh richest person in Singapore, according to *Forbes*.[5]

The legacy of Bengali migration is found in the postcolonial geography of everyday life across the Malay world. For example, in Serangoon, many Bangla-speaking workers visit these areas and shops during weekends and public holidays (Figures A.7 and A.8). The Bangla-speaking diaspora runs mini-marts and restaurants filled with Bangladeshi products and dishes in these areas. In addition to Bengali dishes, those restaurants serve cuisines from other parts of Asia, including Punjabi, south Indian and Chinese food. The Bengali diaspora can taste the most popular Bangladeshi street foods in Singapore and Malaysia. Some outlets of Bangladeshi banks and departmental stores are often found in the Bengali enclaves in Malaysia and Singapore (Figures A.9 and A.10). Customers exchange pleasantries in Bangla, and popular Bangla music is played in shops and restaurants. These places were popularly known as 'Bangla Town' or 'Bangla Bazaar' in Malaysia and Singapore[6] and are considered transnational business places developed by Bangladeshi workers and professionals.

In the cultural domain, interracial marriage led to the emergence of cultural potpourri and created a social space in host countries. For example, M. A. Majid and Ismail Ballah's biracial marriages de-territorialised their ethnic identity over time. The language and territorial memories of the original home either became blurred or redefined in the everyday world of multiracial families during the postcolonial time.[7] Interracial marriages fostered the third space of cultural blending across the boundary of the nation states, which Homi K. Bhabha termed 'hybrid'.[8]

The Bangla-speaking community created cultural space amidst other diasporas in Malaysia and Singapore. The two earliest Bangla organisations, namely the Bangiya Moslem Sammilani, a Muslim-majority organisation from East Bengal, and the Malaysian Bengali Association, a primarily Hindu organisation from West Bengal, were founded in Singapore and Malaysia. These associations practised Bengali culture by organising different events, including Pahela Baishakh's celebration and arranging Bangla music concerts and theatres. Though the two Bangla-speaking communities shared a common cultural space, after 1947 and 1971, they performed sociocultural activities in parallel. However, the sense of 'otherness' has been primarily blurred in recent times; both communities watch Bangla TV channels aired from both West Bengal and Bangladesh and straddle each other's social spaces, although the political space of Bangladesh and India as nation states keep informing the daily debates.

As noted earlier, the existing scholarship on Bengali migration focuses on policies and socio-economic perspectives, such as the impact of remittances in the sending countries. This book fills the gap in existing scholarship and the literature on Bengali's historical mobility in the Malay world. It further contributes to the growing field of transnational mobility and space-making through the lens of the Bengali sojourns in the eastern Indian Ocean world. The misconception is prevalent in the Malay public space that the Bengalis are merely a homogeneous migrant labour pool from South Asia without any historical lineage is hopefully ameliorated to some extent by this book.

There are, however, limitations in this study. The Bengali migration to Brunei was quite unlike Singapore and Malaysia throughout the colonial and postcolonial periods. The unavailability of sources on the Bengali migration in Brunei makes the discussions less elaborate on Bengalis in Brunei. During my field trip, we interviewed some Bangladeshi migrants who had come to Brunei in the late 1980s, married Bruneian women and stayed there. This book has also been skewed towards being more descriptive than analytical, mainly because of the overwhelming pool of unused primary data. I have aimed to use this data to reconstruct a narrative of Bengali migration and diaspora in the Malay world, hoping that this will lead to further specialist work on the subject.

This book opens up multiple research windows onto colonial and postcolonial connections between Bengal and the Malay world and in the field of Asian history in general. How did Bengali transient migrants become a creole community during the colonial time? Tim Bunnell shows how the Malay seamen created transnational space by the Malay Club at Liverpool until its closure in 2007.[9] Like his study, could new studies focus on how the

Bengali seamen created spaces and benefited from Majid's seamen union, for example? Bengali male migrants married Malay women and adopted Malay culture and customs. It was a usual process to embrace the Malay language and culture. Therefore, new research may focus on forming these mixed ethno-religious families and their implications. Did the Bangla culture, through miscegenation, influence Malay culture and shape their politics and public space? These questions have been raised and interrogated, but more remains to be addressed. Further debates will enhance our knowledge of Bengali–Malay entanglement and South Asian migration and the broader area of intra-Asian mobility studies and connected histories in the Indian Ocean world.

Now back to the starting point of this book. The intention of writing this book was seeded when miscegenetic 'Free Bengalis' were found in Penang and Malacca in the *Crossing the Bay of Bengal* by Sunil Amrith. This book is profoundly evident in inter-Asia connectivity, particularly between Bengal and the Malay Peninsula from the early colonial till the late twentieth century. Such connectivity fostered regional trade, commerce, cultural exchange and human mobility. During the colonial period, Bengali migrants were mainly skilled professionals, such as engineers, doctors and legal practitioners. There were also some mine workers and convicts. These migrants created space in Malay sociocultural geography. However, the pattern of Bengali migration significantly shifted from Bengali skilled professionals to short-lived or transient workers during the postcolonial period. The social interactions between the descendants of Bengali colonial migrants and current temporary migrants are nominal, which makes them two worlds within the Malay world.

Notes

1. John Solomon, 'The Decline of Pan-Indian Identity and the Development of Tamil Cultural Separatism in Singapore, 1856–1965', *South Asia: Journal of South Asian Studies* 35, no. 2 (2012): 257–281; Amrith, 'Tamil Diasporas across the Bay of Bengal'; McCann, 'Sikhs and the City'.
2. Molly Moore, 'Number of Immigrants in Brunei 2005–2017', *Statista*, 21 October 2019, https://www.statista.com/statistics/697564/brunei-number-of-immigrants/, accessed 8 November 2020; R. Hirschmann, 'Number of Migrant Workers in Malaysia 2017, by Country of Origin', *Statista*, 6 April 2020, https://www.statista.com/statistics/711974/malaysia-number-of-migrant-workers-by-country-of-origin/, accessed 8 November 2020.

3. *Labor Migration in Asia: Increasing the Development Impact of Migration through Finance and Technology* (London: Asian Development Bank Institute, Organisation for Economic Co-operation and Development, and International Labour Organization, 2018), 6; Md Mizanur Rahman and Lian Kwen Fee, 'Bangladeshi Migrant Workers in Singapore: The View from Inside,' *Asia-Pacific Population Journal* 20, no. 1 (2005): 63.

4. *Financial Express*, 25 February 2019.

5. https://www.forbes.com/profile/muhammed-aziz-khan/?sh=103131f58ec0, accessed 15 February 2021.

6. Sultana, 'The Dynamics of a Multi-Cultural Society', 149; interview with Noorul Islam; interview with A. K. M. Mohsin.

7. Puru Shotam, *Negotiation Language, Constructing Race*, 150.

8. Homi K. Bhabha, *The Location of Culture* (New York; London: Routledge, 1994).

9. Tim Bunnell, *From World City to the World in One City: Liverpool through Malay Lives* (Oxford: Wiley-Blackwell, 2016).

Appendix

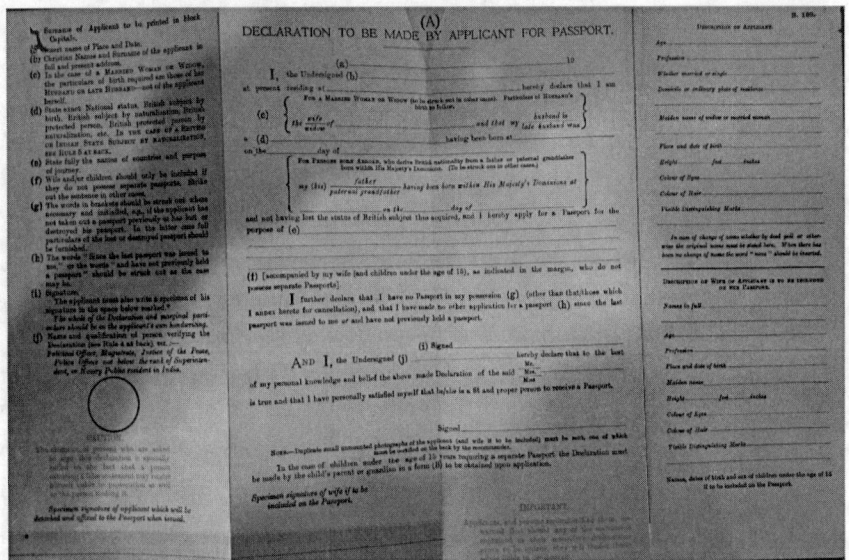

Figure A.1   Passport of a British subject in 1940

Source: National Archives of Bangladesh, Bundle 4, Proceedings B, List 95, Dept. and Br.: Emigration, period 1938–40, Wooden Bundle.

PASSPORT REGULATIONS.

1. Applications for Indian Passports must be made in the prescribed form, printed on the back of these regulations, and submitted either direct or through the local authority—

    (a) in the case of a resident in British India, to the Provincial Government or Local Administration concerned.

    (b) in the case of a resident in an Indian State, to the Political Officer concerned.

2. The charge for an Indian Passport is Rs. 6. (Payable either in Cash or in Postage Stamps).

3. Indian Passports are granted to :—

    (a) British subjects by birth.

    (b) Wives and widows of such persons.

    (c) British subjects by naturalization.

    (d) British-protected persons.

A married woman is deemed to be a subject of the State of which her husband is for the time being a subject.

* 4. Passports are granted upon the production of a declaration by the applicant (in the case of a child under 15 requiring a separate Passport, by the child's parent or guardian) in the prescribed form of application verified by a declaration made by a *Political Officer, Magistrate, Justice of the Peace, Police Officer not below the rank of Superintendent*, or *Notary Public*, resident in India. If possible the declaration should be signed by an Officer of the district in which the applicant is resident. Otherwise the issue of a Passport may be delayed while enquiries are being made from the local authorities.

5. If the applicant for a Passport be a British or Indian State subject by naturalization, the certificate of naturalization must be forwarded with the form of application to the Officer empowered to grant the Passport. It will be returned with the Passport to the applicant through the person who may have verified the declaration.

British subjects by naturalization will be described as such in their Passports, *which will be issued subject to the necessary qualifications.*

6. Small duplicate unmounted photographs (size approximately two and three quarter inches by two inches) of the applicant (and wife, if to be included) must be forwarded with the application for a Passport, one of which must be certified on the back by the person verifying the declaration made in the application form.

7. Indian Passports are not available beyond five years from date of issue. They may be renewed for a further maximum period of five years after which fresh Passports must be obtained. The fee for renewal is Re. 1 for each year, or portion of a year, for which the Passport is renewed.

8. Passports cannot be issued or renewed on behalf of persons already abroad: such persons should apply for Passports to the London Foreign Office or nearest British Mission or Consulate. Passports must not be sent out of India by post.

9. In the case of an applicant for a Passport being unable to write English, a transcription in English should be placed below the applicant's vernacular signature in the form of application. In the case of an illiterate person, a thumb impression should be substituted for a signature on the form of application, which should be certified by the person verifying the declaration.

10. The Passport is only available for travel to the countries named on p. 4, but may be endorsed for additional countries. The possession of a Passport so endorsed does not exempt the holder from compliance with any immigration laws in force in British or Foreign countries, or from the necessity of obtaining a Visa when required.

11. Passports endorsed as valid for the British Empire are also available for travelling to territory under British protection or mandate, not, however, including Palestine or Transjordan, for which the Passport must be especially endorsed, or the Aden Protectorate, for which both an endorsement and a Visa are required.

12. British subjects resident abroad should in all cases register their names and addresses at the nearest British Consulate. Such registration constitutes the most ready means in emergency or difficulty of enabling all proper assistance or advice to be afforded them. Changes of address in or departure from the country of residence should also be notified to the Consulate.

Persons merely passing through a foreign country or making a short stay there are not regarded as residents, and need not register unless their stay exceeds three months.

* FOOTNOTE.—Parda-nashin or gosha women desirous of travelling from India to Malaya, the Straits Settlements, the East Africa Protectorate, Uganda, Zanzibar, Mauritius, the Nyasaland Protectorate and the Union of South Africa are exempted from the necessity of attaching their photographs to their applications for passports, or of appearing in person before the passport issuing authorities.

MFP—666 S&P—(M.1935)—5.12-38—30,000.

Figure A.2   Passport of a British subject in 1940

Source: National Archives of Bangladesh, Bundle 4, Proceedings B, List 95, Dept and Br.: Emigration, period 1938–40, Wooden Bundle.

Figure A.3 Singtel advertised in Bangla to attract the current Bengali migrants

Source: Photo by Gazi Mizanur Rahman, Lembu Road, and Farrer MRT Station, Serangoon, Singapore, August 2018.

Figure A.4 Starhub advertised in Bangla to attract the current Bengali migrants

Source: Photo by Gazi Mizanur Rahman, Lembu Road, and Farrer MRT Station, Serangoon, Singapore, August 2018.

Figure A.5 A Bengali coffee hawker and his customer, 1900

Source: Photo Accession No: 49481, Anthony Wharton Collection, Courtesy of National Archives of Singapore.

Bengali bread seller, Singapore.

Figure A.6   A Bengali bread seller, 1900

Source: Photo Accession No: 28666, Anthony Wharton Collection, courtesy of National Archives of Singapore.

Figure A.7   Bengali migrants on Lembu Road and Desker Road areas in Singapore on Sunday (weekend)

Source: Photo by Gazi Mizanur Rahman, Serangoon, Singapore, August 2018.

Figure A.8   Bengali street food shop at Sengkurong, Brunei

Source: Photo by Gazi Mizanur Rahman, Sengkurong, Brunei, January 2020.

Figure A.9 A Bangladeshi restaurant, Jalan Tun Tan Siew Sin, Kuala Lumpur, Malaysia

Source: Photo by Gazi Mizanur Rahman, Kuala Lumpur, Malaysia, November 2018.

Figure A.10 A Bengali boutique shop, Serangoon area, Singapore

Source: Photo by Gazi Mizanur Rahman, Serangoon Area, Singapore, August 2018.

Glossary

alam melayu	Malay world
Allah-hu-Akbar	Islamic phrase, Allah is the Greatest
amah	domestic assistance
Anugerah Cinta Mutiara	Women of True Beauty Award
Anushilan Samity	Bodybuilding Society, a revolutionary group in Bengal
Arya Samaj Sangam	Association for the Aryan People
baboo/babu	Bengali gentry in the colonial period
Bahasa Melayu	Malay language
Bagha Jatin	Byname of Jatin Mukherjee, a Bengali revolutionary during the early twentieth century. He was described as ferocious like a tiger.
Balak Sena	a young men's wing of the Indian National Army
Balika Sena	a young women's wing of the Indian National Army
Bangalitto	Bengaliness
Bangiya Moslem Sammilani	Bengal Muslim Association
Banglar kantha	the voice of Bengal
Belabab basar	eldest child
Belabab tengah	middle or second child
Belabab damit	youngest child
bhoo-paryatak	world traveller

chaprasi	an attendant, orderly, or messenger in the household of a landowner or of an office
chintz	a printed or hand-painted cotton fabric
corgi	a mercantile term for a score or a bundle of twenty pieces of cloth
dacoity	robbery
Datuk/Dato	a title given to a person upon being conferred with certain orders of honour in Brunei and Malaysia
deshabandhu	friend of the nation
dhoba/dhobis	washerman or washerwoman
doa selamat	a special supplication to Allah
doodhwallah/gowala	herdsmen
dowa	offering prayers in thanksgiving
duffadar	A non-commissioned officer in the former Indian army or police. Presently, this rank is found in village policing at a union council level in Bangladesh.
iftar	the breaking of fasting in the month of Ramadan
imam	person who leads prayers in the mosque
jamadar	a junior officer or a person who supervises a staff of servants
janazah	funeral prayer
jawi pekan/jawi peranakan	offspring of a Malay mother and a Chinese or Indian father
jeta junaza	living tomb
jugantar	a secret revolutionary group in Bengal
kala pani	a taboo referring to ill fortune because of crossing a sea
kampung/kampong	village or community in the Malay world
kangany	a form of labour recruitment under British colonial rule in parts of Southeast Asia

khalur	a bicycle carrier
kling	The word might be corrupted from Kalinga, a region of Odisha and northern part of Andhra Pradesh. The people who came from Kalinga might have been known as *kling*.
lascar	a sailor from the Indian subcontinent, Southeast Asia and the Arab world
mahalla	a settlement or unit of a residential area
makan	eat/eating
manus	human beings
Mayur nreetha	peacock dance
meelad shareef	observance of the supplication to Allah for the birthday of Prophet Muhammad (Peace Be Upon Him), which is commemorated in the Arabic month of Rabi' al-awwal
merdeka	independence of the Federation of Malaya
Monipuri nreetha	a special dance of the Monipuri ethnic family in Bangladesh and India
Nakshi kathar math	field of the embroidered quilt—a dramatised Bengali verse narrative
Netaji	byname of Subhas Chandra Bose
Pahela Baishakh	Bengali New Year
petugas lapangan	field agent/officer
rai sahib	a title of honour issued during the era of British colonial rule in India
raja	hereditary ruler or king
Sapurey nreetha	snake charming/snake dance
sardar/sirdar	Commander (literally); however, in the nineteenth century, a *sardar* was a leader who worked as an intermediary for indentured labour migration across the Indian Ocean
sareng/sukani	captain of crews or chief of sailors
shikari	hunter

tambi	an office server
temenggung	chief of public security
tindal	a petty officer
tom-toms	native drums
ulki/godna/godena/tattoo	stamping
'Vande Mataram'	A Bangla poem written by Bankim Chandra Chatterjee. The title means 'mother, I bow to thee'.

Bibliography

Primary Source

Manuscripts

National Archives of Malaysia, Headquarters, Kuala Lumpur

Public Archives, State Records

1957/0054480W, Application from Mr Gheewala, Bengali Interpreter of Courts for the Post of Munshi to Selangor Police Force, 17 January 1895.

1957/0101700W, Bengali Cattle Keepers in Petaling Hills Land, Selangor, 11 March 1902. 1957/0269544W, Debiting to Town Improvements Vote $7,000 Being the Estimated Cost of Relief Work at Kampong Bengali, 11 February 1931.

1957/0361064W, Request That a Bangalee [Bengali] Interpreter Be Appointed at Sungai Petani Court, 1 February 1915.

1957/0361245W, Lim Peng Hooi Ketua Pajak Chukai Chukai Baling Teriak Kata Bengali K. G. Laboomall Bawak Masuk Barang2 Perniagaan Dengan Parcel Itu Tiada Mau Bayar Chukai Kepada Nia, 27 February 1915.

1957/0361860W, Asks That ACP (Assistant Corporal Police) Be Instructed to Supply Police Bengali Interpreter When Required by the Courts, 28 April 1915.

1957/0363247W, Applies for the Post of Bengali Interpreter, 25 November 1915.

1957/0597789W, Refusal of the Captain of the S. S. 'Hong Ho' to Allow Passage to a Bengali British Subject Who Was Ill. Applies for Instructions in the Matter, High Commission Office, Malaya, 12 May 1914.

1987/0001642P, Culvert at Jalan Padang Bengali at Telok Ayer Tawar, Province Wellesley (N), 20 May 1963.

1987/0003005P, JKK 48/81 Mengambil Alih Untuk Penyelenggaraan Jalan-Jalan dan Parit di atas lot-lot 1113, Jalan KG Bengali, Butterworth, 24 November 1981.

2007/0034044W, Bengali Mosque Leth Street, Penang, 1958, 31 December 1958.

National Archives of Bangladesh, Dhaka

Wooden Bundle, Government of Bengal and East Pakistan (1858–1964)

Bundle 1, Proceedings A, List 25, Dept and Branch-Emigration, 1860–1867.
Bundle 1, Proceedings B, List 25, Dept and Branch-Emigration, 1889–1930.
Bundle 3, Proceedings B, List 95, Dept and Branch-Emigration, 1936–38.
Bundle 4, Proceedings B, List 95, Dept and Branch-Emigration, 1938–40.
Bundle 6, Proceedings A, List 25, Dept and Branch-Emigration, January 1875–June 1877.
Bundle 14, Proceedings A, List 25, Dept and Branch-Emigration, 1901–04.
Bundle 17, Proceedings A, List 25, Dept and Branch-Emigration, 1911–1929.

Catalogue of Printed Proceedings/A Proceedings: 1858–1955

Dept: General, Br.: Emigration, Vol. no. 102-492, List no. 5.2, 1878–1911.
Dept: Revenue, Br.: Emigration, May 1921–September 1943.
Dept: Commerce, Br.: Emigration, January 1918–November 1920.
Dept: General, Br.: Emigration/and Miscellaneous, January 1911–August 1913.
Dept: Finance, Br.: Emigration, September 1913–December 1916.

National Archives of Singapore, Singapore

Straits Settlements Original Correspondence

Mr M. A. Majid, Indian Employees Bureau: Alleged Difficulties Experienced by Bengali Lascar Seamen in Obtaining Employment in Singapore, Acc. No. 273/639/1-14 (CO), Covering Date - 01/01/1938–31/12/1938, Image number: D2016050717.

Secret-Migrated Archives

FCO 141/14392, Activities of the Indian National Army (INA) and the Indian Independence League (IIL). Secret-Migrated Archives, D2014040111; 01/01/1945–31/12/1946.
WO 203/2298, Malaya: Disposal, Status and Brief History of the INA; 01/08/1945–31/08/1945; Microfilm-NAB 2147.
WO 208/803, Indian Traitors and Fifth Columnists Trained by the Japanese: Formation of Indian Independent League and Indian National Army; 1942–1945; Image: NAB 2575.

Speeches and Press Releases

Addressed by Lee Kuan Yew, 19 February 1966.

Addressed by Lee Kuan Yew, 23 December 1977.

Addressed by Lee Kuan Yew, 14 April 1978.

Oral History Interview

Bhattachary, Kishore. 8 March 2010, Acc. No. 003490.

Bong, Anthony Kim Siong. 18 February 1993, Acc. No. 001398.

Chakravarti, Salil Kumar. 3 August 2007, Acc. No. 003209.

Damodaran s/o K. Kesavan. 9 November 1981, Acc. No. 000127.

Goh, Sin Ee. 8 December 1982, Acc. No. 000225.

Gupta, Sudhansu Ranjan Das. 16 October 2014, Acc. No. 003928.

Jumabhoy, Rajabali. 9 September 1981, Acc. No. 000074.

Kannusamy s/o Pakirisamy. 17 November 1983, Acc. No. 000081.

Karmakar, Ronendra. 10 October 1983, Acc. No. 000343.

Kothair, Girishchandra. 14 October 2013, Acc. No. 003824.

Lourdes, Gabriel. 20 November 1984, Acc. No. 000509.

Menon, Sukumara Ittamuittil. 9 May 1985, Acc. No. 000557.

Naidu, Lakshmi. 27 November 1981, Acc. No. 000110.

Nair, Chengara Veetil Devan. 9 January 1981, Acc. No. 000049.

Palanivelu, Natesan. 10 October 1985, Acc. No. 000588.

Pillay, V. Kanda. 8 December 2006, Acc. No. 003106.

Rajan, Soundara. 25 November 1987, Acc. No. 000845.

Samosir, Nora Anny. 13 May 2010, Acc. No. 001811.

Selvadurai, Pathmanaban. 10 September 2002, Acc. No. 002699.

Singh, Mohinder. 24 June 1985, Acc. No. 000546.

Singh, Seva. 11 April 1984, Acc. No. 000418.

Sinha, Hena. October–November 1983, Acc. No. 000354.

Sivadas s/o Sankaran. 1 September 1995, Acc. No. 001681.

British Library

India Office Records and Private Papers

IOR/F/4/1184/30747, Correspondence of the Bengal Government with the
    Penang Government and the Government of the Dutch East Indies
    Regarding the Removal from Bencoolen of Certain Free Bengalis,
    Emancipated Caffrees and Convicts, September 1826–March 1829.

Interviews (with Gazi Md Mizanur Rahman)

Ali, Mushahid. 19 July 2018, Far East Plaza, Singapore.
Davenport, Dolly Sinha. 23 July 2018, Singapore.
Haque, Anwarul. 25 July 2018, Guild House, National University of Singapore.
Islam, Noorul. 11 July 2018, ANA Book Store, Far East Plaza, Singapore.
Khatoon, Shafiya. 1 August 2018, Universiti Brunei Darussalam, Brunei.
Mohsin, A. K. M. 16 July 2018, Rowell Road, Singapore.

Newspapers (The Year at the Right Represents the First Issuing Place and Date)

Advertiser, Adelaide, South Australia, 1858.
Asia One, Singapore, 1998.
Banglar Kantha, a Bengali newspaper published in Singapore since 2006.
Business Times, Singapore, 1976.
Daily Advertiser, Singapore, 1890.
Daily Mail, Australia, 1903.
Daily Telegraph, Sydney, 1879.
Eastern Daily Mail and Straits Morning Advertiser, Singapore, 1905.
Financial Express, Bangladesh, 1993.
Harian Metro, Malaysia, 1991.
Malaya Tribune, Singapore and Malaysia, 1914.
Mid-Day Herald and Daily, Straits Settlements, Singapore, 1894.
Morning Tribune, Singapore, 1927.
New Nation, Singapore, 1971.
New Paper, Singapore, 1988.
Nikkei Asian Review, Japan, 1876.
Pelita Brunei, Brunei Darussalam, 2010.
Singapore Chronicle and Commercial Register, Singapore, 1824.
Singapore Free Press, Singapore, relaunched in 1946.
Singapore Free Press and Mercantile Advertiser, Singapore, 1835.
Singapore Free Press and Mercantile Advertiser, Singapore (Weekly), 1884.
Star Online, Penang, 1971.
Straits Observer Singapore, Singapore, 1874.
Straits Times, Singapore, 1845.
Straits Times Overland Journal, Singapore, 1868.
Straits Times Weekly Issue, Singapore, 1868.

Sunday Tribune, Singapore, 1933.
Telegraph, India, 1982.
Today, Singapore, 2000.
Toodyay Herald, Western Australia, 1912.
World's News, Sydney, 1901.

Emails

Gerhard Keiper, Political Archive of the Federal Foreign Office, Berlin. 13 May 2019.
Mushahid Ali, Senior Fellow at S. Rajaratnam School of International Studies, Singapore. 26 November 2018.

Government Published Books and Reports

A Bengal Civilian. *De Zieke Reiziger, or Rambles in Java and the Straits in 1852.* London: Simpkin, Marshall and Co., 1853.
Allen, B. C. *Eastern Bengal District Gazetteers: Dacca.* Allahabad: The Pioneer Press, 1912.
Annals of Indian Administration 1856. Serampore: Printed by Marshall D'cruz, 1856.
Annals of Indian Administration in the Year 1859–60. Serampore: Marshall D'cruz, 1860.
Appendix to the Report on the Affairs of the East India Company, Volume 3, External and Internal Commerce of Bengal, Madras, and Bombay. London: The House of Commons, 1831.
Asian Relations: Being Report of the Proceedings and Documentation of the First Asian Relations Conference, New Delhi, March–April 1947. New Delhi: Asian Relations Organization, 1948.
At the Crossroads: Report on the Action Committee on Indian Education. Singapore: Promotion & Sales Center, 1991.
Bartholomew, J. G. *Constable's Hand Atlas of India.* Westminster: Archibald Constable & Company, 1893.
Blue Book for the Year 1888. Singapore: Government Printing Office, 1889.
Blue Book for the Year 1904. Singapore: Government Printing Office, 1905.
Bort, Balthasar. *Report of Governor Balthasar Bort on Malacca 1678.* Translated (from the Dutch) by M. J. Bremner with an introduction and notes by C. O. Blagden. *Journal of the Malayan Branch of the Royal Asiatic Society* 5, no. 1 (1927): 1–232.

Braddell, Roland. *The Lights of Singapore*. London: Methuen, 1934.

Campos, J. J. A. *History of the Portuguese in Bengal with Maps and Illustrations*. Calcutta; London; Sydney: Butterworth & Co., 1919.

Cavenagh, Orfeur. *Report on the Progress of the Straits Settlement, from 1859–60 to 1866–67*. Singapore: Straits Government Press, 1867.

Census of the British Empire 1901. London: Darling & Sons, 1906.

Chakravarti, P. C. 'Economic Conditions'. In *The History of Bengal, Vol. 1, Hindu Period*, edited by R. C. Majumder, 642–669. Dacca: University of Dacca, 1943.

Clay, A. L. *Principal Heads of the History and Statistic of the Dacca Division*. Calcutta: Calcutta Central Press Company Limited, 1868.

Crawfurd, John. *Journal of an Embassy from the Governor-General of India to the Court of Siam and Cochin China: Exhibiting a View of the Actual State of Those Kingdoms*. Vol. 1. London: Henry Colburn and Richard Bentley, 1830.

Dohfar, Ibrahim bin Mohamed. *State of Brunei Annual Report on the Social and Economic Progress of the People of Brunei for the Year 1941*. N.p., 1942.

Earl, Windsor. *The Eastern Seas, or Voyages and Adventures in the Indian Archipelago in 1832–33–34*. London: W. H. Allen, 1837.

Engagement of Non-resident Bangladeshis (NRBs) in National Development: Strategies, Challenges and Way Forward. Dhaka: Economic Relations Division (ERD), Ministry of Finance, Government of Bangladesh, 2018.

Furnivall, J. S. *Netherlands India: A Study of Plural Economy*. New York: Cambridge University Press, 1944.

Gait, E. A. *Census of India 1901, Vol. VI, Bengal, Part I, Report*. Calcutta: Bengal Secretariat Press, 1902.

———. *Census of India 1911, Vol. I, India, Part II, Tables*. Calcutta: Superintendent Government Printing, 1913.

———. *Report on the Census of Bengal, 1901: Chapter I of Administrative Volume with Census Code*. Calcutta: Bengal Secretariat Press, 1902.

General Report on the Administration of the Several Presidencies and Provinces of British India during the year 1859–60. Vol. 1. Calcutta: Bengal Printing Company Limited, 1861.

Graham, Maria. *Journal of a Residence in India*. Edinburgh: George Ramsey & Co., 1813.

Grierson, G. A. *The Administration of the Lower Provinces of Bengal from 1882–83 to 1886–87*. Calcutta: Bengal Secretariat Press, 1887.

Holloway, C. P. *Tabular Statements on the Commerce of Singapore, during the Years 1823–24 to 1839–40 Inclusive. Shewing the Nature and Extent of the*

Trade, Carried on with each Country and State. Compiled from Official Documents. Singapore: Singapore Free Press, 1842.

Hunter, W. W. *A Statistical Account of Bengal.* Vol. 5. London: Trubner and Co., 1875.

Hutton, J. H. *Census of India, 1931, Vol. I, India, Part I, Report.* Delhi: Manager of Publications, 1933.

Indian Emigration (Bengal) Manual 1926. Calcutta: Bengal Government Press, 1926.

John, Horace St. *The Indian Archipelago: Its History and Present State.* Vol. 2. London: Longman, 1853.

Little India: Historic District. Singapore: Urban Redevelopment Authority, 1995.

Lowis, C. C. *Census of India 1901, Vol. XIIA, Burma, Part II, Imperial Tables.* Rangoon: Office of the Superintendent of Government Printing, 1902.

Makepeace, W., Gilbert E. Brooke and Roland St J. Braddell (eds.). *One Hundred Years of Singapore: Being Some Account of the Capital of the Straits Settlements from Its Foundation by Sir Stamford Raffles on the 6th February 1819 to the 6th February 1919.* Vol. 1. London: John Murray, 1921.

Marriott, H. *Report on the Census of the Straits Settlements, Taken on the 10th March 1911.* Singapore: Government Print Office, 1911.

McNair, J. F. A., and W. D. Bayliss. *Prisoners Their Own Warders: A Record of the Convicts Prison at Singapore in the Straits Settlements Established 1825, Discontinued 1873, Together with a Cursory History of the Convict Establishments at Bencoolen, Penang, and Malacca from the Year 1797.* Westminster: Archibald Constable and Co., 1899.

Merewether, E. M. *Report on the Census of the Straits Settlements, 1891.* Singapore: Government Printing Office, 1892.

Nair, P. Thankappan (ed.). *Calcutta in the Nineteenth Century: Company's Days.* Calcutta: Firma K. L. M. Private Limited, n.d.

Nathan, J. E. *The Census of British Malaya, 1921.* London: Dunstable & Watford, 1922.

Newbold, T. J. *Political and Statistical Account of the British Settlements in the States of Malacca, Pinang, and Singapore with a History of the Malayan States on the Peninsula of Malacca.* Vol. 1. London: John Murray, 1839.

O'Malley, L. S. S. *Census of India, 1911, Vol. V, Bengal, Bihar and Orissa and Sikkim, Part I, Report.* Calcutta: Bengal Secretariat Book Depot, 1913.

Parkinson, C. Northcote. *Trade in Eastern Seas 1793–1813.* Cambridge: Cambridge University Press, 1937.

Phipps, John. *A Practical Treatise on the China and Eastern Trade: Comprising the Commerce of Great Britain and India, Particularly Bengal and Singapore, with China and the Eastern Islands.* London: W. H. Allen & Co., 1836.

Report on the Administration of Bengal 1873–74. Calcutta: Bengal Secretariat Press, 1875.

Report on the Administration of Bengal 1884–85. Calcutta: Bengal Secretariat Press, 1886.

Report on the Administration of Bengal 1904–1905. Calcutta: Bengal Secretariat Book Depot, 1906.

Report on the Census of Population 1971. Bandar Seri Begawan: Star Press, 1972.

Report on the State of Brunei for the Year 1911. Singapore: Government Printing Press, 1912.

Report on the State of Brunei for the Year 1924. Singapore: Government Printing Press, 1925.

Report on the State of Brunei for the Year 1947. Singapore: Government Printing Press, 1948.

Report on the State of Brunei for the Year 1923. Singapore: Government Printing Press, 1924.

Report on the State of Brunei for the Year 1946. Kuala Lumpur: Malayan Union Government Press, 1948.

Report on the State of Brunei for the Year 1947. Singapore: Malaya Publishing House, 1948.

Report on the State of Brunei for the Year 1959. Kuala Belait: Brunei Press Limited, 1961.

Report on the State of Brunei for the Year 1961–1962. Kuala Belait: Brunei Press Limited, 1964.

Report on the State of Brunei for the Year 1964. Brunei: Government Printing Press, 1966.

Report on the State of Brunei for the Year 1966. Brunei: Government Printing Press, 1968.

Report on the State of Brunei for the Year 1968. Brunei: Government Printing Press, 1969.

Report on the State of Brunei for the Year 1969. Brunei: Government Printing Press, 1970.

Risley, H. H., and E. A. Gait. *Census of India, 1901, Vol. I, India, Part I, Report.* Calcutta: Office of the Superintendent of Government Printing, 1903.

Smith, Samuel, and Co. *The Bengal Almanac for 1845 with a Companion and Appendix.* Calcutta: Bengal-Hurkaru and Chronicle Press, 1845.

Statistics on Marriages and Divorces, 2017. Singapore: Department of Statistics, Ministry of Trade and Industry, 2017.

Straits Settlements Blue Books 1871. Singapore: Government Printing Office, 1872.

Summary Tables of the Brunei Population Census of 1981. Negara Brunei Darussalam: Ministry of Finance and Economy, 1981.

Taylor, James. *A Sketch of the Topography and Statistics of Dacca.* Calcutta: Military Orphan Press, 1840.

The Acts of the Supreme Government, Part I, 1834 and 1835, in Continuation of the Regulations of Supreme Government from 1793 to 1834. Calcutta: Baptist Mission Press Edition, 1836.

The Bengal and Agra Annual Guide and Gazetteer for 1841, Vol 1. Calcutta: William Rushton and Co., 1841.

The Indian Steam-Ships Act, 1884, as Modified up to the 1st July 1890, Office of the Superintendent. Calcutta: Government Printing, 1890.

The Regulations and Laws Enacted by the Governor General in Council, for the Civil Government of the Whole of the Territories under the Presidency of Fort William in Bengal. Vol. 7. Calcutta: Baptist Mission Press, 1828.

Tufo, M. V. del. *Malaya, Comprising the Federation of Malaya and the Colony of Singapore: A Report on the 1947 Census of Population.* London: Crown Agents for the Colonies, 1949.

Vlieland, C. A. *British Malaya [The Colony of the Straits Settlements and the Malay States under British Protection, Namely the Federated States of Perak, Selangor, Negeri Sembilan and Pahang and the States of Johore, Kedah, Kelantan, Trengganu, Perlis and Brunei: A Report on the 1931 Census and on Certain Problems of Vital Statistics].* London: Crown Agents for the Colonies, 1932.

Warren, Samuel. *The Opium Question.* London: James Ridgway, Piccadilly, 1840.

Published Books and Articles

Aiyar, K. A. Neelakandha. *Indian Problems in Malaya: A Brief Survey in Relation to Emigration.* Kuala Lumpur: The India Office, 1938.

Clifford, Hugh. *Further India: Burma, Malaya, Siam, and Indo-China.* London: Lawrence and Bullen Ltd, 1904.

Cortesao, Armando (trans. and ed.). *The Suma Oriental of the Tome Pires: An Account of the East, from the Red Sea to Japan, Written in Malacca, and India in 1512–1515.* Vol. 1. London: The Hakluyt Society, 1944.

Dutt, Romesh. *The Economic History of India: Under Early British Rule (From the Rise of the British Power in 1757 to the Accession of Queen Victoria in 1837), Vol. 1.* Trench, Trubner: Kegan Paul, 1902.

Furnivall, J. S. *Colonial Policy and Practice: A Comparative Study of Burma and Netherlands India.* Cambridge: Cambridge University Press, 1948.

Leyden, John (trans.). *Malay Annals.* With an introduction by Sir Thomas Stamford Raffles. London: Longman, Hust, Rees, Orme, and Brown, 1821.

Majumder, R. C. *Ancient Indian Colonies in the Far East, Vol. 2, Suvarnadvipa, Part 1.* Dacca: Asoke Humar Majumdar, 1937.

———. 'The Palas'. In *The History of Bengal, Vol. 1, Hindu Period*, edited by R. C. Majumder, 94–166. Dacca: University of Dacca, 1943.

Majumder, R. C., and D. C. Ganguly. 'Bengalis Outside Bengal'. In *The History of Bengal, Vol. 1, Hindu Period*, edited by R. C. Majumder, 670–689. Dacca: University of Dacca, 1943.

Mookerji, Radhakumud. *Indian Shipping: A History of the Sea-borne Trade and Maritime Activity of the Indians from the Earliest Times.* Bombay; Calcutta; London; New York: Longmans, Green and Co., 1912.

Nanjundan, S. *Indians in Malayan Economy.* Delhi: Manager Publications, 1950.

Shellabear, W. G. (trans.). *The Autobiography of Munshi Abdullah Abdul Kadir (1796–1854).* Singapore: Methodist Publishing House, 1918.

Shirras, G. Findlay. 'Indian Migration'. In *International Migrations, Volume 2: Interpretations*, edited by Walter F. Willcox, 591–616. Cambridge, MA: National Bureau of Economic Research, 1931.

Stevens, F. G. 'A Contribution to the Early History of Prince of Wales' Island'. *Journal of the Malayan Branch of the Royal Asiatic Society* 7, no. 3 (108) (1929): 377–414.

Swettenham, Frank. *British Malaya: An Account of the Origin and Progress of British Influence in Malaya.* London; New York: John Lane Company, 1907.

Thompson, Virginia. *Postmortem on Malaya.* New York: The MacMillan Company, 1943.

Williams, Eric. *Capitalism and Slavery.* Chapel Hill: University of North Carolina Press, 1944.

Winstedt, Sir Richard. *Malaya and Its History.* London: Hutchinson House, 1951.

Wright, Arnold (ed.). *Twentieth Century Impressions of British Malaya: Its History, People, Commerce, Industries, and Resources.* London: Lloyd's Greater Britain Publishing Company Ltd, 1908.

————. *Twentieth Century Impressions of Siam: Its History, People, Commerce, Industries, and Resources*. London: Lloyd's Greater Britain Publishing Company, Ltd, 1908.

Books and Periodicals in Vernacular Language (Bangla)

Biswas, Ramnath. *Bhavoghurer Bileth Jatra* [A Wanderer's Journey to Britain]. Calcutta: Dasgupta and Co. Ltd, n.d.

————. *Malaysia Vromon* [Travel to Malaysia]. Calcutta: Prokasok Sattonarayan Bhattacharjo, 1949.

Bangla Academy Bayaboharik Bangla Abhidhan [Bangla Academy Practical Bangla Language Dictionary]. Bangla Academy: Dhaka, 2015.

Chakrabarty, Adhir. 'Bangla o Bahirbissho: Prag Uponibesik Kal' [Bengal and Overseas: Pre-colonial Era]'. In *Itihas Onusshandhan No. 4*, edited by Gautam Chattopadhyay, 51–82. Calcutta: K. P. Bagchi and Co., 1989.

Chattopadhyay, Suniti Kumar. 'Jabodeeper Path e' [On the Way to Java]. In *Probashi, Monthly Magazine*, edited by Ramanando Chattopadhyay, vol. 28:1, 142–145, 266–273, 480–487, 594–602, 761–768. Calcutta: Indian Press, 1335 (BS).

————. 'Jabodeeper Path e' [On the Way to Java]. In *Probashi, Monthly Magazine*, edited by Ramanando Chattopadhyay, vol. 28:2, 270–278, 579–586, 867–888. Calcutta, 1335 (BS).

Das, Anil. 'Bengali Kobi o Bideshi Parjatok der Dristy te Bengalir Banijjo' [Bengali's Trade in the Lens of Bengali Poets and Foreign Travellers]. In *Itihas Onusshandhan, No. 4*, edited by Gautam Chottopadhay, 107–177. Calcutta: K. P. Bagchi and Co., 1989.

Das, Gyanendra Mohon. *Banger Bahire Bangali* [Bengalis Outside Bengal]. Part III. Calcutta: Indian Publishing House, 1931.

Ghosh, Jyotish Chandra. *Bishwa Bhramone Rabindranath* [Rabindranath in World Voyage]. Calcutta: Sri Guru Library, 1942.

Gupta, Ashin Das. *Vanghap Sagar* [The Bay of Bengal]. Calcutta: Pritikxan Publication, 1989.

Secondary Sources (Books, Articles and Chapters)

Abdullah, Muzaffar Desmond Tate, Khoo Kay Kim and Selvamany Gabriel. *The History of Medicine in Malaysia: The Foundation Years*. Malaysia: Academy of Medicine of Malaysia, 2005.

Adams, Caroline. *Across Seven Seas and Thirteen Rivers: Life Stories of Pioneer Sylheti Settlers in Britain*. London: Thap, 1987.

Ahsanuddin, Zahida. *India's Freedom Struggle and the Great INA: Memoirs of Maj. Gen Mohammad Zaman Kiani*. New Delhi: Reliance Publishing House, 1994.

Akyeampong, Emmanuel. 'Slavery, Indentured Labor, and the Making of a Transnational World'. In *A Companion to Diaspora and Transnationalism*, edited by Ato Quayson and Girish Daswani, 163–171. West Sussex: Blackwell Publishing Ltd, 2013.

Alatas, Syed Hussein. *The Myth of the Lazy Native: A Study of the Image of the Malays, Filipinos and Javanese from the 16th to the 20th Century and Its Function in the Ideology of Colonial Capitalism*. London: Frank Cass, 1977.

Alavi, Seema. 'Little Men between Big Empires: Muslim Cosmopolitanism in the Age of Imperial Expansion'. In *Oceanic Islam: Muslim Universalism and European Imperialism*, edited by Sugata Bose and Ayesha Jalal, 100–124. New Delhi: Bloomsbury, 2020.

———. *Muslim Cosmopolitanism in the Age of Empire*. Cambridge, MA: Harvard University Press, 2015.

Alexander, C., Joya Chatterji and Annu Jalais. *The Bengal Diaspora: Rethinking Muslim Migration*. Routledge Contemporary South Asia Series. London; New York: Routledge, 2015.

Ali, Tariq Omar. *A Local History of Global Capital: Jute and Peasant Life in the Bengal Delta*. New Jersey: Princeton University Press, 2018.

Aljunied, Syed Muhd Khairuddin. *Colonialism, Violence and Muslims in Southeast Asia: The Maria Hergogh Controversy and Its Aftermath*. New York: Routledge, 2009.

Ampalavanar, Rajeswary. *The Indian Minority and Political Change in Malaya 1945–1957*. Kuala Lumpur; Oxford; New York; Melbourne: Oxford University Press, 1981.

Amrith, Sunil. *Crossing the Bay of Bengal: The Furies of Nature and the Fortunes of Migrants*. Cambridge: Harvard University Press, 2013.

———. 'Tamil Diasporas across the Bay of Bengal'. *American Historical Review* 114, no. 3 (2009): 547–572.

Andaya, Leonard. 'Massoi and Kain Timur in the Birdshead Peninsula of New Guinea, the Easternmost Corner of the Indian Ocean World'. In *Trade, Circulation, and Flow in the Indian Ocean World*, edited by Michael Pearson, 83–108. Hampshire; New York: Palgrave Macmillan, 2015.

Anderson, Clare. *Legible Bodies: Race, Criminality and Colonialism in South Asia*. Oxford; New York: Berg, 2004.

———. 'The Bel Ombre Rebellion: Indian Convicts in Mauritius, 1815–53'. In *Abolition and Its Aftermath in Indian Ocean Africa and Asia*, edited by Gwyn Campbell, 50–65. London; New York: Routledge, 2005.

Arasaratnam, Sinnappah. *Indians in Malaysia and Singapore*. London; Kuala Lumpur: Oxford University Press, 1970.

Bald, Vivek. *Bengali Harlem and the Lost Histories of South Asian America*. Cambridge; London: Harvard University Press, 2013.

Ballhatchet, Kenneth. *Race Sex and Class under the Raj: Imperial Attitudes and Policies and Their Critics, 1793–1905*. New Delhi: Vikas Publishing House Pvt. Ltd, 1979.

Bamberg, J. H. *The History of the British Petroleum Company: The Iranian Years, 1928–1954*. Vol. 2. Cambridge: Cambridge University Press, 1994.

Bates, Crispin. 'Introduction: Community and Identity among South Asians in Diaspora'. In *Community, Empire and Migration: South Asians in Diaspora*, edited by Crispin Bates, 1–45. New York: Palgrave Publishers Ltd, 2001.

———. 'Some Thoughts on the Representation and Misrepresentation of the Colonial South Asian Labour Diaspora'. *South Asian Studies* 33, no. 1 (2017): 7–22.

———. 'The State and Subaltern Assertion in the Diaspora: Towards a Pan-South Asian Identity?' In *The Politics of Citizenship, Identity, and the State in South Asia*, edited by Harihar Bhattacharyya, Anja Kluge and Lion König, 256–273. New Delhi: Samskriti, 2012.

Bates, Crispin, and Marina Carter. 'Enslaved Lives, Enslaving Labels: A New Approach to the Colonial Indian Labor Diaspora'. In *New Routes for Diaspora Studies*, edited by Sukanya Banerjee, Aims McGuinness and Steven C. McKay, 67–94. Indiana: Indiana University Press, 2012.

———. 'Sirdars as Intermediaries in Nineteenth-Century Indian Ocean Indentured Labour Migration'. *Modern Asian Studies* 51, no. 2 (2017): 462–484.

Bayly, C. A., Sven Beckert, Matthew Connelly, Isabel Hofmeyr, Wendy Kozol and Patricia Seed. 'AHR Conversation: On Transnational History'. *American Historical Review* 111, no. 5 (2006): 1441–1464.

Belle, Carl Vadivella. *Tragic Orphans: Indians in Malaysia*. Singapore: ISAS, 2015.

Bhabha, Homi K. *The Location of Culture*. New York; London: Routledge, 1994.

Bhattacharya, J., and Coonoor Kripalani (eds.). *Indian and Chinese Immigrant Communities: Comparative Perspectives*. Singapore: ISEAS and Anthem Press, 2015.

Boi, Lee Geok. *The Syonan Years: Singapore under Japanese Rule 1942–1945*. Singapore: National Archives of Singapore and Epigram, 2005.

Boomgaard, Peter. *Frontiers of Fear: Tigers and People in the Malay World, 1600–1950*. New Haven; London: Yale University Press, 2001.

Bose, Neilesh (ed.). *South Asian Migrations in Global History Labor, Law, and Wayward Lives*. New Delhi: Bloomsbury, 2020.

Bose, Sugata. *A Hundred Horizons: The Indian Ocean in the Age of Global Empire*. Cambridge, MA: Harvard University Press, 2009.

———. *His Majesty's Opponents: Subhas Chandra Bose and India's Struggle against Empire*. Cambridge, MA; London: Harvard University Press, 2011.

Bose, Sugata, and Kris Manjapra (eds.). *Cosmopolitan Thought Zones: South Asia and the Global Circulation of Ideas*. London, UK: Palgrave Macmillan, 2010.

Brown, Judith M. *Global South Asians: Introducing the Modern Diaspora*. Cambridge: Cambridge University Press, 2006.

Buckley, Charles Burton. *An Anecdotal History of Old Times in Singapore*. Kuala Lumpur: University of Malaya Press, 1965.

Bunnell, Tim. *From World City to the World in One City: Liverpool through Malay Lives*. Oxford: Wiley-Blackwell, 2016.

Butcher, John G. *The British in Malaya 1880–1941: The Social History of a European Community in Colonial Southeast Asia*. Kuala Lumpur: Oxford University Press, 1979.

Campbell, Gwyn. 'Introduction: Abolition and Its Aftermath in the Indian Ocean World'. In *Abolition and Its Aftermath in Indian Ocean Africa and Asia*, edited by Gwyn Campbell, 1–25. London; New York: Routledge, 2005.

Chakrabarty, Dipesh. 'Postcoloniality and the Artifice of History: Who Speaks for "Indian" Pasts?' *Representations* 37, Special Issue: 'Imperial Fantasies and Postcolonial Histories' (Winter 1992): 1–26.

———. *Provincializing Europe: Postcolonial Thought and Historical Difference*. Princeton: Princeton University Press, 2000.

Chakravarti, Ranabir. 'Early Medieval Bengal and the Trade in Horses: A Note'. *Journal of the Economic and Social History of the Orient* 42, no. 2 (1999): 194–211.

———. 'Overseas Trade in Horses in Early Medieval India: Shipping and Piracy'. In *Prachi Prabha, Perspectives in Indology: Essays in Honour of*

Professor B. N. Mukherjee, edited by D. G. Battacharya and Devendra Handa, 343–360. New Delhi: Sundeep Prakashan, 1989.

Chan, Chai Hon. *The Development of British Malaya 1896–1909*. Kuala Lumpur; New York: Oxford University Press, 1964.

Chanderbali, David. *Indian Indenture in British Malaya: Policy and Practice in the Straits Settlements*. Leeds: Peepal Tree Press, 2008.

Chattopadhyay, Tapan. *The INA's Secret Service in Southeast Asia: Its Background, Infrastructure, Resources and Activities during World War II*. Kolkata: Readers Service, 2011.

Cheah, J. S. 'Approaching 100 Years of Medical and University Education in Singapore'. *Journal of the Singapore Medical Association* 44, no. 1 (2003): 1–4.

———. 'History of Medicine in Singapore'. *Singapore Medical Journal* 38, no. 6 (1997): 273–274.

Chew, Sing. 'The Southeast Asian Connection in the First Eurasian World Economy, 200 BCE–CE 500'. In *Trade, Circulation, and Flow in the Indian Ocean World*, edited by Michael Pearson, 27–54. Hampshire; New York: Palgrave Macmillan, 2015.

Chuah, Osman Abdullah, Abdul Salam M. Shukri and Mohd Syukri Yeoh. 'Indian Muslims in Malaysia: A Sociological Analysis of a Minority Ethnic Group'. *Journal of Muslim Minority Affairs* 31, no. 2 (2011): 217–230.

Coedes, G. *The Indianized States of South-East Asia*. Edited by W. F. Vella and translated by Susan Brown Cowing. Honolulu: University of Hawaii Press, 1968.

Conceicao, Joe. *Singapore and the Many-Headed Monster: A Look at Racial Riots against a Socio-Historical Background—A New Perspective on the Riots of 1950, 1964 and 1969*. Singapore: Horizon Books, 2007.

Cox, Howard, and Stuart Metcalfe. 'The Borneo Company Limited: The Origins of a Nineteenth Century Networked Multinational'. *Asia Pacific Business Review* 4, no. 4 (1998): 53–69.

Daniels, Timothy P. *Building Cultural Nationalism in Malaysia: Identity, Representation, and Citizenship*. New York; London: Routledge, 2005.

Dannecker, Petra. 'Bangladeshi Migrant Workers in Malaysia: The Construction of the "Others" in a Multi-Ethnic Context'. *Asian Journal of Social Science* 33, no. 2 (2005): 246–267.

———. 'Transnational Migration and the Transformation of Gender Relations: The Case of Bangladeshi Labour Migrants'. *Current Sociology* 53, no. 4 (2005): 655–674.

Datta, Ansu. *From Bengal to the Cape: Bengali Slaves in South Africa from 17th to 19th Century*. Bloomington: Xlibris Corporation, 2013.

Datta, Arunima. *Fleeting Agencies: A Social History of Indian Coolie Women in British Malaya*. Global South Asians. Cambridge: Cambridge University Press, 2021.

———. '"Immorality", Nationalism and the Colonial State in British Malaya: Indian "Coolie" Women's Intimate Lives as Ideological Battleground'. *Women's History Review* 25, no. 4 (2016): 584–601.

———. 'Social Memory and Indian Women from Malaya and Singapore in the Rani of Jhansi Regiment'. *Journal of the Malaysian Branch of the Royal Asiatic Society* 88, no. 2 (309) (2015): 77–103.

Davenport, Dolly Sinha. *Between Heaven and Earth: A Singapore Story in Flower*. Singapore: Flame of the Forest Publishing Pte Ltd, 2015.

Davis, Kingsley. *The Population of India and Pakistan*. Princeton: Princeton University Press, 1951.

Dick, Howard, and Peter J. Rimmer. *Cities, Transport and Communications: The Integration of Southeast Asia since 1850*. New York: Palgrave Macmillan, 2003.

Drea, Edward, Greg Bradsher, Robert Hanyok, James Lide, Michael Petersen and Daqing Yang. *Researching Japanese War Crimes Records: Introductory Essays*. Washington, DC: Nazi War Crimes and Japanese Imperial Government Records Interagency Working Group, 2006.

Eade, John. 'Bangladeshi Community Organization and Leadership in Tower Hamlets, East London'. In *South Asians Overseas: Migration and Ethnicity*, edited by Colin Clarke, Ceri Peach and Steven Vertovec, 317–331. Cambridge: Cambridge University Press, 1990.

Eaton, Richard M. Introduction to *Slavery and South Asian History*, edited by Indrani Chatterjee and Richard M. Eaton, 1–16. Indiana: Indiana University Press, 2006.

———. *The Rise of Islam and the Bengal Frontier, 1204–1760*. Los Angeles: University of California Press, 1993.

Emmer, P. C. 'The Meek Hindu: The Recruitment of Indian Labourers for Service Overseas, 1870—1916'. In *Colonialism and Migration: Indentured Labour Before and After Slavery*, edited by P. C. Emmer, 187–208. Dordrecht: Martinus Nijhoff Publishers, 1986.

Engerman, Stanley L. 'Contract Labor, Sugar, and Technology in the Nineteenth Century'. *Journal of Economic History* 43, no. 3 (1983): 635–659.

Farrer, D. S. *Shadows of the Prophet: Martial Arts and Sufi Mysticism*. Singapore: Springer, 2009.

Faruque, Md Omar. *International Instruments and Bangladeshi Migrant Workers' Rights*. Dhaka: Refugee and Migratory Movements Research Unit, 2006.

Fernando, M. R. 'Continuity and Change in Maritime Trade in the Straits of Melaka in the Seventeenth and Eighteenth Centuries'. In *Trade, Circulation, and Flow in the Indian Ocean World*, edited by Michael Pearson, 109–128. Hampshire; New York: Palgrave Macmillan, 2015.

Foucault, Michel. *Power/Knowledge: Selected Interviews and Other Writings 1972–1977*. Brighton: Harvester Press, 1980.

García, Dan Rodríguez. 'Mixed Marriages and Transnational Families in the Intercultural Context: A Case Study of African/Spanish Couples in Catalonia'. *Journal of Ethnic and Migration Studies* 32, no. 3 (2006): 403–433.

Gardner, Katy. *Age, Narrative and Migration: The Life Course and Life Histories of Bengali Elders in London*. Oxford; New York: Berg, 2002.

———. *Global Migrants, Local Lives: Migration and Transformation in Rural Bangladesh*. Oxford: Oxford University Press, 1995.

———. *Narrative, Age and Migration: Life History and the Life Course amongst Bengali Elders in London*. Oxford: Berg, 2002.

Ghee, Lim Kean. *The History of Medicine and Health in Malaysia*. Perak: Sin Boon Beng Printing Snd. Bhd, 2016.

Ghosh, Devleena. 'Under the Radar of Empire: Unregulated Travel in the Indian Ocean'. *Journal of Social History* 45, no. 2 (2011): 497–514.

Ghosh, K. K. *The Indian National Army: Second Front of the Indian Independence Movement*. Meerut: Meenakshi Prakashan, 1969.

Gin, Ooi Keat. *Historical Dictionary of Malaysia*. Maryland; Toronto; Plymouth: Scarecrow Press, Inc, 2009.

Ginsburg, Norton, and Chester F. Roberts Jr. *Malaya*. Seattle: University of Washington Press, 1958.

Gopal, Nalina. 'A Sea of Change, an Ocean of Memories: Migration and Identity'. In *Singapore Indian Heritage*, edited by Rajesh Rai and A. Mani, 146–283. Singapore: Indian Heritage Centre, 2017.

Goswami, Manu. *Producing India: From Colonial Economy to National Space*. Chicago: University of Chicago Press, 2004.

Gupta, Sunil. 'The Bay of Bengal Interaction Sphere (1000 BC– AD 500)'. *Bulletin of the Indo-Pacific Prehistory Association* 25, *The Taipei Papers (series 3), Proceedings of the 17th Congress of the Indo-Pacific Prehistory Association Taipei, Taiwan, 9 to 15 September 2002* (2005): 21–30.

Hall, D. G. E. *A History of South East Asia*. Hampshire; London: McMillan Education Ltd, 1981.

Hall, Kenneth R. *A History of Early Southeast Asia: Maritime Trade and Societal Development, 100–1500*. Maryland: Rowman & Littlefield Publishers, 2011.

Harper, T. N. 'Globalism and the Pursuit of Authenticity: The Making of a Diasporic Public Sphere in Singapore'. *Sojourn: Journal of Social Issues in Southeast Asia, Southeast Asian Diasporas* 12, no. 2 (1997): 261–292.

Hean, Loh Oun. *Industrial Relations in Singapore: Practice and Perspective*. Singapore: World Scientific Publishing Co. Pte Ltd, 2018.

Hee, Limin. *Constructing Singapore Public Space*. Singapore: Springer Science, 2017.

Hefner, Robert W. Introduction to *The Politics of Multiculturalism: Pluralism and Citizenship in Malaysia, Singapore, and Indonesia*, edited by Robert W. Hefner, 1–58. Honolulu: University of Hawai'i Press, 2001.

Hirschman, Charles. 'The Meaning and Measurement of Ethnicity in Malaysia: An Analysis of Census Classifications'. *Journal of Asian Studies* 46, no. 3 (1987): 555–582.

Ho, Tak Ming. *Doctors Extraordinaire*. Perak: Perak Academy, 2006.

Hoerder, Dirk. 'Crossing the Waters: Historic Developments and Periodizations before the 1830s'. In *Connecting Seas and Connected Ocean Rims: Indian, Atlantic, and Pacific Oceans and China Seas Migrations from the 1830s to the 1930s*, edited by Donna R. Gabaccia and Dirk Hoerder, 12–41. Leiden; Boston: Brill, 2011.

Hooker, Virginia Matheson. *A Short History of Malaysia: Linking East and West*. Crows Nest, NSW: Allen & Unwin, 2003.

Hossain, Ashfaque. 'The World of the Sylheti Seamen in the Age of Empire, from the Late Eighteenth Century to 1947'. *Journal of Global History* 9, no. 3 (2014): 425–446.

Hoyt, Sarnia Hayes. *Old Malacca*. Kuala Lumpur; Oxford; Singapore; New York: Oxford University Press, 1993.

Hwa, Cheng Siok. 'Land Tenure Problems in Burma, 1852 to 1940'. *Journal of the Malaysian Branch of the Royal Asiatic Society* 38, no. 1 (207) (1965): 106–134.

Iqbal, Iftekhar. 'Reclaiming the Crossroads between India and China: A View from the River'. *Economic and Political Weekly* 49, no. 51 (2014): 20–23.

———. 'The Bengali Muslim: Language and Space-Making at the Ocean's Margins'. In *Oceanic Islam: Muslim Universalism and European Imperialism*, edited by Sugata Bose and Ayesha Jalal, 176–198. New Delhi: Bloomsbury Publishing, 2020.

———. 'The Space between Nation and Empire: The Making and Unmaking of Eastern Bengal and Assam Province, 1905–1911'. *Journal of Asian Studies* 74, no. 1 (2015): 69–84.

Iriye, Akira. *Global and Transnational History: The Past, Present, and Future.* Basingstoke: Palgrave Macmillan, 2013.

Islam, Muinul. 'Bangladeshi Migration: An Impact Study'. In *The Cambridge Survey of World Migration*, edited by Robin Cohen, 360–366. Cambridge: Cambridge University Press, 1995.

Ismail, Abdul Majid. 'The History of Early Medical and Health Services in Malaysia'. *Malaysian Historical Society* (December 1974): 6–15.

Izzuddin, Mustafa. *The Dawoodi Bohras of Singapore: Migration, Mercantilism and Culture in the Indian Diaspora.* Singapore: NUS Press, forthcoming.

Jackson, Isabella. 'The Raj on Nanjing Road: Sikh Policemen in Treaty-Port Shanghai'. *Modern Asian Studies* 46, no. 6 (2012): 1672–1704.

Jones, Geoffrey. *Merchants to Multinationals: British Trading Companies in the Nineteenth and Twentieth Centuries.* Oxford: Oxford University Press, 2000.

Jones, Russell (ed.). *Loan-Words In Indonesian and Malay.* Central Jakarta: Yayasan Pustaka Obor Indonesia, 2008.

Jumabhoy, R. *Multiracial Singapore.* Singapore: Tak Seng Press, Pte Ltd, 1970.

Kastoriano, R. 'Immigration, Transnational Communities and Citizenships'. *Journal Revue Internationale des Sciences Sociales* 165 (2000): 353–359.

Kaur, Amarjit. 'Hewers and Haulers: A History of Coal Miners and Coal Mining in Malaya'. *Modern Asian Studies* 24, no. 1 (1990): 75–113.

——. 'Indian Ocean Crossings: Indian Labor Migration and Settlement in Southeast Asia, 1870 to 1940'. In *Connecting Seas and Connected Ocean Rims: Indian, Atlantic, and Pacific Oceans and China Seas Migrations from the 1830s to the 1930s*, edited by Donna R. Gabaccia and Dirk Hoerder, 134–168. Leiden; Boston: Brill, 2011.

——. *Wage Labour in Southeast Asia since 1840: Globalisation, the International Division of Labour and Labour Transformations.* New York: Palgrave Macmillan Ltd, 2004.

Kaur, Arunajeet. *Sikhs in the Policing of British Malaya and Straits Settlements (1874–1957).* Saarbrücken: VDM Verlag Dr Müller, 2009.

Khatun, Samia. *Australianama: The South Asian Odyssey in Australia.* London: Hurst Publishers, 2018.

Kheng, Cheah Boon. *Malaysia: The Making of Nation.* Singapore: Institute of Southeast Asian Studies, 2002.

Khondker, Habibul Haque. 'Bengali-Speaking Families in Singapore: Home, Nation and the World'. *International Migration* 46, no. 4 (2008): 178–198.

——. 'Sociological Reflections on the Diasporic Bangladeshis in Singapore and USA'. In *The South Asian Diaspora: Transnational Networks and*

Changing Identities, edited by Rajesh Rai and Peter Reeves, 124–150. London; New York: Routledge, 2009.

Kim, Khoo Kay. 'Malay Attitudes towards Indians'. In *Indian Communities in Southeast Asia*, edited by K. S. Sandhu and A. Mani, 266–287. Singapore: Times Academic Press and ISEAS, 1993.

Kobayashi, Atsushi. 'The Role of Singapore in the Growth of Intra-Southeast Asian Trade, c. 1820s–1852'. *Southeast Asian Studies* 2, no. 3 (2013): 443–474.

Koh, Tommy Thong B., Timothy Auger, Jimmy Yap and Wei Chian Ng (eds.). *Singapore: The Encyclopedia*. Singapore: Didier Millet, 2006.

Kratoska, Paul, and Ben Batson. 'Nationalism and Modernist Reform'. In *The Cambridge History of Southeast Asia, Vol. 2, The Nineteenth and Twentieth Centuries*, edited by Nicholas Tarling, 249–318. Cambridge: Cambridge University Press, 1992.

Kuah, Khun Eng. *Social Cultural Engineering and the Singaporean State*. Singapore: Springer Nature Pte Ltd, 2018.

Kulke, Hermann. 'Rivalry and Competition in the Bay of Bengal in the Eleventh Century and Its Bearing on Indian Ocean Studies'. In *Commerce and Culture in the Bay of Bengal*, edited by Om Prakash and Denys Lombard, 17–35. New Delhi: Manohar, 1999.

Kyshe, J. W. Norton. 'A Judicial History of the Straits Settlements 1786–1890'. *Malaya Law Review*, 'Special Issue to Commemorate: The One Hundred and Fiftieth Anniversary of Singapore' 11, no. 1 (1969): 38–180.

Labor Migration in Asia: Increasing the Development Impact of Migration through Finance and Technology. London: Asian Development Bank Institute, Organisation for Economic Co-operation and Development, and International Labour Organization, 2018.

Landau, Jacob M. *Pan-Islam: History and Politics*. London: Routledge, 2015.

Latif, Asad-ul Iqbal. *India in the Making of Singapore*. Singapore: Singapore Indian Association, 2008.

Lebra, Joyce. *The Indian National Army and Japan*. Singapore: ISEAS, 2008.

———. *Women against the Raj: The Rani of Jhansi Regiment*. Singapore: ISEAS, 2008.

Lee, Y. K. 'The Founding of the Medical School in Singapore in 1905'. *Annals Academy of Medicine Singapore* 34, no. 6 (2005): 4–13.

Lees, Lynn Hollen. *Planting Empire, Cultivating Subjects*. Singapore: Cambridge University Press, 2017.

Lefebvre, Henri. *The Production of Space*. Translated by Donald Nicholson-Smith. Oxford: Basil Blackwell, 1991.

Lemire, Elise. *'Miscegenation': Making Race in America*. Philadelphia: University of Pennsylvania Press, 2002.

Leng, Ang Seow. 'A History of the Singapore Police Force: Men in Blue'. In *BiblioAsia*, edited by Veronica Chee 11, no. 3 (October–December 2015): 26–31; National Library Board, Singapore.

Levitt, P. 'Migrants Participate across Borders: Towards an Understanding of Forms and Consequences'. In *Immigration Research for a New Century*, edited by N. Foner and R. G. Rumbaut, 459–479. New York: Russell Sage Foundation, 2000.

Lieberman, Victor. *Strange Parallels: Southeast Asia in Global Context, c. 800–1830, Vol. 2, Mainland Mirrors: Europe, Japan, China, South Asia, and the Islands*. Cambridge: Cambridge University Press, 2009.

Liu, Gretchen. *Singapore: A Pictorial History 1819–2000*. London: Curzon, 2001.

Lloyd, I., and Wendy Moore. *Malacca*. Singapore: Time Edition, 1986.

Loo, Yat Ming. *Architecture and Urban Form in Kuala Lumpur: Race and Chinese Spaces in a Postcolonial City*. Surrey; Burlington: Ashgate Publishing Limited, 2013.

Louis, L. J. 'Recovery from the Depression and the Seamen's Strike 1935–6'. *Labour History* 41 (November 1981): 74–86.

Low, James. *The British Settlement of Penang*. With an introduction by James Jackson. Singapore: Oxford University Press, 1972.

Ludden, David. 'Cowry Country: Mobile Space and Imperial Territory'. In *Asia Inside Out: Itinerant People*, edited by Eric Tagliacozzo, Helen F. Siu and Peter C. Perdue, 75–100. Cambridge, MA: Harvard University Press, 2019.

———. 'Presidential Address: Maps in the Mind and the Mobility of Asia'. *Journal of Asian Studies* 62, no. 4 (2003): 1057–1078.

Lwin, Thet. 'Indians in Myanmar'. In *Rising India and Indian Communities in East Asia*, edited by K. Kesavapany, A. Mani and P. Ramasamy, 485–499. Singapore: Institute of Southeast Asian Studies, 2008.

Mahajani, Usha. *The Role of the Indian Minorities in Burma and Malaya*. Bombay: Vora & Co., Publishers Private Ltd, 1960.

Maideen, Haja. *The Nadra Tragedy: The Maria Hertogh Controversy*. Malaysia: Pelanduk Publications Sdn Bhd, 1989.

Manderson, Lenore. *Sickness and the State: Health and Illness in Colonial Malaya, 1870–1940*. Cambridge: Cambridge University Press, 1996.

Mani, A. 'A Century of Contributions by Indians in Negara Brunei Darussalam'. In *Rising India and Indian Communities in East Asia*, edited by K. Kesavapany, A. Mani and P. Ramasamy, 171–195. Singapore: ISEAS, 2008.

Mann, Michael. *South Asia's Modern History: Thematic Perspectives*. London: Routledge, 2015.

Mapril, José. 'Making a "Bangladeshi Diaspora": Migration, Group Formation and Emplacement between Portugal and Bangladesh'. *Migration Letters* 18, no. 1 (2021): 13–24.

Mayer, Thomas. 'Egypt and the General Islamic Conference of Jerusalem in 1931'. *Middle Eastern Studies* 18, no. 3 (1982): 311–322.

McCann, Gerard. 'Sikhs and the City: Sikh History and Diasporic Practice in Singapore'. *Modern Asian Studies* 45, no. 6 (2011): 1465–1498.

Mclane, John R. *Land and Local Kingship in Eighteenth-Century Bengal*. Cambridge: Cambridge University Press, 1993.

Medrano, Anthony D. 'The Edible Tide: How Estuaries and Migrants Transformed the Straits of Melaka, 1870–1940'. *Journal of Southeast Asian Studies* 51, no. 4 (2020): 579–596.

Metcalf, Thomas R. *Imperial Connections: India in the Indian Ocean Arena, 1860–1920*. Berkeley; Los Angeles; London: University of California Press, 2007.

Mialaret, Jean-Pierre. *Hinduism in Singapore: A Guide to the Hindu Temples of Singapore*. Singapore: D. Moore for Asia Pacific Press, 1969.

Milner, Anthony. *The Malays*. West Sussex: Wiley-Blackwell, 2008.

Mongia, Radhika. *Indian Migration and Empire: A Colonial Genealogy of the Modern State*. Durham: Duke University Press, 2018.

Morgan, David O., and Anthony Reid. *The Eastern Islamic World Eleventh to Eighteenth Centuries*. Cambridge: Cambridge University Press, 2010.

Morrah, Patrick. 'The History of the Malayan Police'. *Journal of the Malayan Branch of the Royal Asiatic Society* 36, no. 2 (202) (1963): 1–172.

Mukherjee, Rila. 'Ambivalent Engagements: The Bay of Bengal in the Indian Ocean World'. *International Journal of Maritime History* 29, no. 1 (2017): 96–110.

———. 'Introduction: Bengal and the Northern Bay of Bengal'. In *Pelagic Passageways: The Northern Bay of Bengal before Colonialism*, edited by Rila Mukherjee, 1–262. Delhi: Primus Books, 2011.

——— (ed.). *Pelagic Passageways: The Northern Bay of Bengal before Colonialism*. Delhi: Primus Books, 2011.

———. *Strange Riches: Bengal in the Mercantile Map of South Asia*. New Delhi: Foundation Books, 2006.

———. 'The Struggle for the Bay: The Life and Times of Sandwip, an Almost Unknown Portuguese Port in the Bay of Bengal in the Sixteenth and

Seventeenth Centuries'. *Revista da Faculdade de Letras: Historia* 9 (2008): 67–88.

Murfett, Malcolm M., John N. Miksic, Brian P. Farrell and Chiang Ming Shun. *Between Two Oceans: A Military History of Singapore from 1275 to 1971.* Singapore: Marshall Cavendish Editions, 2011.

Nasution, Khoo Salma. *The Chulia in Penang: Patronage and Place-Making around the Kapitan Kling Mosque 1786–1957.* Penang: Areca Books, 2014.

Nathan, S. R. *An Unexpected Journey: Path to the Presidency.* Singapore: Editions Didier Millet, 2011.

———. *S. R. Nathan: 50 Stories from My Life.* Singapore: Editions Didier Millet, 2013.

Northrup, David. *Indentured Labor in the Age of Imperialism 1834–1922.* Studies in Comparative World History. Cambridge: Cambridge University Press, 1995.

Parmer, J. Norman. 'Health and Health Services in British Malaya in the 1920s'. *Modern Asian Studies* 23, no. 1 (1989): 49–71.

Pearson, Michael. *The Indian Ocean.* London; New York: Routledge, 2003.

Pieris, Anoma. *Hidden Hands and Divided Landscapes: A Penal History of Singapore's Plural Society.* Honolulu: University of Hawai'i Press, 2009.

Pine, Frances. 'Migration as Hope: Space, Time, and Imagining the Future'. *Current Anthropology,* 'Crisis, Value, and Hope: Rethinking the Economy' 55, no. S9 (2014): S1–S154. https://doi.org/10.1086/676526. Accessed 12 February 2023.

Prakash, Om. *European Commercial Enterprise in Pre-colonial India.* Cambridge: Cambridge University Press, 1998.

Priori, Andrea, and José Mapril, 'Banglascapes in Southern Europe: Im-mobilities, Emplacements, Temporalities'. *Migration Letters* 18, no. 1 (2021): 1–11.

Puru Shotam, Nirmala Srirekam. *Negotiation Language, Constructing Race: Disciplining Difference in Singapore.* Berlin; New York: Mouton de Gruyter, 1998.

Rahman, Md Mizanur. *Bangladeshi Migration to Singapore: A Process-oriented Approach.* Singapore: Springer, 2017.

———. 'Colonising the Penal Capital: Locating the Bengali Convicts in Cosmopolitan British Malaya'. *Asian Studies, The Twelfth International Convention of Asia Scholars (ICAS 12), ICAS Conference Proceedings,* vol. 1 (June 2022): 569–582. https://doi.org/10.5117/9789048557820/ICAS.2022 .066. Accessed 18 June 2022.

———. 'Transnational History and Colonial Records: Locating Bengali Mobility in the British Malaya'. *Journal of Maritime Studies and National Integration* 3, no. 2 (2019): 97–112.

Rahman, Md Mizanur, and Lian Kwen Fee. 'Bangladeshi Migrant Workers in Singapore: The View from Inside'. *Asia-Pacific Population Journal* 20, no. 1 (2005): 63–88.

Rai, Rajesh. *Indians in Singapore, 1819–1945: Diaspora in the Colonial Port City*. Delhi: Oxford University Press, India, 2014.

———. 'Nestled in a Faraway Land: Early Indian Settlements in Singapore'. In *Singapore Indian Heritage*, edited by Rajesh Rai and A. Mani, 284–301. Singapore: Indian Heritage Centre, 2017.

———. 'Sepoys, Convicts and the "Bazaar" Contingent: The Emergence and Exclusion of "Hindustani" Pioneers at the Singapore Frontier'. *Journal of Southeast Asian Studies* 35, no. 1 (2004): 1–19.

Rashid, Faridah Abdul. *Biography of the Early Malay Doctors 1900–1957 Malaya and Singapore*. Bloomington: Xlibris Corporation, 2012.

———. *Research on the Early Malay Doctors 1900–1957 Malaya and Singapore*. Bloomington: Xlibris Corporation, 2012.

Ray, Animesh. *Maritime India: Ports and Shipping*. New Delhi: Munshiram Manoharlal Publishers Pvt. Ltd, 1993.

Reid, Anthony. *Imperial Alchemy: Nationalism and Political Identity in Southeast Asia*. Cambridge: Cambridge University Press, 2010.

———. *Southeast Asia in the Age of Commerce 1450–1680, Vol. 2, Expansion and Crisis*. New Haven; London: Yale University Press, 1993.

——— (ed.). *Southeast Asia in the Early Modern Era: Trade, Power and Belief*. Ithaca; London: Cornell University Press, 1993.

Reynolds, E. Bruce. 'The Indian Community and the Indian Independence Movement in Thailand during World War II'. In *Southeast Asian Minorities in the Wartime Japanese Empire*, edited by Paul H. Kratoska, 170–190. Oxon: Routledge, 2002.

Ricci, R. (ed.). *Exile in Colonial Asia: Kings, Convicts, Commemoration*. Honolulu: University of Hawai'i Press, 2016.

Riddick, John F. *The History of British India: A Chronology*. Westport: Praeger, 2006.

Risley, H. H. *The Tribes and Castes of Bengal: Ethnographic Glossary*. Calcutta: P. Mukherjee, 1998.

Robertson, Roland. *Globalization: Social Theory and Global*. London: Sage Publications, 1992.

Rothermund, Dietmar. *An Economic History of India: From Pre-colonial Times to 1991*. New Delhi: Routledge, 1993.

Roy, Haimanti. 'Paper Rights: The Emergence of Documentary Identities in Post-Colonial India, 1950–67'. *Journal of South Asian Studies* 39, no. 2 (2016): 329–349.

Roy, Tirthankar. *The Economy of South Asia: From 1950 to the Present*. London: Palgrave MacMillan, 2017.

Sadka, Emily. *The Protected Malay States 1874–1895*. Kuala Lumpur: University of Malaya Press, 1968.

Salmon, Claudine. 'Bengal as Reflected in Two South-East Asian Travelogues from the Early Nineteenth Century'. In *Commerce and Culture in the Bay of Bengal, 1500–1800*, edited by Om Prakash and Denys Lombard, 383–402. New Delhi: Manohar, 1999.

Sandhu, K. S. 'Indian Immigration and Settlement in Singapore'. In *Indian Communities in Southeast Asia*, edited by K. S. Sandhu and A. Mani, 774–787. Singapore: Institute of Southeast Asian Studies, 1993.

———. 'Indian Settlements in Melaka'. In *Melaka: The Transformation of a Malay Capital c. 1400–1980, Vol. 2*, edited by Kernial Singh Sandhu and Paul Wheatley, 174–211. Kuala Lumpur; Oxford; New York: Oxford University Press, 1983.

———. *Indians in Malaya: Some Aspects of their Immigration and Settlement (1786–1957)*. Cambridge: Cambridge University Press, 1969.

———. 'Tamil and Other Indian Convicts in the Straits Settlements, A.D. 1790–1873'. *Proceedings of the First International Conference Seminar of Tamil Studies, Kuala Lumpur, International Association for Tamil Research* 1 (1966): 197–208.

Sarker, Rayhena. 'Migration and Employment: A Study of Bangladeshi Male Migrant Workers in Malaysia'. In *International Migration in Southeast Asia: Continuities and Discontinuities*, edited by Kwen Fee Lian, Md Mizanur Rahman and Yabit bin Alas, 125–148. Singapore: Springer, 2016.

Sarkissian, Margaret. 'Armenians in South-east Asia'. *Crossroads: An Interdisciplinary Journal of Southeast Asian Studies* 3, nos. 2/3 (1987): 1–33.

Sengupta, Nilanjana. *Singapore My Country: Biography of M. Bala Subramanion*. Singapore: World Scientific Publishing Co., Pte Ltd, 2016.

Sengupta, P. R. *Malaysia and Bengali Doctors 1907–2012: A Personal Perspective*. Bloomington: Xlibris, 2013.

Sethia, Tara. 'The Rise of the Jute Manufacturing Industry in Colonial India: A Global Perspective'. *Journal of World History* 7, no. 1 (1996): 71–99.

Shennan, Margaret. *Out in the Midday Sun: The British in Malaya 1880–1960*. London: John Murray, 2000.

Siddique, Sharon, and Nirmala Puru Shotam. *Singapore's Little India: Past, Present, and Future*. Singapore: Institute of Southeast Asian Studies, 1990.

Siddique, Sharon, and Nirmala Shotam-Gore. *Serangoon Road: A Pictorial History*. Singapore: Educational Publications Bureau, 1983.

Siddiqui, Tasneem. *International Labour Migration and Remittance Management in Bangladesh*. Dhaka: Refugee and Migratory Movements Research Unit, 2009.

Singh, D. S. Ranjit. 'Indians in East Malaysia'. In *Indian Communities in Southeast Asia*, edited by K. S. Sandhu and A. Mani, 568–584. Singapore: Times Academic Press and Institute of Southeast Asian Studies, 1993.

Skinner, C. (trans. and ed.). *Ahmad Rijaluddin's Hikayat Perintah Negeri Benggala* [A Narrative of the State of Bengal]. Koninklijk Instituutvoor Taal-, Land- enVolkenkunde [Royal Netherlands Institute of Southeast Asian and Caribbean Studies]. The Hague: Martinus Nijhoff, 1982.

———. 'The Author of the Hikayat Perintah Negeri Benggala'. *Bijdragen tot de Taal-, Land- enVolkenkunde* 132, nos. 2/3 (1976): 195–206.

Smith, T. E. 'Immigration and Permanent Settlement of Chinese and Indians in Malaya: And the Future Growth of the Malay and Chinese Communities'. In *South East Asia: Colonial History, Vol. 3, High Imperialism (1890s–1930s)*, edited by Paul H. Kratoska, 255–267. London; New York: Routledge, 2001.

Solomon, John. *A Subaltern History of the Indian Diaspora in Singapore: The Gradual Disappearance of Untouchability 1872–1965*. London; New York: Routledge, 2016.

———. 'Review of *Indians in Singapore, 1819–1945: Diaspora in the Colonial Port City* by Rajesh Rai'. *Journal of South Asian Studies* 38, no. 3 (2015): 536–538.

———. 'The Decline of Pan-Indian Identity and the Development of Tamil Cultural Separatism in Singapore, 1856–1965'. *South Asia: Journal of South Asian Studies* 35, no. 2 (2012): 257–281.

Steinberg, David Joel (ed.). *In Search of Southeast Asia: A Modern History*. Singapore; Hong Kong; Oxford; New York: Oxford University Press, 1985.

Stenson, M. *Class, Race, and Colonialism in West Malaysia*. Vancouver: University of British Columbia Press, 2011.

Stone, Horace. *From Malacca to Malaysia, 1400–1965*. London: Harrap and Co. Ltd, 1966.

Subrahmanyam, S. 'Notes on the Sixteenth Century Bengal Trade'. *Indian Economic Social History Review* 24, no. 3 (1987): 265–289.

———. 'Persianization and Mercantilism: Two Themes in Bay of Bengal History'. In *Commerce and Culture in the Bay of Bengal, 1500–1800*, edited by Om Prakash and Denys Lombard, 47–85. New Delhi: Monohar, 1999.

Sultana, Nayeem. 'The Dynamics of a Multi-cultural Society along the Straits of Malacca: Networking and Integration of Migrant Bangladeshis in Malaysia'. In *The Straits of Malacca: Knowledge and Diversity*, edited by Solvay Gerke, Hans-Dieter Evers and Anna-Katharina Hornidge, 137–152. LIT Verlag: ZEF Development Studies, 2008.

Tarling, Nicholas. *Piracy and Politics in the Malay World*. Nendeln/Liechtenstein: KRAUS Reprint, 1978.

Thaib, L., and Bharuddin Che Pa. 'Regional Cooperation: Malay World and the Formation of ASEAN Community'. *Global Journal of Human Social Science* 13, no. 2 (2013): 9–16.

Theng, Tan Pheng. 'A Conspectus of the Labour Laws of Singapore'. *Malaya Law Review* 10, no. 2 (1968): 202–229.

Theodore, N., and N. Martin, 'Migrant Civil Society: New Voices in the Struggle over Community Development'. *Journal of Urban Affairs* 29, no. 3 (2007): 269–287.

Tinker, Hugh. *A New System of Slavery: The Export of Indian Labour Overseas, 1830–1920*. London; New York: Oxford University Press, 1974.

Trocki, Carl A. 'Political Structures in the Nineteenth and Early Twentieth Centuries'. In *The Cambridge History of Southeast Asia, Vol. 2, The Nineteenth and Twentieth Centuries*, edited by Nicholas Tarling, 79–127. Cambridge: Cambridge University Press, 1992.

Turnbull, C. M. *A History of Singapore 1819–1988*. Singapore; Oxford; New York: Oxford University Press, 1989.

———. *A History of Modern Singapore, 1819–2005*. Singapore: National University of Singapore Press, 2009.

———. *A Short History of Malaysia, Singapore and Brunei*. Singapore: Graham Brash, 1981.

———. 'Convicts in the Straits Settlements 1826–1867'. *Journal of the Malaysian Branch of the Royal Asiatic Society* 43, no. 1 (217) (1970): 87–103.

———. 'Melaka under British Colonial Rule'. In *Melaka: The Transformation of a Malay Capital c. 1400–1980, Vol. 1*, edited by Kernial Singh Sandhu and Paul Wheatley, 242–282. Kuala Lumpur: Oxford University Press, 1983.

———. 'Regionalism and Nationalism'. In *The Cambridge History of Southeast Asia, Vol. 2, The Nineteenth and Twentieth Centuries*, edited by Nicholas Tarling, 585–642. Cambridge: Cambridge University Press, 1992.

Uddin, Md Sharif. *Stranger to Myself: Diary of a Bangladeshi in Singapore*. Edited by Theophilus Kwek. Singapore: Landmark Books, 2017.

Ullah, A. K. M. A. *Rationalizing Migration Decisions: Labour Migrants in East and Southeast Asia*. London: Ashgate, 2010.

Van Amersfoort, H., and J. Doomernik, 'Emergent Diaspora or Immigrant Communities? Turkish Immigrants in the Netherlands'. In *Communities across Borders: New Immigrants and Transnational Cultures*, edited by P. Kennedy and V. Roudometof, 55–68. London: Routledge, 2002.

Vann, Michael G. 'When the World Came to Southeast Asia: Malacca and the Global Economy'. *News Letter, Association for Asian Studies* 19, no. 2 (2014): 20–25.

Vertovec, Steven. 'Indian Indentured Migration to the Caribbean'. In *The Cambridge Survey of World Migration*, edited by Robin Cohen, 57–63. Cambridge: Cambridge University Press, 1995.

Wah, Yeo Kim. 'A Study of Three Early Political Parties in Singapore, 1945–1955'. *Journal of Southeast Asian History, Singapore Commemorative Issue 1819–1969* 10, no. 1 (1969): 115–141.

———. *Political Development in Singapore, 1945–55*. Singapore: Singapore University Press, 1973.

———. 'The Communist Challenge in the Malayan Labour Scene, September 1936–March 1937'. *Journal of the Malaysian Branch of the Royal Asiatic Society* 49, no. 2 (230) (1976): 36–79.

Welif, Rik Van. 'Slave Trading and Slavery in the Dutch Colonial Empire: A Global Comparison'. *NWIG: New West Indian Guide/Nieuwe West-Indische Gids* 82, nos. 1/2 (2008): 47–96.

Whitehead, Angus. 'Review of *Stranger to Myself: Diary of a Bangladeshi in Singapore* by MD Sharif Uddin'. *Asiatic* 12, no. 1 (2018): 219–223.

Wise, James (ed.). *Notes on the Races, Castes and Trades of Eastern Bengal*, with an introduction by Ananda Bhattacharyya. London; New York: Routledge, 2017.

Yaacob, Fatini. *Natrah: In the Name of Love*. Translated by Maryam Abdullah, Zurhaida Mohd Ismail and Flora Emilia Abdullah. Kuala Lumpur: Institut Terjemahan Negara Malaysia and Penerbit Universiti Teknologi Malaysia, 2011.

Yang, Anand A. *Empire of Convicts: Indian Penal Labor in Colonial Southeast Asia*. California: University of California Press, 2021.

————. 'Indian Convict Workers in Southeast Asia in the Late Eighteenth and Early Nineteenth Centuries'. *Journal of World History* 14, no. 2 (2003): 179–208.

Conference and Working Papers

Alexander, C., Shahzad Firoz and Naaz Rashid, 'The Bengali Diaspora in Britain: A Review of the Literature'. Working Paper, Bangla Stories, London, 2010.

Chowdury, A. M. 'Bengal and Southeast Asia: Trade and Cultural Contacts in Ancient Period'. Paper presented at the conference for the Integral Study of the Silk Roads: Roads of Dialogue, Bangkok, Thailand, 21–22 January 1991.

Deming, Sarah. 'The Economic Importance of Indian Opium and Trade with China on Britain's Economy 1843–1890'. Economics Working Papers no. 25, Whiteman College, Washington, USA, Spring 2011.

Unpublished Dissertations

Chakraborty, Titas. 'Work and Society in the East India Company Settlements in Bengal, 1650–1757'. PhD dissertation, University of Pittsburgh, 2016.

Chanderbali, David Sinjeet. 'Indian Indenture in the Straits Settlements, 1872–1910: Policy and Practice in Province Wellesley'. PhD dissertation, Australian National University, Canberra, 1983.

Khan, Latiffa. 'Indians in Malaya, 1900–1945'. MA dissertation, University of Hong Kong, 1963.

Lanman, Ingelise Lamont. 'The Fabric of Malay Nationalism on the Malay Peninsula, 1920–1940'. PhD dissertation, University of California, 1988.

Murtagh, Benjamin. 'The Portrayal of the British in Traditional Malay Literature'. PhD dissertation, University of London, 2005.

Pirbhai, Mariam. 'The Multiple Voices of Indenture History: The South Asian Diasporic Novel in English'. PhD dissertation, Universite de Montreal, 2003.

Rajendra, Nagendiram. 'The Straits Settlements 1867–1874'. MA thesis, Australian National University, Canberra, 1976.

Sandhu, Kernial Singh. 'Indian Migration and Population Change in Malaya, c. 100–1957 A.D.: A Historical Geography'. MA dissertation, University of British Columbia, Vancouver, 1961.

Sultana, Nayeem. 'The Bangladeshi Diaspora in Malaysia: Organizational Structure, Survival Strategies and Networks'. PhD dissertation, ZEF, Centre for Development Research, University of Bonn, 2008.

Thangavel, Jensrani. 'The Indian National Army and the Singapore-Malayan Indians 1942–1945'. BA dissertation, Nanyang Technological University, Singapore, 1979.

Tschacher, Torsten. 'The Impact of Being Tamil on Religious Life among Tamil Muslims in Singapore'. PhD dissertation, National University of Singapore, 2006.

Electronic Sources/Websites

Allen, Richard B. 'Asian Indentured Labor in the 19th and Early 20th Century Colonial Plantation World'. *Oxford Research Encyclopedia of Asian History*, 29 March 2017, https://doi.org/10.1093/acrefore/9780190277727.013.33. Accessed 14 April 2021.

Amrith, Sunil. 'Islam in the Bay of Bengal: Between Tamil and Malay Worlds'. Public lecture, Tufts University, 14 November 2011. https://corpora.tufts. edu/catalog/tufts:MS165.002.001.00006?transcript. Accessed 14 October 2017.

Bangladesh Population. *Worldometers*, 2018. http://www.worldometers.info/ world-population/bangladesh-population/. Accessed 15 January 2018.

'Bangladeshis Third in Availing Second Home in Malaysia'. *Financial Express*, 25 February 2019. https://thefinancialexpress.com.bd/trade/bangladeshis-third-in-availing-second-home-in-malaysia-1551078329. Accessed 15 February 2021.

BATA Malaysia. https://batamsia.wordpress.com/about/. Accessed 25 May 2019.

'Bata Shoe (Singapore) Pte Ltd'. SingaporeInfopedia, An Electronic Encyclopedia on Singapore's History, Culture, People and Events, National Library Board, Singapore, https://eresources.nlb.gov.sg/infopedia/articles/ SIP_892_2005-01-26.html. Accessed 25 May 2019.

'Bengali Language'. Britannica. https://www.britannica.com/topic/Bengali-language. Accessed 25 June 2019.

'Bengali-speaking South Asian'. Joshua Project. https://joshuaproject.net/people _groups/10790/MP. Accessed 12 February 2023.

Berthet, Samuel. 'Boat Technology and Culture in Chittagong'. *International Water History Association* 7, no. 2 (2015). DOI: 10.1007/s12685-015-0133-y.

Bureau of Manpower, Employment and Training (BMET). Statistical Reports, Ministry of Expatriates' Welfare and Overseas Employment, Government of the People's Republic of Bangladesh. http://www.old.bmet.gov.bd/BMET/stattisticalDataAction#. Accessed 22 October 2016.

Census of India 2011. 'Distribution of the 22 Scheduled Languages'. http://censusindia.gov.in/Census_Data_2001/Census_Data_Online/Language/Statement3.htm. Accessed 15 January 2018.

Chand, Meira. 'Warrior Women: The Rani of Jhansi Regiment'. *biblioasia*, National Library Board, Singapore. https://www.meirachand.com/wp-content/uploads/2019/10/Jhansi-Regiment.pdf. Accessed 21 March 2018.

Chew, Ernest. 'Pioneers of Early Colonial Singapore 1819–1850'. http://www.sabrizain.org/malaya/library/rtc.pdf. Accessed 15 July 2020.

Chue, Danny. 'S. C. Goho and Wartime Singapore'. Singapore Memory Project, Memory of Danny Chue, 2015. https://www.singaporememory.sg/contents/SMA-a296a831-46de-4118-8816-90a6506a5bdf. Accessed 7 July 2018.

Cornelius-Takahama, Vernon. 'Tan Sri Datuk Professor Ahmad Ibrahim'. SingaporeInfopedia, National Library Board, Singapore, https://eresources.nlb.gov.sg/infopedia/articles/SIP_529_2005-01-07.html. Accessed 7 July 2020.

'General Assembly Hears Appeal for Bangla to Be Made an Official UN Language'. General Assembly of the UN, New York, 27 September 2010. https://news.un.org/en/story/2010/09/353662-general-assembly-hears-appeal-bangla-be-made-official-un-language. Accessed 20 September 2017.

Gunasegaran, Palmini. 'Lady with Drive'. *Star Online*, 26 April 2003. https://www.thestar.com.my/authors?q=%22Palmini+Gunasegaran+Pictures+Courtesy+Of+Datuk+Dr+Madhuri+Majumdar%22. Accessed 1 Jan 2019.

Gupta, Mousumi Biswa Das. 'Ramnath er Bishho Vormon' [World Travel of Ramnath]. *Banik Barta*, 6 October 2017. https://www.revolvy.com/page/Ramnath-Biswas. Accessed 13 June 2018.

Hirschmann, R. 'Number of Migrant Workers in Malaysia 2017, by Country of Origin'. 6 April 2020, *Statista*. https://www.statista.com/statistics/711974/malaysia-number-of-migrant-workers-by-country-of-origin/. Accessed 8 November 2020.

'Malaysian Bengalee Association'. https://www.mba.org.my/history.php. Accessed 20 March 2017.

Mamun, Muntasir, and Ujjal Ashrafuzzaman. 'Legend of the East Ramnath Biswas Who Wheeled before WII'. *Trino (Adventure Quarterly)* 3, no. 1 (March 2012): 48–55. http://www.downtheroad.org/India-Nepal-Subcontinent

/TRINO-8TH-TOUR%20BIKING-INDEPENDENCE%20DAY%20
ISSUE.pdf. Accessed 25 March 2018.

Moore, Molly. 'Number of Immigrants in Brunei 2005–2017'. *Statista*, 21
October 2019. https://www.statista.com/statistics/697564/brunei-number-
of-immigrants/. Accessed 8 November 2020.

'Muhammed Aziz Khan', *Forbes*. https://www.forbes.com/profile/muhammed-
aziz-khan/?sh=4f0347328ec0. Accessed 15 February 2021.

'NSmen and NSFs Honoured at Istana as Reception Caps Year-Long Home
Team NS50 Celebrations'. *Today*, 3 November 2017. https://www.today
online.com/singapore/nsmen-and-nsfs-honoured-istana-reception-caps-
year-long-home-team-ns50-celebrations. Accessed 23 June 2018.

Ong, S. H. 'Majumder Scholarship Fund'. *Ipoh Echo (Archives), Ipoh's Community
Newspaper, Ipoh Food, Ipoh Media*, 16 March 2013. http://www.ipohecho.
com.my/v2/page/58/. Accessed 28 June 2018.

Rahman, Nor-Afidah Abd. 'Ramakrishna Mission Singapore'. National Library
Board, Singapore. https://eresources.nlb.gov.sg/infopedia/articles/SIP_410
_2005-01-18.html, . Accessed 28 June 2018.

'RAM NATH BISWAS, the Globe Trotter'. *Bhattacharyasofsylhet*, 6 December
2011. http://bhattacharyasofsylhet.blogspot.com/2011/12/revised-family-tree
.html. Accessed 2 Jan 2017.

'S. C. Goho and Wartime Singapore'. Memory of Danny Chue, Singapore
Memory Project, 2015. https://www.singaporememory.sg/contents/SMA-
a296a831-46de-4118-8816-90a6506a5bdf. Accessed 15 January 2018.

Sport Singapore. 'Singapore Hockey Olympians Reunite to Get Behind New
ActiveSG Hockey Academy'. 15 July 2017. https://www.sportsingapore.
gov.sg/newsroom/media-releases/2017/7/singapore-hockey-olympians-
reunite-to-get-behind-new-activesg-hockey-academy. Accessed 19 July 2019.

Sundralingam, S. 'Datuk Dr Madhuri Majumder'. *Ipoh Echo (Archives), Ipoh's
Community Newspaper, Ipoh Food, Ipoh Media*, 16 March 2013. http://www.
ipohecho.com.my/v2/2013/03/16/datuk-dr-madhuri-majumder/. Accessed
26 March 2018.

Teng, Sharon. 'Singapore Labour Party'. SingaporeInfopedia, National Library
Board, Singapore. https://eresources.nlb.gov.sg/infopedia/articles/SIP_2018
-01-26_111726.html. Accessed 7 July 2019.

'The Cattle Trade and Related Cottage Industries'. In *Little India Heritage Trail*.
Singapore: National Heritage Board, Ministry of Culture, Community and
Youth, 2018. https://www.roots.sg/visit/trails/Little-India-Heritage-Trail-
Walk-of-Faiths. Accessed 27 August 2019.

Tomizawa, Roy. 'From Silver to Gold in Singapore: Tan Howe Liang to Joseph Schooling'. *The Olympians*, 5 May 2017. https://theolympians.co/2017/05/05/from-silver-to-gold-in-singapore-tan-how-liang-to-joseph-schooling/. Accessed 15 May 2018.

Veda, Vedic Knowledge Online. http://veda.wikidot.com/malay-words-sanskrit-origin. Accessed 25 June 2019.

Zamri, Norena Abdul Karim and Adam Abdul Karim Zamri. 'In Lens of the Odd: Constructing the Otherness in Malaysian History, the Role of Financial Development and Manufacturing Sector Expansion on Emission Reduction for Sustainable Economic Development in the World's Biggest Emitter Asia'. *International Journal of Advanced Science and Technology* 29, no. 10s (2020): 8207–8213; http://sersc.org/journals/index.php/IJAST/article/view/24272. Accessed 24 November 2020.

Index